THE GROUNDHOPPER GUIDE TO
SOCCER IN ENGLAND

THE GROUNDHOPPER GUIDE TO

SOCCER IN ENGLAND

Meet the clubs. See them play. Eat, drink, and sing with the locals.

2021–22 SEASON

PAUL GERALD

Bacon and Eggs Press
Portland, Oregon

THE GROUNDHOPPER GUIDE TO SOCCER IN ENGLAND, 2021-22 SEASON

Bacon and Eggs Press, Portland, Oregon

© 2021 by Paul Gerald

Editing and design by Indigo: Editing, Design, and More

ISBN: 978-1-7375660-0-7

In memory of everybody we lost to this terrible pandemic, and in the hope that we all learned something so we will handle the next one much better.

CONTENTS

Consider this book an invitation.

Whether you have been to soccer games in England, only watched them on TV, dreamed about seeing them in person, or just recently heard from your kids that a game at (insert big club here) *must* be a part of your English vacation, you can think of me as standing in English Soccer World and telling you it's great fun in here.

I've been to more than a hundred games at sixty-plus clubs all over the country, and I want you to know that it's not dangerous, it's not difficult (though it might be expensive), and I think it will remind you of what sports were like in your youth. Remember when television hadn't completely taken over the experience? Remember when rowdy visiting fans filled a corner of the stadium? When going to a game didn't take up the whole day? When the loud-speakers weren't blaring music all the time, when dance teams weren't gyrating, when replays and ads and cheering instructions weren't constantly emanating from a giant TV screen?

That's English soccer—with more singing.

So I am inviting you to come over and check it out. More than that, I am inviting you to visit an England that you wouldn't otherwise see. Specifically, I hope you will leave London, leave the big six clubs, and go find a true English soccer experience. I know you (and most certainly your kids) want to see Chelsea, Arsenal, Man U, Man City, Liverpool, or Tottenham. Those places are great. But I really want to get you to Charlton, QPR, Millwall, or Fulham. Better yet, I want to get you out of the capital entirely—to Sheffield, Nottingham, Brighton, Norwich, Newcastle, Leeds…I could go on.

So many people are fixated on seeing The Best—or even worse, on seeing what they've seen on TV or what their friends saw on their trips. What I am saying is that Leeds vs. Millwall will be much more entertaining (and cheaper) than seeing Man U sleepwalk through a game at a silent Old Trafford. In fact, any local derby at any level, or a top-of-the-table clash in any league, or even a relegation scrap in League One will be more fun than many home games at the big six. And there's a decent chance that your neighbors in the stadium will be surprised to have a foreigner sitting with them. They will also be pleased if you know a little something about where you are, what you're looking at, and what the locals are singing.

For that is my real invitation: to not just go to a game or two but to learn about the town you're visiting and learn the club's songs, history, and traditions. In other words, I want you to be a proper football fan, if only for a day. This is what I am trying to help you do with this book.

There are many great places to visit all over England, and there are many places where even the locals will wonder why you're there. But going to a football game is such a great way to be, as American writer Rick Steves always says, a temporary local. Really, it's meeting the people—and hearing them sing and curse and tell stories—that I think you'll remember most.

Halftime tea at Derby County; it's not always so civilized.

I want you to have the soccer adventure of your dreams, but I also invite you to expand those dreams. If it's a big six club you want to see, I can help. But I want to get you on the terraces, with a Bovril and a basket of chips, singing your guts out and yelling, "Who are ya" at the wankers in the away end. Because that's where I'll be and what I'll be doing.

Come and join me.

No matter how often I write a book, I always come to this awful, embarrassing moment in which I say to myself, *Why, oh, why, did I not keep a better list of people whom I wish to thank?* For they are legion, and I am certain I have lost some of their names. I apologize.

Of course, I begin with the O'Sullivans of South London, whom I call my English family although they are in fact American, Irish, and English—proper Londoners nonetheless. They are my emotional and physical base when in the great city, and they cannot be thanked enough. Back home in Portland, many thanks have to go to Rebecca Schreiber and Andrew Tice for being great friends, meeting for coffee and those 7:00 a.m. English kickoffs, contributing to the "How to Read the Referee" and "How to Speak Soccer" sections, and holding my hand when the Timbers have a late one-goal lead. We really are gonna open that soccer bar, you two!

Also, special thanks go to Angie and Allen Johnson, new fellow Timbers sufferers who helped keep me sane during this damned pandemic with friendship, charm, and terrible movies.

I also have actual employees to thank! Alethea Smartt has been a rock and an inspiration, providing the brains, efficiency and organizational skills I so sorely lack. And Brian Reinhardt has been helping tremendously with creating and managing all sorts of website content. I thank both for putting up with me, working hard, and helping to paddle this little boat farther than I could ever get it alone.

Thanks to all the folks at Champions Travel—Trevor Anderson, Ciaran Ward, and Michelle Long—for working with me on the hospitality packages—by which I mean putting up with my annoying questions and general ignorance. Thanks also to Tony Broekens and Atze Bosma at P1 Hospitality.

Over in England, I have encountered so many fine people that I really do feel sad about the ones I forgot to write down. Still, a list must be attempted. Thank you, Spike and Nick, for taking me to my first West Bromwich Albion game. Steve Alison is a wonderful Millwall ambassador. To my charming neighbor at The Hawthorns on my second visit, may you get back to Wembley someday. Elle and Lily were absolutely charming hosts at Everton. Thanks to Scott Bemment for making me feel like a true Mackem that day at Stamford Bridge, and to all the other Sunderland fans I continue to hear from since that night at Old Trafford. And RIP Stephen Quinn; you went too soon, marra. Thanks to James Clark for being my guide to the world of Leeds United. Thanks to John for a wonderful afternoon chat about Barnsley and football at the visitor center in Nailsworth; the next veggie burger is on me. Thanks also to Jean at BeatlesWalk.com for showing me around Liverpool and to Sara O'Donnell for coming out to see me talk at the library and then letting me help plan her husband's big surprise trip. Thanks to Susan and Sam Foster for letting me be a part of a memorable trip and a night at White Hart Lane. Thanks to Alan Pickard for the Steel City derby ticket and the pregame lemonade. And boy did I enjoy hanging out with Larry Shire and his family at Craven Cottage.

Thanks, of course, to all the folks who have joined my "Groundhop" tours: Frank, Cheryl and Devin Armstrong; Adele Clements, Sue and Alex Schierer, Brad Brown, Mike Clark, Bruce Winkelstein, Al Holston, Stephen Windell, Bev Rumer, and Mark Peterson.

Back at home, Alethea Smartt gave invaluable advice in the early going of the book project and joined Groundhopper Guides as our first employee! She also did all the editing on this edition of the book. Jeff Pietka offered much wizardry on tours, guiding, and consulting. Once I actually wrote the book, Vinnie Kinsella at Indigo: Editing, Design, and More laid it out beautifully and Olivia Hammerman put a lovely cover on it.

And also just a general thanks to all the people I hear from via email, social media, and so on. I love being part of this banter, and I love helping everybody with their footy adventures. Hearing from you helps as well, and I really appreciate it.

Keep it coming, and I'll see you at the grounds!

In the old days of 2019, I was always getting to new clubs and grounds, and I kept adding club profiles to the book. As you might imagine, as I write this in the summer of 2021, it's been a while since I did that. So I am still on 103 games at 61 different clubs and 63 different grounds, including Wembley and the old grounds at Tottenham and Brentford.

So there is nothing new to report this time, since the 2020-21 edition. We have, however, gone through everything here and updated all the leagues, schedule information, and whatever we could find about the women's teams at each club. So what you hold here is up to date for the 2021-22 season.

My goal for the new season is to finish "the 92" by attending a game at every club in the top four tiers of professional football in England. So next year's book will look very different.

I hope you'll come along at groundhopperguides.com.

With my usual croissant and flat white, I settle onto the train with the standard five or so minutes to spare. I relax into my seat, the CrossCountry service eases out of Birmingham New Street, and another Saturday football outing is underway.

Onboard, it's the same crowd as every week. Ladies going shopping, old couples sitting quietly, families sometimes bickering, pods of teenagers going who knows where and all staring at their phones, somebody already asleep. Then there are always groups, or maybe just pairs, of twenty- to forty-something men with beers talking football.

Listening to little snippets here and there, I realize that on my train to Nottingham there are at least two other clubs represented that I can see, even though the English fan tends to hide his supporter status in public. We've got Birmingham City people headed for Derby, West Brom people headed for Nottingham, and then another crest on a cap…is that Coventry City? I search on my phone and confirm the Sky Blues are on their way up to Peterborough for some League One action.

A train through England on a Saturday morning is an odd sort of river fed by many streams and then spreading out again into a delta of football grounds. You lose some flow in Burton but pick up a dad and son headed to Leicester. In Derby, you lose the Nottingham-bound, and on the platform you spot some Forest fans who must live down south somewhere. For now, they're nodding at some West Brom folk, but in about two hours, they will all be calling each other wankers (and worse).

Back on the train, you hear all the soothing sounds of football. "Fancy our chances today?" "How do you reckon our new manager will do?" "That new Spanish midfielder is starting today." "What was he thinking, playing them kids in that game?" "You see that goal by that Bristol City lad?"

It feels festive and communal, with games happening all over the place. It's ninety-two professional clubs in a country about seven hours long by train. We're not at home watching on TV, but we will keep an eye on our phones for the "scores from around the country." Everybody is pulling for their club but also keeping an eye on somebody else who might help out by beating a rival or a competitor for playoff positions. On the way back to Birmingham after my game, we would pick up the Birmingham City stragglers fresh off a frustrating loss but enjoying Forest's 2–0 first-half lead over Aston Villa in the 5:00 p.m. kickoff.

On the train, it's civilized and old-fashioned, even though we all know at the ground it will be obscenity and carnage. You can practically see the kids studying the adults for how to talk about the game, how to act. The younger adults are respectful and mostly calm now, but if they are getting a little rowdy, you'll see some of the older guys looking over that way wistfully, remembering something lost, even as the non-footballers on the train will mumble to themselves, ruffle their paper with a flourish, and maybe even share an eye roll and a shake of the head. I always smile at that one; every society needs somebody mildly offensive, and England has football fans.

For us, Saturday means our tribe gathers and mixes and then disperses again, every week, all over the country. Our journey for the day is geographical but also emotional, from cautious optimism or crouched fear regarding our club and honest good wishes regarding the others—unless it's a rival, of course—to despair or joy, followed by resignation or relief.

We might see magic. We might see crap. We might be thinking promotion at the end of the day, or maybe about our next manager. But whatever happens we'll be back on the train, having another beer, talking about this goal or that decision, comparing notes with the other clubs' folks as we roll back to wherever we came from.

Next week our boys will play at home, but somebody else will be out on the road doing the same thing. We all wander around the country hoping for three points, good times, a proper sing-song, and maybe a bit of footballing magic.

INTRODUCTION

Ground: a place where football games occur

+

Hopper: one who hops from place to place

=

Groundhopper: one who visits football grounds as a neutral; a soccer tourist

or

Me and you.

Especially if you are American, you are going to catch some crap—or I should say, "get some stick"—from English people about the word *soccer*. Here, I will arm you for self-defense and also cover a very brief history of the game in England and around the world.

THE OLD DAYS

Take yourself back to, say, 1850 in England. All over the country, people are kicking around a ball or a pig's bladder or something else and calling this activity football. Some form of this had been going on for centuries, but it became focused at this point in clubs and at schools.

Since nobody was in charge, there were no agreed-upon rules. Each set of rules, or code, had slight variations in number of players, length of game, way to score, and so on. They were generally sorted into two camps. In one, using hands was not allowed, nor was "hacking" one another to the ground. The most common of these were known, due to their geographical origins, as the Cambridge Rules and the Sheffield Rules. In another version, you could hold the ball and hack each other down; these came from a place called Rugby.

Eventually, it was decided that having proper competitions required a common set of rules, so the Football Association was formed in London in 1863. It took several days and required a series of votes—I should point out this happened in a tavern—but the "no hands, no hacking" crowd won, and the Laws of the Game were written. But the "hands and hacking" crowd wanted to play their way, so in 1871 they formed the Rugby Union.

From this point forward, there were two official versions of the game: Rugby Football and Association Football. Soon enough, nicknames emerged to simplify things: rugger and soccer. So *soccer* comes from *association* and was invented by English people. Remember that.

THE DAMN WORD *SOCCER*

So why do Americans (and many others) call it soccer? Because as both Rugby and Association Football were spread around the world by British soldiers and sailors, different parts of the world liked different versions. For whatever reason, rugby football took hold in the United States, Canada, Ireland, Australia, South Africa, and New Zealand, while association football pretty much took over the rest of the world. This is where two parallel stories diverge.

In the United States, rugby football was so much more popular that it just became *football*. And then it occurred to us that it would be more fun to throw the ball forward and safer to wear helmets, and after a few decades of change, American football was created. Its nickname was gridiron, and for a while in the early 20th century, you would still see that word in publications here and there.

Left: the original rules of the game. Right: the Manchester newspaper uses the "s word" in the 1950s.

Meanwhile, in England, people actually used the word *soccer* a fair amount until about 1980. By that time, association football had become so much more popular than rugby football that they simply reverted to *football* and *rugby*.

In the 1970s, we Americans "discovered" this thing called association football and decided it was cool. We formed a professional league and started paying attention to the World Cup. Since by this time our football had become the king of our sporting world, we had to call this "new" game something else. Obviously, we settled on its old English nickname, soccer.

As you will discover, this utterly infuriates many English people. They don't seem to care that the Aussies, Kiwis, Canucks, and Irish call it soccer as well. There is something about the combination of this game, that word, and us Yanks that sets them off. For a while, it really annoyed them that we were getting to be better at it than they were; we were getting out of our groups in the World Cup while they weren't, and our record against them in World Cups was one win and one draw. But ever since the United States whiffed on the 2018 World Cup and England made the semifinals, we don't get to use that stick against them anymore.

Americans should try to have some sympathy for them though. Imagine that Great Britain started a basketball league called the Hoops League or a football league called the Gridiron Association. Americans would give them crap about that, right?

In this book, as you will see, I switch all the time between soccer and football, as well as between England, Great Britain, and the UK. I really don't care what we call any of it.

SPREADING AROUND THE COUNTRY

As the game spread, local competitions started to form. We'll stick with England but assume that the following happened in every country, everywhere.

First, local sets of clubs and schools formed little leagues and associations. Then a national league was formed; in England this was the Football League in 1888, with twelve original members who all still exist today: Blackburn Rovers, Burnley, Bolton Wanderers, Accrington, Everton, Preston North End, Aston Villa, Derby County, Notts County, Stoke City, West Bromwich Albion, and Wolverhampton Wanderers. Note that all of those are from Birmingham or farther north; English football began as a Northern Thing.

The leagues multiplied and formed layers connected by promotion and relegation—but in the old days, that was based on being voted into different leagues. Now it's about winning and losing; more on that in the "Structure" chapter.

Meanwhile, the Football Association decided to have a national competition, so in 1871 they formed the FA Cup. Again, this kind of competition happens all over the world and is referred to as a domestic Cup competition. Every country has at least one; in the States it's called the US Open Cup, in Spain it's the Copa del Rey, in Italy the Coppa Italia, etc.

Today there are nine levels of leagues in England and more than seven hundred clubs that participate in the FA Cup. More on that in the "Structure" chapter as well.

THE WORLDWIDE GAME

At some point, countries decided to get their best players together and have a game. And eventually there was a need for a worldwide governing body to run all of this. Enter the Fédération Internationale de Football Association, or FIFA, an international crime syndicate that poses as soccer's world governing body. (A dozen or so of its leaders have been indicted by the United States for bribery, tax evasion, and general scumbaggery.)

FIFA, which runs the World Cup, is divided into several regions, which you can think of as crime family turfs: UEFA in Europe, CONCACAF in North America, CONMEBOL in South America, and so on. (Let's just skip what those stand for, shall we?) Within each of these regions, there are three types of competitions:

- A qualifying tournament for the World Cup
- A country-versus-country competition held every few years
- A club championship held every year

In Europe, these are known as World Cup qualifying, which takes almost two years to work out; the European Championships, or Euros, next to be held in summer 2021; and the UEFA Champions League. The last will be covered in more detail in a bit. Versions of all three of these competitions exist wherever you live as well.

Soon we are going to take a deeper dive into the leagues and Cups of English football, but first, now that we've covered the words soccer and football, let's look at some other important words.

Having discussed the word *soccer*, allow me a word about *English*. There are, in fact, a couple of clubs in here that are Welsh, and one would do well to not tell Welsh (or Scottish) people they are English. But Swansea City, Cardiff City, and several other clubs play in the English football league system; when a Welsh league was formed in 1992, these clubs declined an invitation to join. Therefore, for our purposes here, they are playing soccer in England.

Next, there is this issue of England, Britain, Great Britain, and the UK. In short, Britain is all the islands, Great Britain is the biggest island, and England is one of the four countries (kind of) in the United Kingdom, which is a political entity which occasionally considers tearing itself apart. As with *soccer* and *football*, I shall switch back and forth between them all the time.

Now, among the many things that cannot be separated from the experience of English football—passion, history, singing, stories, characters, traditions, and beer—one should be touched upon quickly before we proceed: cursing.

This is no casual thing; I am talking about serious, sustained, committed cursing. *Shit* and its British cousin *shite* are completely unavoidable, but they're only the beginning. *Wanker* is kind of a cute entry in the category; a wanker is simply one who masturbates (wanks), and you will see a lot of "wanker signs" at games. Hearing *fuck* in public as often as you will may well be a shock; get used to it. Beyond that, it's all the usual stuff, although British folks do like to use *bastard* a lot, generally preceded by *fat, Scottish, dirty northern*, or *soft southern* generally proceeding it.

And there is the word, well, *cunt*. I cringe to even type it, as I grew up in a country where its use is utterly taboo. Not so where you're headed. Especially at Millwall.

I will limit the use of these words as much as I can, but the simple fact remains that if you attend a soccer game in England, you will hear someone—many someones—yell or sing that some useless cunt and/or their support is fucking shit. In fact, our next Story Time entry, which starts on page 32, is a prime example.

Grim but true. And on we go.

WHAT THE PANDEMIC HAS DONE TO FOOTBALL

As we head into the 2021-22 season, there is a sense of people coming out of their homes, looking around, and asking if it's okay to be out here. England is, as I write this, about to re-open and let stadiums be full again. Travel restrictions are being lifted. So I suppose we are about to have a "normal" season.

Still, the effects of the pandemic are everywhere, and mainly on balance sheets. Football clubs have rarely been money-making operations, especially when the field is tilted by the lure of television money and twisted by the entry of foreign owners looking to make a quick buck by "flipping" what is, for the locals, a part of their community and heritage.

Add a roughly 18-month shutdown to that mix, and things are going to break. Bury FC and Macclesfield Town FC are no longer with us; each has been replaced by a fan-owned "phoenix club" now trying to climb the league ladder. Even bigger clubs like Wigan Athletic, Derby County and Sheffield Wednesday are teetering. A 2021 report said at least half of English clubs are in financial trouble.

This threat to the ever-shaky business model of football has led some to propose radical changes, like the European Super League that would let the biggest clubs always play in Europe, or FIFA proposing a World Cup every two years, or doing away with promotion and relegation in England.

For now, it seems safe to come out and go to games. Whether we recognize what we're looking at in a few years is anyone's guess.

As we continue our tour of English soccer, let's now move on to the structure of this new world we're exploring. By this I mean the leagues, the system that connects them all, and the Cups.

THE LEAGUE PYRAMID

To grasp the structure, as well as the size, of English football, one should always keep in mind a pyramid. At the top are two leagues made of four levels containing ninety-two fully professional clubs. Just below that is another league with twenty-four semiprofessional clubs, and after that it gets kind of confusing.

At the very top is the Premier League. This is a twenty-team league with all the clubs you've certainly heard of: Arsenal, Chelsea, Manchester United, Liverpool, and so on.

The next league down is called the English Football League, and it has three levels with twenty-four teams each. The names here are odd: the Championship is the top tier of the Football League but the second tier of the overall pyramid. Below that are League One and League Two, which are called leagues but are part of the Football League. (Hang on, it gets even weirder in a minute.)

To summarize, these are the top four levels, which are the nearly exclusive focus of this book:

1. Premier League—20 clubs
2. The Championship—24 clubs
3. League One—24 clubs
4. League Two—24 clubs

There are actually nine levels to this pyramid, with each step below level 5 containing more leagues and clubs than the one above. Everything below level 4 is called non-league football, and the vast majority of it is fully amateur. At the top of this level is the National League, with twenty-four clubs. That's level 5 of the pyramid—and yes, the National League is part of what's called "non-league football." British English is weird. Level 6 is two twenty-four-team leagues called the National League North and National League South, and I will show mercy on both of us and not go any farther down the pyramid than that.

The total number of clubs in this pyramid varies a bit from year to year, but a safe bet is that it's over seven hundred.

Each league determines its champions the same way: A season consists of every team in the league playing every other team twice—home and away. (So the Premier League season has thirty-eight games, for example; the Championship has forty-six.) You get three points for a win, one for a draw, and "fuck-all" for a loss. At the end of the year, whoever has the most points is the champion. So there is no postseason playoff. Well, there sort of is. We'll get to that.

The most exciting finish ever was the 2011–12 season, when Manchester City won the league by scoring a goal with about thirty seconds left in the very last game of the year—taking it away from their rivals Manchester United to win it for the first time in forty-six years. It's basically the greatest thing that ever happened in English football…unless you're a United fan.

The 2020-21 season wasn't quite normal, of course. It started a month late but ended on time for the Premier League and Football League. In the National League and below, a second Covid-related shutdown in the spring led to those seasons being abandoned. Leagues One and Two, along with the National League, finished up eventually. But all the leagues below that just declared the whole season null and void, for the second year in a row. In the club chapters that follow, for those leagues I have just listed the club's position in the table when the season ended.

CONNECTING IT ALL: PROMOTION AND RELEGATION

A club can play its way up, or down, through the leagues.

Let's start with the Premier League. At the end of each season, the three worst clubs get relegated down to level 2, the Championship, for the entire next season. I know "going down to the Championship" sounds odd, but they're going from the Premier League to the top level of the Football League. Likewise, the bottom three clubs in the Championship go down to League One.

The bottom four in League One go down to League Two, and the bottom two from League Two drop out of the Football League and into the ("non-league") National League, at level 5.

Of course, clubs go up as well. From the Championship, the top two go up to the Premier League automatically, and the next four go into a playoff.

Yes, England has playoffs, and they can be thrilling, even though they are for the last promotion spot. Number 3 plays number 6, and number 4 plays number 5—one game at each ground, total goals win. Then the two winners play a final at Wembley Stadium in London for the final promotion spot. The same thing happens in League One, with clubs competing for a spot in the Championship. League Two sends four clubs up to League One—three automatically, the fourth via playoff. The National League sends two to League Two: the champion and the winner of a playoff between clubs two through five.

Head hurt? Mine too. Let's leave England for a minute.

"GETTING INTO EUROPE"

So where do the top teams in the Premier League go with no other league above them? Simple: to Europe.

There is a second-tier European championship called the Europa League, and the fifth-place English team goes there, along with the FA Cup winner. The League Cup winner will go to the new UEFA Europa Conference League. It's all actually a bit more complicated than this (what happens if the FA Cup winner also finishes second in the league?) but let's pause for a "cuppa."

It's all about silverware, the biggest of which are the FA Cup (left) and Premier League (right, in its Manchester City Sky Blue from 2019).

THE CUPS

Tournaments in England are called Cups. The biggest and oldest—this year's is number 141—is the FA (or Football Association) Cup. It basically includes the entire pyramid; this year's Cup includes 737 teams. It starts in August with a series of preliminary qualifying rounds, and there is neither a bracket nor seeding. You take everybody in level 9, throw them into a basket, and start pulling out names. The first team is at home, the second away. If you draw, you play again at the other place. If that is a draw, you have penalty kicks.

After every round, the losers are done, and the winners get an ever-larger paycheck and go back into the basket, where they are joined by everybody in the next level up. I am simplifying to keep things moving. You're welcome.

The FA Cup starts to get really fun with the fourth qualifying round in mid-October and the first round proper in early November. By this time you've got all those level 5 and 6 clubs going at it, along with several from down below who have survived this far. These are clubs with a goalie who is also the club custodian or something, and they play in a stadium with like 435 seats. And remember, whoever comes out of that basket first plays at home, so some of these games are practically in cow pastures. Just to pick a random game from the 2017–18 fourth qualifying round: National Leaguers Macclesfield Town, known as the

Silkmen, got a 5–0 win at Stourbridge, known as the Glassboys, of the Northern Premier League Premier Division (level 7) before a crowd of 1,152!

After that, the pros come in and start cleaning up, but the first round proper (early November) and second round proper (early December) still have tiny clubs known as "minnows" playing clubs from League One and League Two. The Championship and Premier League clubs go in for the third round proper on the first weekend of January—an absolutely fantastic time to be there, aside from the weather. In 2019, I got to see Chichester City from tier 8 play at League One Tranmere Rovers; they lost, 5–1, but their lone goal will go down in club lore. Also, the clubs split the ticket sales evenly, so when a little club plays a big club, they would love to win of course, but a tie means a replay, and either a guaranteed sellout at home or a huge payday on the road. Imagine Yeovil Town getting almost half the gate from Old Trafford!

Sometimes you get tasty matchups like rivals who aren't in the same league at the moment. For example, Portsmouth and Southampton hate each other with a passion, but they are in different leagues and haven't played for years. If they get drawn together in the FA Cup, look out—and try to get a ticket. Visiting teams also get more tickets in the Cups, so in the 2017–18 third round proper, Liverpool and Everton got drawn together, leading to 8,000 Everton fans packing into Anfield (instead of the usual 3,000) to watch a thrilling 2–1 Liverpool win. Bonus Merseyside derby!

All of this leads up to the FA Cup final at Wembley Stadium in May. In the old days, this was the only game all year broadcast live on television, and it was simply the biggest day in all of football. It's still a big deal but now is more like the ceremonial end to the English football season.

By the way, the winner of the 2020–21 FA Cup was Leicester City, the first in their 137-year history. They had previously lost four Finals but had not been there since 1969.

These days, a lot of top teams treat the FA Cup as a second-rate tournament because staying in their current league or getting into Europe means more money. So a lot of them play reserves. For our purposes, tickets are cheaper, and they can be really fun games.

Speaking of second-rate tournaments, there is another Cup you should know about: The League Cup is just for the top ninety-two clubs, and it's even less important than the FA Cup. It's officially known as the Carabao Cup because it is sponsored by a Thai energy drink company (*carabao* actually translates as "red water buffalo"). It has previously been known as the Capital One Cup, the Carling Cup, and even the Milk Cup. Whatever you want to call it, Man City have won it four straight times.

Below that is the League Trophy, for League One and League Two, as well as others, all the way down into the world of regional amateur Cups, but let's move on.

PROMOTIONS, RELEGATIONS, AND EUROPEAN PLACES

From the Premier League down to the Championship:

- Sheffield United
- West Bromwich Albion
- Fulham

From the Football League Championship up to the Premier League:

- Norwich City
- Watford
- Brentford

From the Championship down to League One:

- Wycombe Wanderers
- Sheffield Wednesday
- Rotherham

From League One up to the Championship:

- Hull City
- Blackpool
- Peterborough United

From League One down to League Two:

- Bristol Rovers
- Swindon Town
- Rochdale
- Northampton Town

From League Two up to League One:

- Cheltenham Town
- Cambridge United

- Bolton Wanderers
- Morecambe

From League Two down to the National League (aka "non-league football")

- Grimsby Town
- Southend United

From the National League up to the Football League Two:

- Sutton United
- Hartlepool United

In the UEFA Champions League:

- Manchester City
- Liverpool
- Chelsea
- Manchester United

In the UEFA Europa League:

- Leicester City
- West Ham United

In the UEFA Europa Conference League:

- Tottenham Hotspur

You think it's fun watching this stuff on TV? Wait till you are at the ground seeing (and hearing) it in person!

Just to get you excited—and to point out some of the differences from my home country—here are some of the ways in which England does this stuff better than we Americans do.

SMALL STADIUMS

You may have watched, say, Arsenal on television and gotten the impression their stadium is gigantic. And it is—by English standards. It holds just over 60,000 people, meaning it is smaller than every American NFL stadium but one.

The biggest club stadium in England is Old Trafford, home of Manchester United, with about 75,000 seats. (There are at least three dozen college football stadiums in the United States bigger than that.) Otherwise, even some of the biggest names in the country have stadiums much smaller than you might think. Chelsea? 41,000. Liverpool? 54,000. Everton? 40,000. Crystal Palace? 26,000. Even in the Premier League, they go as small as 22,000 at Burnley. In most places in England, you're going to feel right on top of things.

GAMES IN THE MIDDLE OF TOWN

Americans are used to football stadiums located in suburbs and surrounded by parking lots. Basketball arenas are usually found either in the same environment or in soulless developed zones where no one goes except on game day. Most of us older folks, though, can remember when we walked through a neighborhood to get to the stadium, and that is mostly what English soccer is like.

Consider Chelsea: They are one of the biggest clubs in the world, with a cabinet full of trophies and a roster full of international stars. But their stadium, Stamford Bridge, is surrounded by homes and is about a two-minute walk from a Tube station in the middle of a busy neighborhood in South West London.

Many of these stadiums are being replaced now, and sadly some of the new ones tend to lack in atmosphere and charm. Seeing a match at one of the old stadiums in a town is one of the treats of this whole experience. (See page 352 for a list of the best.)

COVERED SEATING

The English season runs August to May, and for what seems half that time, it's raining and cold. But not to worry—almost all the seats are covered! Unless the wind is really blowing and you're down in front, you'll be dry. Not warm, necessarily, but that's why they have Bovril.

NEIGHBORHOOD RIVALRIES

You want rivalries? In the top two English leagues alone, 11 of the forty-four teams are in Greater London.

You can walk from Queens Park Rangers to Fulham to Chelsea and not go five miles. Tottenham and Arsenal are four miles apart in North London.

Still in just the top two leagues, there are four clubs in Greater Birmingham and two each in Manchester and Liverpool. There are also many other pairs of clubs, like Nottingham Forest and Derby County, which are in different towns but only sixteen miles apart.

BIG CROWDS OF VISITING FANS

In the States, in almost every sport, when the visiting team scores, you hear nothing but crickets. In the Premier League, the away team has to be given 3,000 tickets or 10 percent of the total seats if the stadium holds fewer than 30,000. In the Championship, it's 2,000 or 10 percent if under 20,000. These numbers all go up for a Cup game.

This, combined with the relatively small distances between clubs, means there are always visiting fans at the game, and most spend the whole game singing their guts out. You have noise all the time, you have banter among the fans, and if it's a rivalry, the place will be crackling with energy.

DAMN LITTLE JUMBOTRON NONSENSE

In America, attending a game is like sitting inside a TV broadcast with dance squads. They pipe in music, ads, constant sponsor announcements—the whole deal. In England, when the game starts, that is all there is: the game. They have a bit of pregame and halftime programming, but no interruptions during the game and only the occasional replay on the big screen. You will almost never see any kind of controversial replay on the screen either. I am only aware of one dance team in the entire country, the Crystals of Crystal Palace, but everyone seems to pretend they don't exist.

In fact, there are club stadiums with no scoreboard! Liverpool only added one in 2017, in fact.

SINGING AND CHANTING

At most stadiums, especially if the home team is doing at all well, the crowd provides a constant roar of singing and chanting. The visiting fans seem to take it as their job to keep up the noise, no matter what is happening. Even if the game is crap, the fans will just decide to have a go at one another. When it's a good game between two top teams, the atmosphere will simply blow your mind.

In fact, one of my favorite hobbies is trying to make out what people are singing. Unlike in many countries, where there is a lot of coordinated singing, in England it's almost entirely spontaneous. Nobody is in charge, the songs are tied to the action on the field, and sometimes it's quite funny what they come up with.

Awaiting kickoff at Queens Park Rangers; you're never far from the other fans at an English soccer game.

BUMS IN SEATS

"Bums in seats" is the English expression for selling tickets. But the way I use it here is to say that when the game starts, people are in their seats and *watching the game*. There is often not much conversation beyond talk about the game; people rarely leave, except toward the end of each half to beat the beer or exit lines; there are no vendors selling food and drink blocking the aisles. It's almost like being at a tennis match, except it's fun.

PEOPLE PAY SERIOUS ATTENTION

In England, if there is a breakaway opportunity and the final shot goes just wide or never happens, the whole stadium will be screaming at the useless piece of shite who didn't make that run at the back post or the wanker whose bad touch screwed up the whole thing. Or they may be listing the players' other recent sins or maybe grudgingly admitting their center back made a nice recovery run there.

In other words, the level of knowledge is quite high, as are the levels of attention being paid, passion, proximity, convenience, and sound. Welcome to English soccer.

The Ball Is Round: A Global History of Soccer by David Goldblatt. This is a comprehensive history of the game, which is to say it's massive, thick, tough to get through, incomparable, and indispensable.

The Game of Our Lives by David Goldblatt is honestly *the* book about English soccer. It picks up where *The Ball is Round* leaves off and focuses entirely on England and the UK over the last 30 years.

Fever Pitch by Nick Hornby. Two dumb movies (one of them American about the Boston Red Sox) have been made from this, but the real story is about our irrational relationship with the sport, not a Hollywood romance.

Hooper's Revolution by Dennie Wendt is a fun, silly novel based on the premise that soccer in America really is a communist plot, and it takes a hulking centerback from East Southwich Albion to save the day.

Dictionary of Football Club Nicknames in Britain and Ireland by Shaun Tyas. You might not think this topic rates 350 pages, but the author proves you wrong—and also introduces you to names like the Cider Army and the Wurzels.

Football Clichés by Adam Hurrey. Let's put it this way: the opening chapter is called "101 Ways to Score a Goal (or Not)" and explains very important distinctions like an impudent chip versus an exocet.

How Soccer Explains the World by Franklin Foer. Each chapter takes you to a different place and explains how soccer touches on a current theme: Brazil for corruption, Italy for the "new oligarchs," America for the culture wars.

Savage Enthusiasm by Paul Brown. A history of football fans—how they have evolved and why they (by which I mean we) care so much.

Bloody Confused!: A Clueless American Sportswriter Seeks Solace in English Soccer by Chuck Culpepper. A veteran sportswriter has lost all passion for the subject and so turns it into a job to be analyzed. And then he encounters Portsmouth FC. Hilarity ensues.

Who Are Ya?: The TalkSport Book of Football's Best Ever Chants by Gershon Portnoi. It's really hard to write about songs (trust me), but this book is at least a humorous and entertaining entry into the world of soccer singing.

The London Football Companion: A Site-by-Site Celebration of the Capital's Favourite Sport by Ed Glinert. Though it's almost ten years old, this book still holds up as a history of not only the game and the clubs in the capital but also the locations of random events in its history.

Turf Wars: A History of London Football by Steve Tongue. Another run at London, this one takes a bigger view and is written by a longtime professional journalist. It's also a bit more recent, having been published in 2016.

What We Think About When We Think About Soccer by Simon Critchley. A philosopher and Liverpool fan goes deep to answer the basic question about all of this: Why?

WEBSITES TO CHECK OUT

When Saturday Comes: wsc.co.uk. A fine all-purpose football magazine.

The Football Pink: footballpink.net. Another magazine, this one focusing mostly on history.

The London Football Guide: tlfg.uk. If somebody is playing soccer in London this week, dude has it.

The Londonist: londonist.com. An all-London blog that knocks out a dozen posts and videos every day.

Yanks Abroad: yanks-abroad.com. Tracking all the Americans playing all over the world.

Football Ground Guide: footballgroundguide.com. One of many such "away day" sites in the UK telling you how to get there and where it's safe for visiting fans to drink.

Football Ground Map: footballgroundmap.com. Create a free account, then log all the places you've been and learn about new ones to visit.

The 100 Grounds Club: 100groundsclub.blogspot.com. You think you've been to some clubs? The host of this blog has been to more than six hundred!

Goalden Times: goaldentimes.org. A worldwide football magazine with high-quality writing.

ON YOUTUBE

Groundhopper Guides: Our channel is packed with educational and entertaining videos, and we update it regularly.

Copa 90: Game reports, tactics discussions, fan experiences, club profiles, and more.

Copa 90 Stories: More specific content telling stories of supporter culture.

Football Away Days: Fun videos of fans being fans. Lots of hopping.

Tifo Football: If you want whiteboard videos explaining different teams' tactics.

You can find links to all of these, as well as new ones I come across, at groundhopperguides.com/links.

Let's briefly discuss the ladies, as they are almost always called in England. I enjoy talking about something America kicks ass at.

Women's soccer in England is roughly fifty years old. It was around before that—in fact, it was quite popular around World War I—but incredibly, the Football Association banned women's and girls' soccer being played on club members' grounds from 1921 until 1971. This effectively killed the game for decades.

In 1969 the Women's FA came about, and when the ban was lifted in 1971, the women's game came under the control of the national associations around Europe. The first Women's World Cup was held in 1991 and was won by the USA; they got their fourth in 2019. Since 1993 there has also been a Women's FA Cup in England. Arsenal have won it a record fourteen times, and Manchester City are the current champions from 2020, and have won it three of the past four years. The 2020-21 tournament is ongoing, with quarterfinal matches set to resume in late September. The final is scheduled for December 5, 2021 at Wembley Stadium. I should point out that the women's champion club receives less money than a men's first-round winner.

In England, women's teams are associated with the preexisting men's clubs. This means the financial system makes a lot more sense than in the United States, and the clubs are starting to throw some of that money around. Many of the top US international players have moved to English and European clubs to have the opportunity to play more games. For the 2021 season, the National Women's Soccer League in the United States has only ten clubs, with just three of those—including the Portland Thorns, the best-supported women's team in the world—associated with an existing MLS club.

In England, there is a pyramid of leagues, just as in the men's game, with the top two being the FA Women's Super League and FA Women's Championship. The third tier is the Women's Premier League, northern and southern divisions; the fourth tier is each of those split into two regional divisions; after that, it gets really small and really regional.

Typically, a club's women's team plays at the men's team practice facility or a smaller local club's ground. At the lower levels, it can be hard to track down fixture lists and game information, but wherever I can, I have listed them in the club profiles in this book.

If you are lucky enough to fly into London on a clear day and pass over the central part of the city, you are treated to one of the great city views on earth. You can also see quite a few football stadiums, if you know where to look.

The easiest way to start, assuming you fly over the northern part of the city (which seems to usually happen), is to look for massive Wembley Stadium on the north side of town. It's notable for its giant arch and bright-red seats.

Other locations of note for grounds spotters flying into the city:

- Bonus points for spotting The Hive, home of Barnet FC, just north of Wembley. Look for a bunch of soccer fields—one with a helicopter pad and hideous orange seats.
- Way up north and west of Wembley, you might see, in the middle of a residential area, the distinctive red and yellow seats at Vicarage Road, home of Watford FC.
- The Emirates, Arsenal's home, is also on the north side. It looks like a big, silver oval with a hole on top. It's massive and easy to spot. Nearby is their old stadium, much of which still exists. It got turned into apartments.
- The new Tottenham Hotspur Stadium is also in North London, northeast of Wembley and due north of Arsenal. It looks like a spaceship landed in a neighborhood.
- Stamford Bridge (Chelsea) is pretty central on the southwest side of the city and next to a big park with a keyhole-shaped structure in it. The blue seats have Chelsea on them in all capital letters.
- Fulham's Craven Cottage is right on the Thames, west of the center of London, and usually has something about Florida written on top of it. There is now a new stand right on the river.
- Due north of Craven Cottage is Queens Park Rangers' Loftus Road, a small rectangle with blue seats and two red roofs.
- Over on the east side of the city, look for the sprawling Olympic Park and West Ham's perfectly oval London Stadium with a bizarre-looking swirly red sculpture next to it.
- If you can spot the famous O2 Arena (it looks like a circus tent) on a bend in the Thames east of town, look just to the southeast for Charlton's The Valley, with cafc in huge letters on red seats.
- Just on the southeast side of the central city and south of the river, look for Millwall's home. It's between a railroad junction and a housing project, with The Den written in yellow on blue seats.

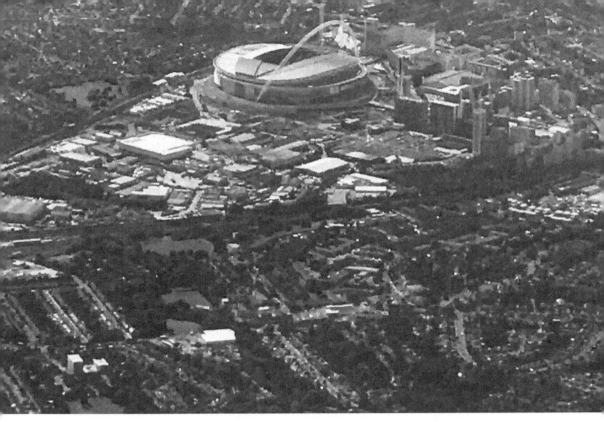

Wembley Stadium is easy to spot from the plane because of its famous arch.

- Especially if you're flying into Gatwick, you should see Selhurst Park, home of Crystal Palace. It's a rectangle whose sides don't match; one is huge and flat, one is tall and curved. The seats say Eagles.
- On final approach into Heathrow, if coming from over the main city, look for Brentford's new stadium, a silver structure surrounded by tall office buildings next to a major highway.
- Very near Brentford's ground is the national rugby stadium, the 82,000-seat Twickenham Stadium. But that's for another book.
- Farther southwest, look for the new Plough Lane at AFC Wimbledon, tightly hemmed in by housing.

I have a guide to this with a map and photos on my website at tinyurl.com/overlondon.

I stepped off the train, onto the platform, and into what I assumed would be the usual London-area train station: people coming and going, lively street down below, and if I was lucky, a coffee shop on the platform. This was particularly true as I had only come one stop from bustling London Bridge.

But South Bermondsey station is just a platform with nothing on it but a tiny, three-sided wind shelter. On both sides are dark rooftops above mostly dark windows. On both sides are dark rooftops above mostly dark windows. A damp wind whipped across the scene. In the distance I could see what I had just left—the shining and colorful towers of Central London—but here I felt, and largely was, alone and away from everything.

I had come to see a game at Millwall Football Club, which is to say I had somehow traveled back in time to when football was local and personal, intense, and at times a bit horrifying.

Beyond the station, where a special walkway "for away supporters only" was guarded by two police officers, I saw a single strip of a handful of shops: Indian food, barber, burgers, and a chippy. I decided to head for the ground and look for something else along the way.

I instead saw an RV park, a trucking firm, a tire shop, more dark side streets…and then the ground. Heading in to pick up my ticket, I saw a group of around a hundred supporters waiting by the player and staff entrance, and I thought, *It's nice that they still line up to welcome their heroes.* Later I would chuckle at this bit of naïveté.

I got my ticket and headed the other way on the street to look for food. I found instead more industry. Taking out my phone, I saw there was a rated chippy nearby, so I headed for that. After fifteen minutes' walking past housing estates, I found a solid place called Express, where I emerged from the chaos within carrying a proper and tasty cod and chips.

I decided to eat and then walk, only to realize I had forgotten to grab a fork. *Not going back in there, thanks!* So I ate with my hands, barbarian style, on a side street, and felt a bit conspicuous—or I would have, but for wave after wave of young men, beers in their hands, stumbling and weaving and singing their way toward the football ground, and occasionally sending out group volleys of long "Miiiiiiiiiiiiiiiilllll." I dug into my fish shamelessly and even shot some "what are you looking at" glances at non-footy locals.

Following the colors as always, I traversed a walkway littered with the same kind of chippy boxes I was eating from. Graffiti on the walls, a towering factory of some sort behind a fence, overflowing rubbish bins, another tire shop—not exactly a romantic approach.

I got to my seat, down low on the side as always with a good view of the away fans. On this night it was Queens Park Rangers, from just a few miles away across London, and I was hoping for a little derby atmosphere. Before kickoff, things felt rather sweet around me, with old friends and regulars greeting each other, checking in about their holidays, wondering how the team will fare. The usual.

Waiting for their man at The Den.

Speaking of the usual, the PA system played the Clash's "London Calling," which is apparently required by an Act of Parliament at all games in the capital, and the crowd belted out "I live by the river!" Also required. I felt nearly at home.

The teams came out, and the PA played the Millwall version of one of those old '80s soccer songs, "Let 'Em Come." It's got lines about jellied eels and glasses of beer and everything. The crowd sang along in great voice with the last line, "Let 'em all come down…to The Den!" I thought, *I love it when they sing these old-fashioned songs!* Then they busted out the last bit of "Hey Jude," replacing those words with "Millwall"—but they somehow managed to say their club's name without pronouncing a single letter *l*.

I was grateful to be among an honest, enthusiastic football crowd for an evening London derby.

That was the last happy thought I had for a while, because just after the music ended, everyone around me began to sing, even louder than they had before:

Ole, ole ole ole,
You cunt!
You cunt!

Now, I have heard people say *cunt* before, and I used to work on a fishing boat, so I wasn't offended. But with that ringing in my ears, I had a hard time reconciling what I was seeing two rows in front of me, which was a man, sixtyish, standing on his seat, looking around to encourage the singers to new levels, screaming himself hoarse already…and right next to him what appeared to be his grandchildren! They were two girls and couldn't have been north of fourteen. For all the *cunts* and *wankers* and *bastards* and *fuck-offs* flying around them, I have to say they didn't look upset, worried, or even surprised. I guessed this is what they do at Millwall.

A quick glance at Twitter informed me this wasn't a standard pregame ritual. I saw a video of that crowd I had seen waiting for the coach earlier, with the opposing manager walking off and that whole ensemble singing the same cunt song at him. He was playing along, with a hand to an ear, and when he actually disembarked, there was a moment when I thought the crowd might go for him. And I had thought they were waiting for their heroes!

Off to the web I went to determine that it wasn't "ole" they were singing, it was "Ollie," short for Ian Holloway, who had committed two unforgivable sins in combination: he was in charge at Millwall in a bad year that saw them relegated to League One, and (perhaps worse) he had arrived here from South London rivals Crystal Palace. The former was a disaster, the latter would be something like Hillary Clinton on the Republican ticket, and the combination made Holloway, in Millwall World, a proper cunt who needed to be reminded of his cunt status.

All. Night. Long.

There was, in fact, a game that evening. Millwall scored a goal, QPR didn't, the action was fairly even, neither of them was likely to go up or down that season, and it's vaguely possible that someone outside of South or West London gave a crap. Where I stood, the goal only served to let the Millwall fans get the upper hand on the QPR lot in the end and mix in a song about how Holloway is "gonna hide in the dugout."

QPR sang that Millwall's support is fucking shit, and Millwall responded with wanker signs and a mocking cheer. Millwall did their famous song "No one likes us, we don't care," and QPR responded with "No one likes you, 'cause you're shit." QPR taunted Millwall when some of "us" thought a side-netter was a goal, and Millwall taunted Holloway with "You're gettin' sacked in the morning."

Then some fool in the QPR end—this is my favorite—decided to stand on a rail, raise his arms, and invite an entire stand of Millwall supporters to "come on, ya fuckers," to the massive amusement of those across the way. The amusement was greatly heightened when a steward led him down the tunnel, but not before he ran out and gave them one more "come on!" gesture.

I spent much of my evening trying to catalog the various adjectives that I heard used before *cunt.* They included—and this is truly a partial list—*fat, ugly, useless, goddamn, fucking, horrible, horrific, lazy,* and *poofy.* That last one pretty much means "gay," because hey, might as well do the double.

It ended at 1–0, pulling Millwall up to about fifteenth in the table, but the crowd was joyous. Not only did they beat the wankers from across town, they got to remind that cunt

Ollie where he stands over and over, and they joined in with a musical selection post-match: "Down to The Den," "Rockin' All Over the World," and "Sweet Caroline." Well after the game was over, a last few Millwallers in the upper section were still standing on rails, giving the fuckers in the end a "come on!" or two. Half-hearted wanker signs were all the response QPR could muster as they shuffled off down the ramps.

As for me, I stuck around to take some stadium pictures and wound up helping out with a picture of ten groundhopping Belgians who were still shaking their heads at what we had just seen. Then I headed into the night, back to the windswept platform, onto the train where supporters seemed to have become human again, and down to South London to my safe, civilized English friends' home.

All along the way, there were really two of me having a bit of a disagreement. One said, "I need never return to this shithole again," while the other called it a proper old-fashioned football experience. That one also rejected many of the decency advances of late (aka political correctness) and thought Ollie's greeting hilarious, but the other considered it absolutely juvenile. What on earth makes "adults" act this way? One said atmosphere, the other said vulgarity. One said honest and real, the other said role-playing. One said, "When's the next real derby?" the other said, "Fuck you, never again."

But both of me agreed that, at the end of the night, it's just football, and it's just fucking Millwall.

Postscript: A version of this story on my website got around 20,000 visits. The nearly universal response among Millwall supporters was "You actually get us, and we know you'll be back." Among non-Millwall people, it was "They're fucking animals, aren't they?"

MAKING PLANS

When looking for the best time to go to England for some games, use these pages to find a high concentration of games: midweek, Cup and European ties, and so on.

Barring a massive resurgence in Covid cases, we think this will be a fairly normal season in terms of the schedule.

Even in normal times, though, two main factors bring schedule changes as the season rolls along:

- Premier League and Championship games, all set initially for Saturday at 3:00 p.m., will be moved for television broadcast to other times on Saturday, to Sunday, and maybe even to Friday or Monday evening. This typically happens about six weeks before the weekend in question. I keep a list of these dates for the Premier League at tinyurl.com/epltelly.
- As teams advance in the FA Cup, League (Carabao) Cup, or European competitions, some of their league games may move—sometimes by a day or two, sometimes by weeks.

Still, the structure is here, accounting mainly for Cups, European competitions, and stretches when the Premier League and Championship don't play due to international breaks. I have also listed when there are games during the week—an excellent way to see more games during a shorter trip.

There is a graphic representation of all this at groundhopperguides.com/calendar.

KEY:
- League and Cup games will show here as being on one day, but they will actually be played over several days that weekend.
- "Midweek" means Tuesday and/or Wednesday.
- Football League = Championship, League One, League Two.
- "European games" means Champions League Tuesday and Wednesday, Europa League and Europa Conference League Thursday.

If you don't see a weekend listed here, assume all the leagues are playing.

AUGUST 2021
7: Football League starts
10: League Cup First Round

17: Midweek Football League

14: Premier League Starts

24: League Cup Second Round

SEPTEMBER 2021

4: International Break; Leagues One and Two only

14-16: European Group stages, midweek Football League

21: League Cup Third Round

28-30: European Group stages, midweek Football League

OCTOBER 2021

9: International Break; Leagues One and Two only

19-21: European Games, midweek Football League

26: League Cup Fourth Round

NOVEMBER 2021

2-4: European Group Stages, midweek Football League

6: FA Cup First Round (Leagues One and Two enter)

13: International Break; Leagues One and Two only

23-25: European Group Stages, midweek Football League

30: Midweek Premier League

DECEMBER 2021

6: FA Cup Second Round, Premier League, Championship

7-9: European Group Stages, midweek Football League

14: Midweek Premier League

21: League Cup Quarterfinals

26: Boxing Day, all leagues play

28: All leagues play

JANUARY 2022:

1: All leagues play

4: League Cup Semifinals

8: FA Cup Third Round (Premier League and Championship enter)

11: League Cup Semifinals

FEBRUARY 2022

5: FA Cup Fourth Round, Football League

8-9: Midweek all leagues

15-16: Champions League Round of 16

17: Europa League Playoffs

22-23: Champions League Round of 16, midweek Football League

24: Europa League Playoffs

27: League Cup Final at Wembley

MARCH 2022

1: FA Cup Fifth Round

8-10: European Round of 16

15: Midweek Football League

15-17: European Round of 16, midweek Football League

19: FA Cup Quarterfinals

26: International break, Leagues One and Two only

APRIL 2022

5-7: European Quarterfinals

12-14: European Quarterfinals

15: Good Friday Football League games

16-17: FA Cup Semifinals at Wembley

18: Easter Monday Football League games

26-28: European Semifinals

30: League One last day

MAY 2022

3-5: European Semifinals

7: Championship and League Two last day

14: FA Cup Final at Wembley

21: League One Playoff Final at Wembley

22: Premier League last day

26: Europa League Final in Seville, Spain

28: Champions League Final in St. Petersburg, Russia

28: League Two Playoff Final at Wembley

29: Championship Playoff Final at Wembley

Look for regular updates at groundhopperguides.com.

TOP DERBIES THIS SEASON

Nothing beats a derby match, when two sets of supporters who loathe each other find themselves in the same ground for ninety minutes of yelling, screaming, singing, and occasionally even some good soccer.

With the usual disclaimer that actual dates might change a bit for television or Cup ties, especially in the Premier League, here are the best rivalry games to watch for this season in the top two tiers:

Premier League:
- Manchester Derby, City vs. United: November 6 at United, March 5 at City
- Merseyside Derby, Liverpool vs. Everton: November 30 at Everton, April 23 at Liverpool
- North London Derby, Tottenham vs. Arsenal: January 15 at Tottenham, September 26 at Arsenal
- Crystal Palace vs. Brighton and Hove Albion: September 27 at Palace, January 15 at Brighton
- Tottenham vs. Chelsea: January 22 at Chelsea, September 19 at Tottenham
- Liverpool vs. Manchester United: March 19 at Liverpool, October 23 at United
- West Ham vs. Chelsea: April 23 at Chelsea, December 4 at West Ham
- West Midlands Derbies, Aston Villa vs. Wolverhampton: October 16 at Villa, April 2 at Wolverhampton
- Leeds vs. Manchester United: August 14 at Manchester United, February 19 at Leeds

Championship:
- West London (QPR vs. Fulham): October 16 at Fulham, April 2 at QPR
- East Midlands (Derby County vs. Nottingham Forest): January 22 at Forest, August 28 at Derby County
- South Wales (Cardiff City vs. Swansea City): April 2 at Cardiff, October 16 at Swansea
- West Lancashire (Blackpool vs. Preston North End): October 23 at Blackpool, March 19 at Preston
- West Midlands (Birmingham vs. West Bromwich Albion): October 16 at West Brom, April 2 at Birmingham

If you aren't set on a particular club, then how do you decide which game to see? I use the following questions as a guide to making this decision.

WHERE WILL YOU BE?

If you're in London, you will have tons of choices. To get a sense of this, check out the amazing blog *The London Football Guide* (tlfg.uk). In other cities, you will have fewer options but still more than you might think.

Vacationing in Bath, for example? There are two clubs twelve miles away in Bristol (City and Rovers). There are some other common tourist destinations with clubs: Oxford, Cambridge, Norwich, and Nottingham, for example.

In Manchester or Liverpool? There are about two dozen clubs within an hour or two by train. In Newcastle? Several to choose from.

I have a helpful and up-to-date map of the top six levels of the pyramid at groundhopper guides.com/clubs.

WHEN WILL YOU BE THERE?

With four main leagues, two domestic Cup competitions, and three European competitions, plus the occasional international break when a lot fewer clubs play, tracking the schedule can be a challenge. I have a complete look at this season's schedule on page 39.

If you're looking at a schedule—especially for the Premier League—more than about six weeks before the game, you will see they are all scheduled for 3:00 p.m. Saturday. But at some point the TV folks will move one to noon, another one or two to 5:00 p.m., a couple to Sunday, maybe one to Monday—all on about six weeks' notice. And they could be moved to a whole different week for a Cup game! So you have to pay attention.

HOW WILLING ARE YOU TO TRAVEL?

Let's say you're in London but are willing to take a little trip to get out of the city and see a game. While English people think a two-hour train ride is a long journey, I say you can have breakfast in London, be in another town for a 3:00 p.m. game, and be back in London by dinner. So places like Sheffield, Bristol, even Hull, Norwich, the South Coast, or South Wales are all more accessible than you might think.

If you're wondering about train times, London to Birmingham is about ninety minutes, Manchester is about two hours, and Liverpool is about two and a half.

UP FOR THE LOWER LEAGUES?

If you want to see a smaller, more accessible club (and have an easier time with tickets), check out a Championship game, or League One, or go really small-time with League Two. That is truly a family, neighborhood experience. In these lower leagues, there are nearly two dozen clubs around Greater London, for example. Chances are you'll be the only foreigner there, a real change from the big Premier League clubs.

HOW WILL THE ATMOSPHERE BE?

I want to see everybody eventually, but I prioritize games with a good atmosphere. Here are some factors I look for:

- How close are the two teams? Just plug their names into Google Maps and check the distance. This will determine how many visiting fans will be there and how much singing there will be.
- Is it a rivalry (or a "derby")? Usually this corresponds to distance but not always. You wouldn't think Brighton and Crystal Palace are rivals, but they are. Check the club chapters here or the clubs' Wikipedia pages for their main rivals.
- Where are the two teams in the table? If they are both up high, this means it's a high-stakes game. If they are both down low, it's a relegation scrap! Either can be exciting, with the crowd really into it.
- Is it a potential giant-killing Cup game? In other words, is a big club visiting a small one or vice versa? This makes for some good action—and perhaps something historic, like seeing Sunderland win at Manchester United in front of 9,000 of their fans, which I got to do once.

HOW OLD IS THE GROUND?

I love the old grounds, so I always check the Wikipedia page of the club I'm considering to see if they are still in the old place (like Everton), if there has been a lot of remodeling (like Liverpool), or if it's one of the new, generic places (like Reading).

I have a list of the best old grounds on page 352.

WHAT ELSE IS THERE TO DO IN TOWN?

Maybe your whole group doesn't want to go to the game, so what else would they do in town? Or what will you do before and after?

In London this is a breeze; same for Manchester or Liverpool (especially if somebody is into The Beatles). But maybe you want to hit the coast, hence Brighton, Bournemouth, Southampton, or Portsmouth. If you're headed north, maybe going to Scotland, swing through Newcastle for one of the clubs in the North East (Durham and its famous cathedral are just down the road as well). Nottingham is awesome, with two clubs and all the Robin Hood stuff. Bristol, near Bath, is a great little city.

Just check the town on Wikipedia or TripAdvisor and see what you come up with. If you can find a nearby game with visitors who are also from nearby and two pretty good teams, available tickets, a cool old ground, and something else to do in town—or a decent combination of any of these—you have yourself a winner. Go forth and enjoy.

Remember to keep an eye on the schedule for changes!

(Of course, you can also pay me for a consultation, and I'll do all this work for you—and even help with tickets! Check out tinyurl.com/soccertrips for more.)

So here we are at the big question: How do you get tickets to actually see these games?

There is a lot to discuss here, so I will try to winnow it down for you. Let's start with some basics.

HOW CLUBS ALLOCATE TICKETS

Let's say that Groundhopper FC has a home game coming up. First, all the season ticket holders of course get their seats automatically. Then about six weeks out, they will get a chance to buy another ticket or two, depending on how big a game it is. (You'll see references to Category A and B matches, for example.) After a week of that, paid club members get a chance to buy a ticket, or maybe more, again depending on the match.

This is where loyalty points come in. Every time a member buys a ticket, they earn points. Those with the most points go first, so Groundhopper FC might say that, starting five weeks out, the number of points required to get tickets drops every few days. As you might imagine, if you are brand-new to this—even if you're a member—you won't have any points. So you have to wait for general sale, which usually happens as little as a few weeks before the game—if the members didn't snap everything up.

Many clubs also have a ticket exchange on their website that allows season ticket holders who can't make a game to resell their tickets. Sometimes this is handled by a third-party website, but either way, access to this area is restricted to paid members. I've gotten single tickets this way to see some of the big boys, but two or more together is really hard.

If you're trying to buy from a club, it's critical to pay attention to on-sale dates. You might have to dig around on the club website to find them, but sometimes being a day late means not getting a ticket. Don't forget the time zone difference!

NOT ALL CLUBS OR MATCHES ARE THE SAME

Imagine four levels of difficulty—and by difficulty, I really mean cost. No game is impossible to get into, but some will be crazy expensive. We'll get to that in a bit. The four levels are:

1. **Two of the big six playing each other.** This would be Arsenal, Chelsea, Liverpool, Manchester City, Manchester United, and Tottenham Hotspur. None of these will come anywhere close to general sale. Virtually all Champions League games also sell out before reaching general sale.
2. **A big six club at home against a non–big six club.** Here, you might get a general sale, or a begging call to the ticket office might pay off, but your level of difficulty goes up with each ticket you want. Tickets for Europa League group games and meaningless Champions League group games share this level of difficulty.

3. **Derbies and big-at-little Cup games.** No matter which club is hosting a big rival or one of the big boys in a Cup, tickets will be really hard. You might get one, *maybe* two, but more than that together won't happen.
4. **Everything else.** Anything not in a category above is basically a walk-up, but you still might want to buy ahead of time to make sure and to pick your seats. (See "Where to Sit" on page 50.)

WHAT DOES IT COST?

To get into a Premier League match, assuming you can even get a ticket from the club, expect to pay something along the lines of £35 to £50. In the lower leagues, you typically pay about £25 to £40. Kids are usually around £10 to £15. For Cup games, I have seen regular tickets as low as £10, and sometimes for Cups they run a "kids for a quid" promotion that makes for a real family atmosphere.

HOSPITALITY PACKAGES

This is basically a seat plus something else, like a hotel room, food, booze, lounge access, a stadium tour, a city bus tour, and so on. Sometimes it's a regular seat; sometimes it's a padded seat; sometimes it's actually in a suite or box. The story here is that, technically, it is illegal to resell a football ticket in the UK *at any price*. Any tickets resold have to be part of a package, and both the package and the seller have to be approved by regulators.

All clubs sell hospitality directly to the public, and costs are all over the place, depending on who is playing whom. Check club websites or call their offices for info.

Approved brokers also buy blocks of these for every home game and then resell them either straight to the public or through another level of reseller. And as it happens, I am an official reseller, through a different broker, of hospitality packages for many clubs in England and Europe. So get in touch at groundhopperguides.com!

The cost of these, again, is all over the place. For a big six club at home, expect to pay $200 or more if they're not playing a big six and $400 or more if they are. For Champions League or Cup semifinals and finals, everything is about $500 and up. And yes, those are all per person.

CUPS: EASIER TO GET INTO

If you're determined to, say, get into Old Trafford to see Manchester United, you might not care who they're playing. Unless you can afford hospitality, you won't see them play Liverpool or Chelsea, but you have a decent chance at some of the lower-level games (category 2 above).

One thing to watch for here is Cup games. They tend to be during the week and, at least in earlier rounds, against smaller opponents. I got killer seats at Old Trafford for about £40 for a League Cup game on a Tuesday night in January. It was a semifinal leg, but it was the David Moyes season, and the fans were losing faith. Also, the opponents were Sunderland, not one of

Liverpool home hospitality ticket—a prized piece of paper!

the heavyweights of the sport. But Sunderland brought 9,000 fans to the game and won in a penalty shootout, so it was easily one of the most memorable sporting experiences of my life.

That's another fun thing about Cup games: There will be more away fans due to Cup rules. Keep in mind, though, that if a big club is playing a small club at home, they will probably rest a lot of their stars.

One more thing on Cup tickets: pay attention to when the draws for each round are announced; it's usually right after the previous round is finished.

BUYING AWAY TEAM TICKETS

Some folks ask me, "If I want to see Chelsea but can't get a ticket at Stamford Bridge, why not go see them someplace else?" There are two answers to this.

One, you will never in a thousand lifetimes get an away ticket from Chelsea unless a very good friend of yours has been to a ton of Chelsea away games. This has to do with the loyalty point scheme above, and you will never get enough points. I know longtime season ticket holders at big clubs who can't get to away games.

Otherwise, you can go see Chelsea play away by buying a ticket from the home club and sitting in the home end. Understand, though, that if you or your sixteen-year-old Chelsea-nut son wears Chelsea colors and/or cheers when they score a goal, you will be removed from the stadium for your own protection. They do not mess around with opposing fans mixing together.

THE SECONDARY MARKET

Now we're on to StubHub and their ilk. Here you should know a new word: those whom we call scalpers, they call touts.

Understand that almost any ticket you buy on any website like this is an illegal purchase. (At premierleague.com, there is a long list of unapproved ticket sales websites.) This doesn't mean you'll get ripped off or in trouble, but it does mean you will have limited recourse if you do get ripped off—especially if you figure this out at the turnstile. You might get your money back, but you'll miss the game. The exception is that a few clubs work with StubHub or someone else to handle their resale business.

I have worked with a lot of people on getting tickets, and many of them wind up going with the secondary market because of the cost of hospitality packages. I never hear from most of them again, so I assume it went okay. But every now and then, I hear one of these complaints:

- "The seats were terrible and not where I thought they would be."
- "I didn't get the tickets until right before the game, and we were all freaking out."
- "I had to meet the guy afterward to give the card back."
- "I got ripped off."

My one and only experience with any kind of secondary market was using Craigslist to get into a Liverpool home game in the FA Cup against Plymouth Argyle of League Two. That was in 2015, and even then, I only did it because it was a season ticket holder who walked through the gates with us (we used her cards to get in then handed them back). She then stood with us in her seats, taught us songs, and showed us a great time. We bought her a few pints for her trouble.

If you've decided which game to go to and figured out how to get tickets, you should think about where to sit—assuming you have any choice in the matter, which outside the Premier League, you almost certainly will.

For some people, this is pretty simple: the best seats possible, typically defined as close to the center stripe and close to the pitch. I would argue, though, that being too close to the pitch is not ideal, because you want to have a wider view of the action. You want to see the passing angles, have an uncluttered view of the far side of the pitch, and so on.

Some people prefer sitting behind a goal, mainly because there's a lot of action there, and you could see a goal scored right in front of you. Also, if you're into such things, the most vocal and rowdy home fans are usually behind a goal.

I take some of these things into account—I do prefer being between the goals instead of behind one—but the main thing I look for when picking a seat is one with a good view of the away fans.

This may not have occurred to you, but—especially at bigger clubs—there will be up to 3,000 away fans packed into a corner together singing their guts out all night. At a lower-league club, there could be just as many and in a smaller stadium. At Cup games there could be more.

After all, the singing and atmosphere are part of what you will enjoy about seeing English soccer in person. Why not make the most of it? I like to try and make out what they are singing. I also like to see—and take videos of—away fans in case their team scores in front of them. They go "absolutely mental."

Sometimes, if you can't get a good view of the away fans, you want to sit near them so you can enjoy some of the banter between the home and away fans. This may be the only way to enjoy a crappy game, since the fans will decide the day is a waste and they might as well have a go at one another.

If you can't sit near them or across from them, it can be fun (though tricky) to be amongst them. I have done that a couple of times as a Fulham fan. That can be pretty intense, though, since the away fans tend to be the rowdy ones. Well, they do if they aren't Fulham fans. As I said above, though, getting away tickets is tough at bigger clubs.

I use footballgroundguide.com to find out where the visitors sit, but sometimes it's shown on the seating chart when you're choosing your tickets. You could also just call the club and tell them where you want to sit.

AT THE GROUND

You want to go to a game, but you don't want to annoy your neighbors or get in trouble, right? So what are some common dos and don'ts at English soccer games?

Here are some I can think of along with some simple suggestions to make it a more enjoyable day.

Get there well before kickoff. You want to catch the pregame pageantry, such as the players coming out and fans singing traditional songs, and you also don't want to be that person coming in after kickoff. In the UK, that person is quite rare. And getting there may well take longer than you think—especially in London.

Don't plan to get up while the game is on. One of my favorite things about English soccer is the lack of people walking around during the game; there aren't even food or drink vendors going around. People sit and pay attention to the game—what a concept.

Remember it is illegal to take alcohol to your seat. You will probably find, as some of my consulting clients have, that you really like this feature.

Study up on the teams you'll be watching, especially the one whose fans you're sitting with. It will add to your enjoyment, but it's also a good way to strike up a conversation with your neighbor. For example, if it's a Manchester City fan, ask if they saw Agüero score *that* goal.

Watch your colors. While studying up, check for the primary colors both of today's opponent and your neighbors' biggest rival. Don't wear either. I made the mistake of wearing a red coat into Everton's Goodison Park once—when they weren't even playing Liverpool. Won't happen again.

If you're cheering against your immediate neighbors...don't. Keep your loyalties to yourself, unless you're surrounded by the same. And don't wear anything official for the wrong team either. You'll probably get tossed—for your own safety.

Put away your colors outside the ground if you're one of the away fans. The only time I felt remotely unsafe at an English soccer game was when I assumed, wrongly, that no Sheffield United fans could possibly have an issue with little ol' Fulham. It was a nervous walk to the station after a bitter draw. Remember the safety rule: it only takes one nut job to cause trouble.

Learn some of the songs. When your neighbors start singing some of their favorites, or even a common classic, stand up and have a go!

Don't ask your neighbors to explain the offside rule (or anything else) to you. Many of them will assume that foreigners are ignorant of the game and culture; don't prove them right! Learn offside before you go. And it's not "offsides."

Toss a (single) friendly line at your neighbor to see if they want to chat. "Fancy your chances?" is a good one to start with. You could also ask about a song or something else, then say, "It's my first time here." If they don't respond to this, leave them alone! If they smile and ask where you're from…game on!

Understand there are different rules for the above at big-time Premier League clubs and lower-league outfits. At clubs like Chelsea and Arsenal, tourists are common, and the locals might be less amenable to chatting. At a place like Blackburn Rovers, you might become something of an attraction. This also happened to me at West Ham's old ground once; I fell in with a group of old-timers cracking each other up while the Hammers got, well, hammered by Man City. They thought it was great having an American to entertain.

The bottom line is that what you think is a fun distraction, for them might be close to life or death. So don't get in their way of enjoying it, but also give them a chance to share it with you.

As you travel around the world of English football, you will meet—or at least see and hear—a lot of people. In my experience, they tend to fall into a handful of categories or types. Allow me to introduce you to them.

THE COACH

This is usually the man (it's always a man) you'll hear the most, barking instructions at the players who, of course, can't hear him and wouldn't listen anyway. He always wants them to run faster, go forward, pass to the open man, cut off every opposition run, intercept every opposition pass, win every ball in the air, win every second ball, switch it, close down every opposing player, drive them all wider, and do more vague things like "do him," "get into him," "get wider," and, above all, "fucking move!"

He summarizes all of this thusly: Do the simple thing, lads!

I have actually calculated that for all of the Coach's instructions to be followed, one would have to replace whichever eleven players he is "cheering" for with the fourteen greatest footballers in history.

Signature Phrase: "For fuck's sake!"

THE SONG STARTER

Also male, he is considerably younger—rarely above thirty. No matter the weather, he will be wearing jeans somehow both saggy and tight, a short-sleeved shirt, and (often) some product in his hair. He arrives on the scene mostly to make noise, which he might refer to as "havin' a go." He seems to bounce a lot. Above all, he despises silence and desires to be heard, and also to instigate noise all around him.

He is a leader among the 20Something Males with Product in Their Hair (see below).

If something has just happened—*something* being defined as an event on the pitch or the arrival of a silent moment—he will call out the first few words to a song or chant. This may be indistinguishable to you as English, especially after it's picked up by the other 20Somethings. The extent to which it spreads into the rest of the crowd determines how much scorn he heaps upon those wankers sitting farther away.

Signature Phrase: I can rarely make it out, to be honest.

THE 20SOMETHING MALE WITH PRODUCT IN HIS HAIR

This character, who can also be simply called a lad, exists in a swarm around the Song Starter. They are utterly indistinguishable as individuals to any human above the age of thirty-two. They travel in packs of three to seven, and they speak very quickly with accents beyond the comprehension of anyone not native to the United Kingdom. They drink, though not terribly heavily; they sing, though not particularly strongly; they pay attention to the game, though not in terribly great detail. In all ways, they move very, very fast—in a blur, really.

The main purposes of the 20Something Male with Product in His Hair are to fill the seats and amplify whatever the Song Starter, as well as the various pack leaders among their numbers, are up to. Their goal, to the extent to which they are individuated, seems to be only to get better at their purposes by observing each other and the pack leaders.

Signature Phrase: Whatever a leader just said.

THE BROODER

The Brooder is, of course, sitting alone. He's also male—roughly 90 percent of the crowd is—and speaks to no one. He doesn't sing, though he might stand on occasion.

He looks at his phone often and, if he is between thirty-five and fifty, may have a blog. He doesn't appear to drink, eat, move around, or even be alive—aside from the fact that his eyes are open and aimed generally toward the pitch. One assumes he is there to watch the game and is thus aware of it, but one can't be sure, for the Brooder mostly appears to simply brood.

Signature Phrase: N/A

THE 30SOMETHING WEARING A CLUB SHIRT

This is, in some ways, the saddest of the characters. He is, of course, a graduate of sorts from the ranks of the 20Somethings with Product in Their Hair, but he has lost his youth, his crew, and his thinness. He is now alone and a bit too old to really be with the lads, though he stands with or near them. But he is also too rowdy to sit with the Pensioners and Middle-Aged Randos.

This character seems to be living in the past, unable or unwilling to step into the future, his identity tied up with the club to an extent that should really make everyone just a bit uncomfortable. His gut hangs out just a bit, and he hasn't bounced for years. Most people seem to try not to notice, much less engage, him.

He is, not surprisingly, the heaviest drinker among the characters.

Signature Phrase, directed at the other team's fans: "Eh, ya fuckin' wankahs."

THE SINGLE FEMALE

This is a certain version of the Brooder, though of course she is female, and therefore less…brooding. She sits alone, thereby attracting the attention of various males, though none of them approach.

One assumes she supports the club because she is known to stand and clap when something positive happens, but she doesn't exactly sing. She pays less attention to her phone than the Brooder and more attention to the game, it would appear, than the 20Somethings. She is probably in her thirties, and it is unclear whether she enjoys the game or the male surroundings more.

Your author is determined to investigate the motivations and desires of the Single Female; further information will be, he hopes, forthcoming.

Signature Phrase: "Yay."

THE DATE

As in the real world, the Date is a combination of youngish male and female. (I recognize, of course, it could be two males or two females, but these would be lost in a pack of 20Somethings.) On rare occasions, the male part of the Date is actually a 20Something with Product in His Hair, but even then, the couple sits apart from the pack—either so she might be safer or so he might be less likely to discourage her interest by calling someone on the pitch a useless cunt.

Occasionally, one can spot the male part of the Date gazing longingly at the 20Something pack. Part of him would rather be in the pack, another part in her—thus the conflict. The female, meanwhile, is better dressed than the average female in the stands, and if she's a Fulham or Cambridge fan, there's an excellent chance she's very attractive—and utterly disinterested in the game.

Signature Phrase: Unknown, as it is whispered between them.

THE MIDDLE-AGED RANDOS

These are, one might assume, simply older versions of the 20Somethings with Product in Their Hair. And they probably used to be in that lot; however, they have gone through an important transition since those days, a transition known as life. In their twenties, they were doing as pack animals do. Now in their forties and fifties, and almost always traveling in pairs, they really just want to meet at the pub, catch a game, cuss, fart, drink perhaps a pint too much, analyze the Single Females and the female parts of the Date, and just basically get the fuck away for an afternoon and be a fucking lad again, for fuck's sake.

Signature Phrase: A sort of resigned groan.

THE PENSIONER

He has been attending games since the old days, and if you want to believe in Santa Claus and/or elves, simply ask him about those old days and wait for him to smile. The Pensioner twinkles. He was a lad when you could stand on the terraces for ten pence, when the players wore work boots and wool socks, the ball weighed five stone, and giants strode the earth. In the United States, this would be the guy at Yankee Stadium who saw Babe Ruth play. All male characters desire to one day be a Pensioner. In fact, the Pensioner is often attended, almost bodyguard-style, by admiring Middle-Aged Randos, perhaps his sons.

The Pensioner also exists in two versions: Happy and Bitter. The Happy version always has supported the team through thick and thin, came here when his dad hoisted him over the turnstiles and now comes with his grandkids, and just loves the club; he probably wants his ashes scattered on the pitch. The Bitter Pensioner is usually a former Coach and would love to explain how today's players are soft, overpaid wankers and how money (and foreigners, if he's been drinking) has ruined the sport.

It is worth noting that in the old days, there were almost certainly Pensioners in the stands, treating everyone to stories of the 19th century.

Signature Phrase: "I was here the day…"

THE MUM

The Mum is actually my favorite character to observe, for like the Pensioner, she exists in two forms, and I love watching to see which she is. Sweet Mum is there with a family, and whether she really gives a crap about the game or not is unclear and irrelevant; she is there because the family is there. She loves her kids, loves family time, and spends most of the game asking the kids if they're having fun, pointing out the "cute" mascot/animal on the pitch that everyone else thinks is a fucking wanker, and keeping an eye on her husband, who without fail is either a 30Something with a Club Shirt On, a Brooder, or a uniquely unhappy Middle-Aged Rando.

And then there is Bitter Mum…I love Bitter Mum. What is beyond awesome about Bitter Mum is that she looks and acts exactly like Sweet Mum, harping on the kids, keeping the dad in check, pointing out the mascot, appearing to pay no attention to the game whatsoever, and then, from nowhere, will turn to a nearby Pensioner or Middle-Aged Rando and scream something like, "Why doesn't our fucking back line fucking push them up the pitch!?!?!" At my next game, I want to sit next to a Bitter Mum.

Signature Phrase: "Look, dear, it's a tiger…. Oh, watch the fucking game, line-o!"

THE KID

Well, your heart kind of breaks, doesn't it? We all used to be the Kid, and maybe the Kid breaks our hearts because part of us still longs for the days when concrete, cigarettes, unwashed men, and stale beer were the smells of pure magic—and now we know it's just awful. The Kid is still in us, somewhere, yet we grieve for him.

Now, when we look at the Kid, we think the poor bastard will grow up thinking this load of shite on the pitch and in the stands is, in fact, the good old days. And when we look back at the changes (aka the fucking up) the game has seen during our lives, then project that into the Kid's future, we think that poor Kid is going to grow up in a world utterly without meaning or inspiration.

Also, the Kid, should she or he take any interest in all this nonsense, will by necessity have to go through all the stages listed above, none of them happy, and even then might wind up as a Bitter Pensioner that no one wants to listen to. And really, if that's the case, what's the fucking point?

A special mention here for the worst possible version of the Kid: the American Leicester City Kid. This poor little bastard fell in love with a second-tier club when they magically won the league in 2016, bought one of their shirts with Vardy on the back, and he could live to be 147 years old without ever seeing it happen again.

Signature Phrase: "Daddy, why is everyone so upset?"

THE TOURIST

She or he must be included here because they are showing up everywhere, and after all, this is being written by one. (In truth, I am something of a cross between the Tourist and the Brooder, and of course, I have a blog.) The Tourist might be American (cough), Japanese, Indonesian, Dutch…from anywhere, really. Just not English, which explains why they are happy to be here.

They also exist in two forms: the Adopted Fan and the Groundhopper. The Groundhopper heard—not from an English football supporter, mind you—that this English football thing is fun, and they were told—probably by an English TV person—that the English league is the best in the world. So they are hopping to all the grounds they can. English people respond to them at clubs like Barnsley by saying, "Why would you come here?" and at clubs like Chelsea with, "Jesus, this isn't even an English club anymore!"

The Adopted Fan often went through some twisted intellectual process in the last ten years or so and wound up as a "fan" of some team whose songs and players and history they don't really know. They chose the team because their country has been represented among the players, or their family came from there eight generations ago, or because they saw them on TV one time and/or liked their shirts. English fans generally respond to them as above, with either "Why do you support this lot?" or "Could you please at least learn the songs?"

Either way, the worst of the Tourists are sweet, naïve, detached, taking selfies, not entirely sure who the visiting team is, speaking a bizarre language that the locals wish would shut the hell up, holding up their just-bought both-team scarves for photos after the game, and thinking that this is all just grand. But wait, who scored more points?

The good Tourist has taken some time to learn a bit about the game and the club, pronounces words the local way, can sing along at times, didn't bring a backpack to the game, and keeps their voice down during play, unless the Pensioner next to them feels like chatting.

May your goal in reading and using this book be to become a good Tourist!

Here are some key words and phrases you will hear as you wander the world of English "footy." This is just a tiny sampler of what I have collected over the years. For more, check my website at groundhopperguides.com/soccer-terms.

For a special section all about ways to say that a game sucked, see page 358.

Against the run of play: One team has been on top, then the other one suddenly scores.

As you were: Just like it was before: "It's as you were at the top of the table after this weekend's games."

Ascendancy: Where a team is if they are doing better in a game.

Asking questions: Forcing the issue in a game, pressuring the others' defense.

At a canter: With ease.

At sixes and sevens: Lost, all over the place; always about a defense.

Brace: Two goals in a game by the same player.

Cap: Appearance for your country in an international game. They used to actually get caps.

Carnage: A super crazy celebration.

Clattered into: Ran into clumsily.

Clean sheet: A shutout.

Clear your lines: Get the ball the hell out of there. Late in the game you'll hear, "Anywhere will do!"

Collector's item: A rare sight, usually a goal by some donkey who never scores.

Comprehensive: Complete, like a 5–1 win.

Consolation: A late goal when you've already lost.

Cover himself in glory: Do well, but always used sarcastically when he didn't.

Cracker: A really good one, usually a game or goal. Adjective form is *cracking*.

Deemed surplus to requirements: Possibly the greatest phrase in soccer. Refers to a player who is no longer needed by his club.

Donkey: A clumsy, poor, and (often) large player.

End: A stand behind a goal; could also just mean "area," like home end or away end.

End-to-end stuff: Wide open, a fun game.

End product: A shot or pass after you've done something good. Most often used in the negative, like "He made a good run there but couldn't find the end product."

Fergie time: Final minutes, supposedly always extended for Sir Alex Ferguson at Manchester United.

Fixtures list: Schedule, which by the way is pronounced SHED-jule.

Flattered to deceive: Seemed like he'd be good, but he flamed out.

Fluffed his lines: Screwed up. Should have scored.

Foothold: What you're getting when you're starting to play somewhat decently in the game.

Gaffer: Manager.

Get a result: Win or draw.

Golazo: A cracking goal, pronounced go-LOT-zo.

Gutted: Super-duper disappointed.

G'wan!: That guttural thing you hear crowds yell when their team suddenly creates a chance. They are actually saying "Go on!" but it has become its own word.

Hair dryer: Getting yelled at by the manager.

Handbags: An almost semi-fight, with men acting like little girls.

Honors even: An impossibly charming way of saying, "It was a draw."

Hoof it: Just kick it up the field without caring where it goes. You'll hear crowds yell a mocking "Hoof!" when this happens, and the announcer will often say "Anywhere will do."

Joy: Success, always found down one side or another, never down the middle for some reason.

Just about: This one is important and confusing. In the United States, it means "almost," but in the UK it means "barely." So if a keeper just about saved that shot, he actually did save it—in England. In America, he didn't. I used to think British announcers were on drugs until I figured this out.

Know about: You take a shot, it bounces off a teammate, and goes in. He gets credit, but we all understand he knew nothing about it.

Level: Score an equalizing goal, aka a leveler.

Limbs: A celebration so mental it was just arms and legs everywhere.

Linked with: As in, linked with a move to a different club. This actually means two reporters at a pub making up something to write about.

Long ball: A boring way of playing, just hoofing it up the pitch. Also known as going Route 1. Generally disrespected.

Making up the numbers: Filling out a league. Some teams compete for trophies, some are fighting to stay up, some are just making up the numbers.

Master class: A really good job, usually with *tactical* in front of it and referring to a manager's performance.

Mental: Crazy, in a good way. Your team scores, you go fucking mental.

Minnows: Tiny clubs when they are playing big clubs. The rest of the time, they're just small clubs.

Neutral: What you are if you don't care who wins. A soccer tourist or a groundhopper is a neutral.

Off!: What the crowd will yell if they think some wanker deserves a red card.

On frame: At the goal, where, for example, a free header should always go.

On the bounce: In a row.

On the front foot: Going for it.

One hand on the trophy: Just about got this competition all wrapped up.

One-way traffic: One team killing another.

Opened his account: Scored his first goal for the club.

Pace: Speed.

Park the bus: Purely defending, not even trying to score, as if parking the team bus in front of the goal you're defending. Disrespected by everyone who isn't currently doing it.

Pegged back: You get a one-goal lead, the other team scores to tie it: you've just been pegged back.

Persistent infringement: An actual, official phrase. You keep fouling people and you'll eventually get a yellow card for this. See "How to Read the Referee" on page 366.

Professional foul: The other team is about to get a breakaway, so you grab or wipe out the guy with the ball. You get a yellow card, which you know is coming, but you don't care. You had to stop that breakaway. That was a professional foul. You'll probably argue the yellow card anyway.

Punter: A fan who doesn't really know what he's talking about—not in a mean way, but more like "Punters always bet on Manchester United."

Purple patch: A good stretch of games. No one knows why.

Put in a shift: Just did his job, nothing extraordinary, but useful.

Regular service resumed: Back to normal, like the big six being in the top six places in the table.

Row zed: Brits say "zed" for *z*, so this means the top row of seats, where a wildly mis-hit shot winds up.

Scenes: Craziness.

Shambolic: Terrible.

Shipped: Allowed, as in goals.

Shite: Shit. Apparently it comes from the Scottish or Irish accent. Whatever; it's more fun to say.

Shout: Request or claim, like a shout for handball or a penalty.

Silverware: A trophy signifying you won a competition.

Sitter: An easy shot that some wanker just missed.

Skin him: Take the ball past that wanker.

Small matter: An ironic way of saying a big matter, like "And then there's the small matter of the FA Cup semifinal this weekend."

Spare someone's blushes: Save them from looking like an ass.

Spoils shared: Another great way of saying it was a draw; not quite as great as "honors even," though.

Stonewall: Definite, always used as "That's a stonewall penalty."

Suck a goal in: When fans behind a goal yell their team into scoring a goal in that end.

Surely now: A team is ahead 2–1 late, they score another goal, and the announcer is certain to say, "And surely now," followed by some version of "They're going to win."

Table: Standings. Also of note: it doesn't lie.

Tails up: On the front foot, going for it.

Talisman: Hero or leader.

Teacups thrown: The manager was angry at halftime. I kind of hope they actually drink tea at halftime.

Unlucky: Something they all need to stop saying. If a player gets an open shot and hits the crossbar, he wasn't unlucky, which is what they always say. He hit it too damn high.

Wanker: One who masturbates. Setting aside that virtually all of us masturbate, this is still considered a mild insult, as in (I suppose) you are masturbating right now instead of doing something useful. Kind of like calling somebody a jack-off. Generally accompanied by the famous wanker sign, which you can probably figure out on your own.

Worldie: A golazo or cracking goal—as in, world class.

"Are the games safe?" is a question I get a lot. I even get asked if I'll be "running with the hooligans" when I go over for games. And the answers are yes to the first question, no to the second.

While there are certainly some rowdy boys here and there, you won't see them often, and I have only felt remotely unsafe one time in more than a hundred games in England.

The whole soccer-hooligans thing is left over from the '70s and '80s, when social factors contributed to huge crowds of young men with not much to do except have a go at one another down at the football ground. They would toss coins and darts into the opposing section, invade the pitch, or fight for territory on the terraces. English fans were bad enough that their clubs were banned from European competition for five years in the 1980s.

The final straw was the Hillsborough disaster, when police screw-ups led to a crush that killed ninety-six Liverpool fans. The government stepped in, and the result was the Taylor report (see page 365), which started the long process of cleaning up the game—some say a bit too much.

When massive TV money arrived with the Premier League in the 1990s, so too did innovations like closed-circuit video and fan ID cards. Rising ticket prices also squeezed out many working-class folks, resulting in an overall more posh, expensive, and some say sterile environment.

It is also much safer. Today, all you have to do is scan the crowd during a TV broadcast, and you'll see women, older folks, families, tourists, everybody. There are still rowdy boys, especially among the away fans, but with ejection and even banning looming over their heads, people tend to keep it within the lines. Just about.

So how do you make absolutely sure you stay safe at an English soccer game? Here are some tips:

- Don't wear the wrong colors. Study up on the opponents and local rivals, and avoid both their colors. In fact, few English fans wear colors of any sort, unless they're at home.
- Don't cheer against your neighbors. This will probably get you tossed from the stadium.
- If you're supporting the visitors, remove your colors before leaving the ground. Remember, it only takes one drunken nut job to start trouble.
- Beware the boundary areas on either side of the away fans. Things can get tense in there, although rarely more than just tense.
- Understand that sitting with the away fans probably means sitting (more likely standing) in the rowdiest area. Of course, this can be fun, as can those boundary areas.

Whenever people ask me about hooligans at soccer games, I show them this picture from Portsmouth FC.

- Also understand that wherever the away fans are outside the stadium, there may be tension. There will probably also be cops on horses. Again, this could be entertaining; just be smart about it.
- Understand that at a derby, or rivalry match, the stakes go way up. Some of these folks get truly irrational at the sight of their "enemies." And once again, this can be a ton of fun—from a distance.
- Also understand that some international games are a different beast. Something about young men, booze, and being in a different country seems to bring out the vulgar if not the violent. If we're talking about England vs. Montenegro at Wembley, I wouldn't worry about it. But England vs. Scotland is (in fact was) something else (see page 162).

Sometimes a game is epic: titans going at it, the highest of stakes, stars all over the pitch. Sometimes there's a big story happening: a fight against relegation, a push for promotion, a hometown boy doing well. Sometimes it's awful: a nil–nil in the rain, with the media using phrases like "dour" and "damp squib" to describe it later.

And sometimes you're just down at the ground with your mates, seeing a game, catching up, having a beer and some banter. For one of those nights, come along with me to Oxford United on a nice-enough September Saturday afternoon. Bradford City was in town for a midtable League One clash, and I was sitting in the home end, ticking another club off the list and hoping for something special. They were good seats, and I was blessed with a great view, some cover from the rain, and two lads behind me who spent the entire evening in constant banter.

Technically, one of them provided most of the volume. His was a running, stream-of-football-consciousness ramble filled with shouts and asides and curses and references to beer and other lads and their wives and travel stories and updates from games around the country. It was the flavor of chatter that can only happen at a small-time club, where the stakes on the pitch are low, the action doesn't interrupt too often, and the whole point is just to be out for the afternoon.

I'll try to mix in some of the commentary as we go, which is how I received it anyway.

* * *

The scene opens with Oxford dominating the opening stages, picking up where they left off with their 3–0 thrashing of "Jills" (Gillingham), where it turned out they actually know how to score some fucking goals. If they keep up like this, the weekend trip to Blackpool might be worth something from a footballing perspective, other than the absolutely mental party it's going to be anyway. A place like Blackpool, you have to just take £100 in cash and swear you won't drink any more than that. And shit, Pool is winning 3–1 away to Plymouth, you know. That's gonna be a tough one, that.

Come on, Robbie! *Skin 'im!*

This Robbie, out on the right wing, he just oozes class, doesn't he? We're getting all our joy down his side. He is clearly too good for this team, and I don't see how we keep him. I could see him playing for England one day, if I'm being honest.

[Robbie proceeds to screw something up, drawing a big "Waheeeeyyyy!" from the away fans and groans from the locals.]

Right, there goes the England squad!

What little home-side noise I heard came from this end of the Kassam Stadium.

But why the fuck is 'e playing this Thomas up front? Oh, Aluko is hurt? Well, Thomas is shite; where's Carroll? Looks like we're back to our non-scoring ways tonight. Was brilliant at Jills, though, weren't it?

[Bradford starts to pick up the pressure a bit.] They're well organized, I must say [their lanky winger gets the ball in the corner of the area], and close him down, for fuck's sake! Don't let him just walk into our area! [He curls an absolute peach into the far upper corner, past a courtesy dive from the keeper, then runs back toward the Bradford fans and leaps into a teammate's arms.] Great goal, that. But Jesus, we're shite.

Did you see that Chelsea are already up, 3–0, in the first half? European game. Fucking pub team they're playing—who's it, Carabang? Caribbean? Caribou? Some fucking thing. Honestly, they should just throw their academy squad out there and give the regulars a rest. Man U is being held, though; come on, Basel! We're all Basel supporters tonight, eh?

[1–0 to the visitors as the second half kicks off.] Honestly, Oxford are such shite we'd take a point right now. This Bradford side are really well organized, tough to break down. By the way, I've got a mate that lives up there, and he says their season tickets are £150 to sit behind a goal. Ya believe that? Ours are £300, for fuck's sake. That's why they get 20,000 a game, and we get 6,000. They'll probably get to the Premier League one day as well.

Fuck me, they hit the post as well!

[At seventy minutes…] We would absolutely take a point right here and now [and then van Kessel takes a really speculative shot from way outside the area, the keeper spills it, and that fucking Thomas pounces and roofs it into the net for the equalizer! Now we're jumping and shouting and hugging.]

I fucking knew that Thomas was a player, mate! Didn't I say so?

Yel-lows! *Yel*-lows! *Yel*-lows!

[A few minutes later, damned if the lads don't score again, this time on a brilliant counter.]

It's fucking Jills all over again! We're gonna win the league!

[Chaos down in the home end. We're all throwing wanker signs and shouting, "Who are ya!" at the Bradford folks, who have no doubt decided that they are shite and will probably get fucking relegated. And deserve it, they're such fucking shite.]

Jesus, Celtic are down five to Barcelona at home, ya know? And fucking Man U got one, from Fellaini. *Fellaini!* He's not even a footballer, that cunt; he's a fucking basketballer.

Come on, you U's! If we win this and get a result at Blackpool, we're top four, ya know.

[And then…in injury time…Bradford come down the right, send in a decent cross, our shite defenders don't deal with it, and they head it home, bottom corner. Fucking 2–2. Bradford fans go mental, the ref blows for full time.]

Honestly, now it feels like we fucking lost. I'da taken a point twenty minutes ago, and now it feels like a loss, doesn't it? Jesus, we're shite.

'Ats alright, boys, well done! Let's clap 'em off. But shit, we threw those points away.

Right, so see you in Blackpool, then? You know that Allen bloke is coming, right? It's gonna be fucking mental. He's always like, "Right then, get yer shots, get yer whiskey, let's fucking *do this!*" Jesus, I hope we get out of there alive—and maybe with a result, eh? Honestly, though, this game tonight…I mean, they did well in stretches, but we're kind of shite.

* * *

And…scene. See you next week.

Postscript: The U's lost in Blackpool at the weekend, 3–1. No word on the party.

THE CLUBS

There are well over seven hundred soccer clubs around England, and in any given season, at least ninety-two of them are fully professional. These are in the Premier League and Football League, and to visit them all—to "do the 92," as they say—is to be a proper groundhopper. As of this writing, I have been to more than sixty of them.

My commitment is to not write about a club in this book until I have seen a game there. I have also prioritized which ones to include in these ways:

1. The entire Premier League and Championship for each season
2. All of the greater London Football League clubs
3. Clubs in a tourist location you might be going to anyway

My other commitment is to update this thing every year and someday find a way to get all ninety-two in here. At this point, I've been to every club in the top two tiers except Blackpool and Peterborough of the Championship, and I've still got to check out Brentford's new stadium. Stay tuned and keep up with my progress at groundhopperguides.com/clubs.

ARSENAL

This club has a magnificent stadium, a trophy-filled cabinet, worldwide support...and a definitely unhappy fan base. Arsenal is a giant club in slow-motion transition.

LOCATION: Islington, North London

CONTACT: arsenal.com, 020 7619 5003, #WeAreTheArsenal

NICKNAMES: The Gunners

WOMEN'S TEAM: Arsenal Women FC is the most successful women's club in the country, having won dozens of trophies since 1987, including a record fourteen Women's FA Cups. Home games are at Meadow Park in Borehamwood, home of Boreham Wood FC (see page 81). See arsenal.com/women for more.

HISTORY: Arsenal is, as you probably already know, one of the biggest and most successful clubs in the country. They were the first club from the South of England to join the Football League in 1893. Since then, they have won the league thirteen times, the FA Cup a record fourteen times, and two (minor) European titles. They were the first London club to reach the Champions League final, which they lost to Barcelona, 2–1, in 2006. They also hold the top-flight record for going forty-nine games unbeaten from May 2003 to October 2004. This included the entire 2003–04 Premier League season, making them only the second team in top-flight history—and the first since 1889—to go a whole season without a loss. This team is known as the Invincibles.

Perhaps the most amazing fact is that they have been relegated only one time, in 1913. They went back up the following year and have been in the top division of English football ever since.

The club was founded in 1886 by munitions workers at an arsenal in South East London—hence their nickname, the Gunners, and the cannon motif all around. In 1913, facing financial difficulties, they moved to North London. There were two problems with this move. One is that the neighborhood already had a team, Tottenham Hotspur, just four miles away; the other is that in 1919 the newly expanded First Division voted in Arsenal over Spurs, which Spurs fans have claimed ever since was because of bribery. The two clubs have never gotten over it. Spurs fans *still* insist Arsenal doesn't belong there, and the North London derby (contested nearly 200 times since the move) is among the most bitter in the country.

The reason they are in transition is the same reason they are currently so big and widely supported: Arsène Wenger, whose shadow seems to still linger over the club though he retired in 2018. The Frenchman became manager of an already-successful club in 1996 and took it to new heights: two league-and-Cup doubles, four FA Cups, and the Invincibles season. He brought in an attacking style; revolutionized training, tactics, and diets; and led the club into their palatial new stadium in 2006…and then he stopped winning things. Maybe he lost his edge, maybe the world caught up, who knows? Since 2004, "all" they have won is five FA Cups, and the last four years they didn't even finish in the top four. Hell, they've finished behind Spurs in the league five years running, which has turned the whole "Mind the Gap" business between the supporters on its head.

For most other clubs, this kind of success would be celebrated; at Arsenal, there was almost a sense of a zombie club waiting for someone to lop off its French head so it could die already and start over. In May 2018 Wenger retired, but under his replacement, Unai Emery, Arsenal finished fifth in the league and went out of the FA Cup after just two games. However, they did make the final of the Europa League. They lost that one to Chelsea, and their fans still don't seem happy.

Former player Mikel Arteta took over in 2019 and got them that season's FA Cup trophy—their record fourteenth—but this year they aren't even playing in Europe, the first time in 25 years.

RIVALRIES: Tottenham, of course, is a rival, but any game against the other big six will be a major affair.

SONGS: There is a traditional pregame chant, left over from the old stadium, with one end singing, "We are the Clock End" and the other responding with "We are the North Bank." And if they score first, you will definitely hear "One-NIL to the Arsenal!" Another is an almost grunting-type, "It's good good good to be a Goonnah."

2020–21 SEASON: 8th in Premier League, FA Community Shield Winner, Quarterfinals League Cup, UEFA Europa League Semifinals

2021–22 SEASON: Premier League (basically forever)

STADIUM: The Emirates is a palace, a canyon, almost a city unto itself. It holds just over 60,000, making it the fourth-largest club football stadium in the country. Every seat is padded, and there are lounges and clubs all over the place. I can't imagine how much money it generates. It cost £390 million to build, and they spent another £130 million converting their nearby former ground into housing.

There are four statues on the sprawling concourse outside: defender Tony Adams, long-ago manager Herbert Chapman, and goal-scoring wizards Thierry Henry and Dennis Bergkamp, the latter in a famous pose of flying through the air and controlling a ball with an outstretched leg.

TOURS: There are several options for tours, the low end being self-guided audio tours (£27) and the high end being a £295 VIP experience with a famous former player. There are also somewhat reduced match-day tours for £35. My recommendation is to get on a Legends Tour (£55); I went with Charlie George, who is quite the character.

TICKETS: I like to tell people that there is no such thing as an Arsenal ticket. What I mean is, if you're a member of the public going on their website for a ticket, you will, as near as I can tell, never purchase one through the normal process unless it's a Cup game or some meaningless Europa League game. The membership requirement (around £34 per year—and you'll need one per person) and loyalty points system basically means if you haven't already bought tickets many times, you aren't going to. For perspective, there are more than 45,000 people on the waiting list for season tickets.

There is a ticket resale process on their website, where season ticket holders can resell to members at face value.

So, what to do? There's the third-party market, which is technically illegal and therefore can be dodgy. There are hospitality packages available from the club for astronomical prices, and from sellers like me for less (see "I Can Help" on page 373). What I have for Arsenal is typically club level, above the away fans, with a beer at halftime and a stadium tour on a different day, with prices from £100 to £400 depending on the opponents.

GETTING THERE: The closest Tube station to the Emirates is Holloway Road on the Piccadilly line. There is also Drayton Park station, right next to the stadium, but it is closed on game days. And Holloway Road will be closed after the game. You might as well be traditional and take the slightly longer walk from Arsenal station, also on the Piccadilly. It will be obvious how to get to the stadium; just follow the colors.

But before you head that way, take a historical tour. The old Arsenal Stadium at Highbury was a block away. Most of it got torn down and turned into housing, but the famous main building from the East Stand is still there. To see it, turn left out of the Arsenal station and follow Gillespie Road. In about a minute, turn right onto Avenell Road. It's just down on the right. The former pitch is now a private garden, but the West Stand is still there, and you can see it from the street. You can usually pass through a gate and into the old pitch area, which is now a garden for the residents; walk past it, through a tunnel, and re-emerge on the main road, just next to the beautiful headquarters of the Arsenal Supporters Club.

After the game, the Tube stations will be insane, so hang out and let them clear. Also consider a walk to Finsbury Park rail station (15 minutes away) for a quicker trip to King's Cross station and Central London. You'll have to walk past Arsenal station to get there, so just check the scene there and decide how to go.

Worth saying again, because it has messed up a lot of people: The Holloway Road Tube station will be closed after the match.

PUBS: The closest pub to the ground is the Drayton Park, located right across the street by the (closed) Drayton Park station. It often lets in away fans and will be mobbed. Over by the Finsbury Park station, look for the Twelve Pins and The Blackstock. And by the Highbury and Islington station a little south, check out The Famous Cock, the Duchess of Kent, and the White Swan. Otherwise, it's pretty residential on the east side of the stadium, and there's a rail line on the west side.

Over past the old stadium, there's a cluster of pubs along Highbury Park Road, with The Gunners looking the best bet for pregame atmosphere.

GRUB: You might be better off eating and drinking in Central London before you head up to the game.

BOREHAM WOOD

Just one of literally dozens of non-league clubs around Greater London, Boreham Wood is a fun and proper footballing day out in the North of London. For perspective, I once sat next to one of their players on a train to the game.

LOCATION: Borehamwood, about an hour north of Central London by train in Hertfordshire. Don't ask me why the town is one word and the club two!

CONTACT: borehamwoodfootballclub.co.uk, 020 8953 5097, #WoodArmy

NICKNAMES: The Wood

WOMEN'S TEAM: None, but their ground is home of the Arsenal Women's team.

HISTORY: The club was formed in 1948, and to recap what's gone on since then is to be drawn into the vast and complicated world of non-league football. As I explained in my guide to English leagues and Cups on page 17, after the top four leagues, the football pyramid becomes broader and broader. At the moment, The Wood play in the National League, which is at level 5, and therefore the top non-league level. And yes, I realize that I just said the National League is in non-league football, but when Brits say "the league," they mean the Football League plus the Premier League. Like so many things here—such as Boreham Wood FC being in Borehamwood—you just have to accept it and move on.

For decades, Boreham Wood moved around through leagues like the Parthenon, the Athenian, and eventually the Isthmian. That one still exists, by the way, and is at level 7 of the pyramid. It covers London and South East England; its counterparts are the Southern League and the Northern Premier League. Boreham Wood didn't even get that far up until the 1970s. Along the way, their main accomplishments, other than winning these tiny leagues, were making it out of the qualifying rounds and into the first round proper of the FA Cup. They did this ten times from 1974 to 2017.

In the 1996–97 season, they actually made the second round proper after beating Rushden and Diamonds FC (what a name!) in the first round. They made the second round again the next season, but on both occasions they lost to league opposition.

Finally, in 2015 they made what is now called the National League after beating Havant and Waterlooville and then Whitehawk (!) in the playoffs. And in 2017–18, in a major breakthrough, they actually beat somebody from the Football League. The victims were poor Blackpool in the FA Cup first round, in a come-from-behind 2–1 win at home.

So The Wood would appear to be on the rise. They spent most of 2017–18 toward the top of the National League and lost the playoff final at Wembley, then in 2019-20 made the playoffs but lost in the semifinals. Last season they were fourteenth.

RIVALRIES: St Albans City, from just eight miles north

SONGS: None that I noticed; I was having too much fun to make notes anyway.

2020–21 SEASON: 14th in National League, 3rd Round FA Cup

2021–22 SEASON: National League (promoted in 2015)

STADIUM: Meadow Park is a lovely little ground with a capacity of 4,500, of which 1,700 are seated. Those are in the two sides, one of which also has the ticket office and dressing rooms. Behind each goal are uncovered concrete terraces, just like the really old days.

TOURS: You would probably be the first to even ask for a tour!

TICKETS: Last season tickets were £20 for adults.

GETTING THERE: What you need is the Thameslink train from King's Cross/St. Pancras to Luton. It's 45 minutes from there to Elstree and Borehamwood. When you come out of the station, take a right down the high street and then, after about 10 minutes, turn left at the biggest McDonald's you'll probably ever see. It should be about a 15-minute walk.

PUBS: Not that it will be overflowing with supporters or anything, but The Wishing Well along the high street is a nice enough little boozer. The Alfred Arms across the street is a better bet for space and food.

GRUB: There are better food options here than you might expect. There's a Nando's, where you can get peri peri chicken; a Prezzo Italian; a Kiyoto Sushi; and the usual assortment of kebab, burger, and chicken places.

AROUND THE GROUND: A funny thing you're likely to notice is that the train station is adorned with photos of movie stars. Why? Because this is kind of like the UK's Hollywood. Borehamwood and its neighbor, Elstree, have been the home of film and TV studios since 1914; many famous British shows have been made here, and so was *The Muppet Show* from 1976 to 1981. Certainly the most famous films to come out of here were *2001: A Space Odyssey*, *The Shining*, *Superman*, the first several Star Wars titles, and the entire Indiana Jones franchise.

Sadly, they don't give tours; I just can't think of anything else to tell you about Borehamwood!

BRENTFORD

What was once a trip to the past for a classic old-school ground is now an up-and-coming story playing out in a brand-new stadium.

LOCATION: In the western part of Greater London, about an hour west of the center by train

CONTACT: brentfordfc.com, 0208 847 2511, #BrentfordFC

NICKNAMES: The Bees, which came about in the 1890s because students from Borough Road College came out to support a classmate playing at Brentford. They started their school cheer, which was "Buck up, Bs," and it stuck.

WOMEN'S TEAM: The Brentford Women are in the Greater London Women's Football League, tier 6 of the pyramid. They play home games at Bedfont Sports Club. Check the website for details.

HISTORY: The club was founded in 1889 but didn't make the Football League until 1920, when they came in with twenty other clubs from the Southern League to form the new Third Division. They got to the First Division in just three years and finished fifth, ushering in their glory years under manager Harry "The Guv'nor" Curtis. They made the FA Cup sixth round and spent several months atop the First Division table; several players got international call-ups.

But World War II interrupted all that. They dropped out of the First Division in 1948, Curtis left in 1949, and by 1954 they were back in the Third Division. They would spend the next sixty years in the third and fourth tiers, save one season in the second tier when they finished last. Financial troubles came in the 1990s, but they rebuilt and saw some success, once coming within a penalty kick of automatic promotion to the Championship in 2013. On the last day of the season, they had Doncaster Rovers at home and were awarded a penalty kick in injury time. Marcello Trotta, on loan from huge rivals Fulham, took the ball from captain Kevin O'Connor but hit the post. Doncaster went right down and scored the winner, putting Brentford in the playoffs, where they lost the final at Wembley.

They recovered in style, though, winning automatic promotion to the Championship the very next season. They consolidated there, finishing in the top half five seasons running, and last year they made the playoff final, a West London derby against Fulham with a place in the Premier League on the line. Fulham won it, 2–0, in extra time, extending the Bees' horrible playoff record: a record nine tries without success.

Last year, though, they made it back to Wembley for the Final and won it, 2-0 over Swansea. So their new stadium will see them in the Premier League for the first time ever.

RIVALRIES: Queens Park Rangers and Fulham, both more or less neighbors on this side of London, are their biggest rivals. Any game with either two of those is a West London derby.

SONGS: There is a pretty rocking, '80s-punk-style anthem called "Come on You Brentford," but I don't recall hearing it on my trip there.

2020–21 SEASON: 3rd in the Championship (playoff winners), 4th Round FA Cup, Semifinals League Cup

2021–22 SEASON: Premier League (promoted in 2021)

STADIUM: Brentford Community Stadium replaces the lovely old Griffin Park, which was the main reason I encouraged people to catch a game at Brentford. They played there from 1904 to 2020, and it was the epitome of an old-school ground. It was also the only ground in the country with a pub at each corner. This hasn't been replicated at the new place, which is a shame.

As for that new place, well, I obviously haven't been there! It has 17,250 seats in a modern configuration, which from the outside looks all silver and a little sterile; here's hoping it gets dressed up a little. It also includes 910 new housing units and promises community activity every day of the year.

TOURS: I assume they will offer these, but they haven't announced anything yet; check the website.

TICKETS: Last year adult tickets went for £25 to £30. No word on this season in the new place.

GETTING THERE: Getting there will be considerably easier than Griffin Park, as Brentford Community Stadium sits next to the Kew Bridge Railway Station on the South Western Railway with service from Waterloo 30 minutes away.

PUBS: You could be a traditionalist and go over to the site of Griffin Park to hit those four famous pubs at each corner. Each is small and charming, and each will probably still be packed with Bees. The Royal Oak has outdoor seating and hotel rooms; same for The New Inn; The Princess Royal is the most traditional and seems to have the best food options; The Griffin has a patio and more standard pub food.

Otherwise, near the new stadium, the Express Tavern near the station looks nice. And there are three lovely-looking options right on the Thames, just minutes away: One Flew Over the Ait, the Steam Packet, and the Bell and Crown, serving local Chiswick Ales.

Clearly, I have some pub research to do!

GRUB: Aside from the pubs, the area around the station has lots of options. And if the club has as much sense as I think they do, they will have good food at their new home.

AROUND THE GROUND: If you're into gardens, the Royal Botanic Garden in Kew is a top attraction, with greenhouses, royal buildings, a pagoda, and woods—and now it's just minutes away across the Thames, via the historic Kew Bridge. A couple of miles west (use the Syon Lane Station) and on the same side of the Thames is Syon Park, one of the last honest-to-goodness "ducal estates" in London; the Duke of Northumberland owns it. The park and gardens are open daily, and the 16th-century house is open Wednesday, Thursday, and Sunday.

The Museum of Water and Steam, minutes from the new ground, is all about London's water supply (steam pumps operate on weekends), and it has a Splash Zone and mini railroad for the kids. The Musical Museum, also near the new place, is apparently world famous for its collection of self-playing instruments.

BROMLEY

A proper day out for some non-league football in South London, Bromley are higher in the pyramid than ever before and just might be popping up into the Football League soon.

LOCATION: Bromley is in the southeastern part of Greater London, about thirty minutes out from the center by train.

CONTACT: bromleyfc.tv, 020 8460 5291, #WeAreBromley

NICKNAMES: The Ravens

WOMEN'S TEAM: Bromley Ladies play in the amateur Greater London Women's Football League Division 1 South, which is at tier 7 of the pyramid. Home games are at Hayes Lane.

HISTORY: I suppose I could go through all the years and all the leagues, but honestly, it's the same history as Boreham Wood, Dulwich Hamlet, and any number of other non-league clubs who have never made the Football League. Bromley was formed in 1892, played in a bunch of London-area leagues, won some obscure Cups and leagues—especially in the 1950s—and recently has made a surge upward.

In 2014–15 they won the Conference South, which is now called the National League South, putting them into the fifth-tier National League for the first time. In 2017–18 they made the final of the FA Trophy (for levels 5–8 of the pyramid) but lost on penalties to Brackley Town.

Basically the best thing they've done was make the FA Cup second round proper a couple of times, and last year they made the National League promotion playoffs, losing in the first round to Hartlepool United.

So they're a non-league club in a mostly residential area of South London. Other than my affection for such places, being non-league isn't all that interesting. One small thing that is interesting about Bromley is that their pitch is artificial surface (see Stadium below). Another is that their club bar is open on nongame days and is actually quite nice.

Yet another interesting thing is that Bromley has a weird way of popping up in the general culture. For example, remember the Monty Python skit about Spam? It was set at the (made-up) Green Midget Café in Bromley. The Pythons also had one about seeing all seven continents from the roof of the *Kentish Times* building in Bromley. When the Sex Pistols were going around raising their particular kind of hell, they had a crew that followed them around under the name the Bromley Contingent, because that's where many of them were from. Among their numbers: Bromley-born Siouxsie Sioux (of "and the Banshees") and Billy Idol.

And finally, there's a Bromley fan who has written three books about his life supporting the Ravens, one of which—*The Bromley Boys*—was made into an independent film of the same name. It's a lovely story about a boy falling for soccer and a girl.

I doubt you'll run into punk rockers or movie stars at a Bromley game, but it's a fun day out in the world of non-league football.

RIVALRIES: I'm told nearby Sutton United is a rival, but I saw them play each other and didn't notice anything too exciting about it.

SONGS: There's a band called Dogstand who recorded several songs about Bromley, including a version of Newcastle United's "Blaydon Races" about walking down the Mason's Hill to see the Bromley Aces.

2020–21 SEASON: 7th in National League, 1st Round FA Cup

2021–22 SEASON: National League (promoted in 2015)

STADIUM: Hayes Lane is your very standard non-league ground—two stands and two terraces—with home supporters who switch ends at halftime to be behind the goal the boys are shooting at. Capacity last year was 5,000, of which 1,300 were seats. Last season they opened a new, 1,450-seat stand in the south end, replacing the beloved Benches End terrace.

But it's the pitch that most people know about; it's a 3G surface, which replaced grass in 2017. It's one of very few in the country, which will become an issue should they ever make the Football League, which still bans artificial turf. But "plastic pitches," as the British like to call them, are becoming more popular in non-league football because, once they are installed, they require less money for maintenance and they allow many more games to be played there. The academy, the youth teams, the women's team, community teams, "soccer camps"—all play at Hayes Lane.

Also, since Sutton United has a plastic pitch as well, people like to call their derby El Plastico.

TOURS: None

TICKETS: Tickets were £15 last year, and no way they sell out unless they make an FA Cup run.

GETTING THERE: The station you want is Bromley South, which is about 20 minutes from London Victoria and 35 minutes from London Bridge. That's a mile from the ground, so either walk it or take bus 119 (Purley Way) or 314 (New Addington) from just outside the station to Hayes Road, about a 5-minute walk from the ground.

PUBS: The best option is right at the ground: the Ravens Bar. It has several TVs and a good beer selection. It also stays open during the game, but since in England you can't drink and watch football in person at the same time, right before kickoff a screen comes down and covers the windows!

There is also a Wetherspoon named the Richmal Crompton right across from the station, and if you're walking from the station to the ground you will go past the Bricklayer's Arms on Mason's Hill Road.

GRUB: The Ravens Bar serves pizza and pasties, and there's the usual fare at the ground. Otherwise, everything is up by the station, especially in the opposite direction from the ground.

CAMBRIDGE UNITED

Yes, it's *that* Cambridge, with the chapels and halls and Nobel Prize winners. When you're out for a visit, cross the "town and gown" divide for a game at this friendly little club.

LOCATION: Cambridge, about an hour north of London's King's Cross station

CONTACT: cambridge-united.co.uk, 01223 566 500, #CamUTD

NICKNAMES: The U's, which is funny to me because Oxford United uses the same thing, but they are not rivals.

WOMEN'S TEAM: Cambridge United Womens FC play in the Women's National League, Division One South East. Their home games are at St Neots Town.

HISTORY: Not much, honestly. They were formed in 1912 but didn't turn professional until 1949. They made the Football League in 1970 and hired an Oxford man (gasp) named Ron Atkinson as their manager. He led them to the Second Division (now called the Championship) in eight years and then left to manage West Brom, Manchester United, Atletico Madrid, and others.

They finished as high as eighth place in the second tier before bottoming out once again and spending four seasons in the Fourth Division. They made another run up the ladder in the early '90s, making the quarterfinals of the FA Cup and League Cup in that decade and making the playoffs in 1992. Had they won that, they would have been founder members of the Premier League.

Instead, they plummeted again, actually going out of the Football League entirely in 2005. This led to financial problems, but in 2014 they beat Gateshead at Wembley to get back into the Football League. They have been in League Two ever since, finishing twenty-first and sixteenth the last two seasons.

What they are best known for is holding Manchester United to a 0–0 draw in a home FA Cup tie and then taking 6,600 fans to the replay at Old Trafford. They lost, 3–0, but are estimated to have earned £1 million from the contest.

RIVALRIES: The biggest rival used to be Cambridge City, but United have left that non-league club behind. Now it's Peterborough, an hour north but a league above them. Lesser rivals are Northampton Town, Colchester United, and Luton Town. But not Oxford, which I think both clubs need to work out. Somebody pick a literary fight at least!

SONGS: Nothing out of the ordinary, except they do the same *"Yel-lows"* that you hear at Oxford United. And yet they are not rivals!

2020–21 SEASON: 2nd in League Two, 1st Round FA Cup, 2nd Round League Cup

2021–22 SEASON: League One (promoted in 2021)

STADIUM: The Abbey Stadium, especially since it's in historic and beautiful Cambridge, sounds much nicer than it is. It's a couple of miles out from the town center, next to a shopping center, and there is no abbey to be found nearby. It holds 8,127, roughly half of which are seated. The club sold the ground during a difficult financial period in 2004, and they still have not bought it back—although the supporters tried to make that happen themselves. There are also vague plans to redevelop or replace it.

The away fans will be in the seated South Stand and the hometown rowdies on the North Terrace. If you want to be on the side, you can sit in the Main Stand or stand on the Habbin Terrace, behind which is a somewhat sad beer garden.

TOURS: No tours are available at this stadium.

TICKETS: Tickets are £20 for adults, £5 to £15 for under-21s.

GETTING THERE: Take Citi bus 3 (St. Andrews Christ College) from the town center. It's about a 20-minute trip from near the train station and cost me £2.60 return in 2018.

PUBS: The club has a friendly little pub on the premises, and just down the main (Newmarket) road is a pub called The Wrestlers that, oddly, serves Thai food. Otherwise, hit one of many amazing pubs in town. The Tram Depot offers high-quality basic pub fare, but the real gems in town are the old places. For example, The Eagle is where Watson and Crick announced their discovery of DNA.

GRUB: Nothing special at the ground

AROUND TOWN: I mean, it's Cambridge! I suggest you start with a walking tour that includes college visits if they are open and a punting (pole boat) trip on the River Cam. After that, just wander around and get some lunch—perhaps at The Eagle, though it is generally mobbed—before heading out to the game. There is also a nice little market in town on Saturdays, which is when most games are.

CHARLTON ATHLETIC

Almost a forgotten team in London, especially since they have been out of the Premier League since 2007, Charlton is nonetheless a fun day out: an easily reached, family-friendly club in a part of London that might surprise you with its visitors' options.

LOCATION: South East London, fifteen minutes east of London Bridge station by train

CONTACT: cafc.co.uk, 020 8333 4000, #CAFC

NICKNAMES: The Addicks—and that's not a British spelling of *addicts*. Apparently it's based on the pronunciation, in a South East London accent, of *haddock*, which back in the day a local fishmonger gave to the team as a reward. Sometimes you'll also hear them called the Red Robins.

WOMEN'S TEAM: Charlton Athletic Women's FC play in the FA Women's Championship, tier 2 of the pyramid. Home games are a little bit east at VCD Athletic's ground, The Oakwood, in Crayford.

HISTORY: Charlton started in 1905 as a youth team but soon turned senior and then professional. They made the Football League in the 1920s and, in the '30s, became the first team to ever achieve consecutive promotions.

For the three years just before the war, they were in the top four in the league. Just after the war, they were briefly one of the biggest clubs in the country—they lost the 1946 FA Cup final but won it the next year. In fact, their stadium, The Valley, was then the biggest in the league, with some attendances over 70,000. But they went down in 1956 and didn't get back for thirty years. By the early '80s, serious financial trouble had arrived. They went bankrupt ("into administration"), and for the 1985–86 season they had to move into a stadium-sharing agreement with archrivals Crystal Palace because The Valley was deemed unsafe.

Still, they made the First Division that year, lasted a few years, and finally moved back into The Valley during the 1992–93 season. Credit for that has to go to the supporters, who kept up the pressure, cleaned the stadium themselves, and formed a whole political party just to pressure the local council into approving renovations.

By 2000 their yo-yo was back on the up, and they spent six seasons in the Premier League, then got relegated twice, leaving them in League One. They got back to the Championship for a few years, but were relegated after the 2019-20 season.

Sadly, the most interesting thing of note in recent history has been what amounts to a war between the club's fans and their current owner, the Belgian Roland Duchâtelet. Fans blame him for their recent troubles and have formed a group, Coalition Against Roland Duchâtelet, or CARD, to try to make him go away. There were some creative protests, like a funeral march for the "heart and soul of the club," joint protests with other clubs who also hate their owners, and interrupting games by, among other things, throwing pink plastic pigs onto the pitch. Duchâtelet sold the club in 2019, but the whole deal descended into financial and legal chaos. A new owner was finally confirmed in early 2020, but then Charlton got relegated anyway. Tough days for Addicks supporters.

RIVALRIES: Their south-of-the-river neighbors Millwall and Crystal Palace are rivals; so is Wimbledon to a lesser extent. Any game between Charlton and either of those is considered a South London derby. Millwall is less than four miles away, Palace about eight. Charlton fans consider Millwall the main enemy, but the other clubs rank Charlton as the third-most hated.

SONGS: The teams come out to a happy, clap-along, big-band-era tune called "Red Red Robin" by Billy Cotton. Otherwise, they have one about being "kings of the south" and hating Palace "because they're all mouth." There is also one called "Wanky Millwall" to the tune of "Battle Hymn of the Republic." This is a good place to point out that their accent is hard to make out (at least to me); among other things, *Charlton* comes out as CHAH-lun.

2020–21 SEASON: 7th in League One, 1st Round FA Cup, 2nd Round League Cup

2021–22 SEASON: League One (relegated in 2020)

STADIUM: The Valley was a real revelation to me when I went there. Here was a League One club that I knew almost nothing about, and the neighborhood seemed ordinary bordering on dull, so to see a 27,000-seat stadium appear seemingly out of nowhere took me by surprise. It seems bigger than that inside. It also has a steeper pitch to the seats than most stadiums, so I could see how it could be loud if it was ever filled.

Almost all of what's here has been rebuilt since 1992. The north end behind a goal is still called the Covered End because that's the one it replaced. There sit the rowdies and, uniquely, the band. Many clubs have drummers; Charlton has that and trumpeters. Away fans will be in the opposite south end, named for Jimmy Seed, their 1947 Cup-winning manager.

TOURS: Tours are available every Thursday; call the club for details.

TICKETS: Last year tickets ranged from £17 to £31. I seriously doubt they sell out anything except an FA Cup draw with a big club or maybe a derby.

GETTING THERE: The Valley is one of the easier grounds to reach in this whole book; it's about a five-minute walk, if that, from Charlton railway station. Service runs there from London Bridge and Charing Cross.

PUBS: The Rose of Denmark, close to the station, is a good choice. The Royal Oak on Charlton Lane, on the other side of the stadium from the station, is a small, local pub that draws a lot of home supporters and might do a barbecue if the weather is good. And probably worth a walk of fifteen minutes or so is the Anchor and Hope, with good food and outdoor seating right on the Thames.

GRUB: Near the station is a Frankie and Benny's and an outlet of Prezzo, an Italian chain. For fish and chips, there are the Seabay and the probably better Fresh Fry Bar. There is also, on Charlton Church Lane, a classic old-school London café (or just "caff") called The Valley Café. Go get something smothered in gravy before the game and you'll have a very English day.

AROUND THE GROUND: To say that this part of London isn't on the main tourist route would be a wild understatement. However, each of the following is fairly nearby and could well complement a footballing day in this part of town:

- The Emirates Air Line sounds like an airline, but it's actually a gondola over the Thames.
- The Royal Observatory includes the Greenwich Prime Meridian.
- The National Maritime Museum is nearby.
- The Cutty Sark is a mid-19th-century clipper ship you can tour; it has a museum about the tea trade and an amazing, semi-creepy collection of bowsprits from old ships. You thought it was just a whiskey, didn't you? There is also an even older Cutty Sark pub nearby.
- All of the above are along the Thames Path.

CHELSEA

Chelsea are one of the giants of the league, with a roster full of international stars, in a surprisingly small stadium tucked into a very cool London neighborhood.

LOCATION: Just west of London's center and on several transport lines

CONTACT: chelseafc.com, 0371 811 1955, #CFC

NICKNAMES: The Blues. Also the Pensioners because of a long association with the Royal Chelsea Hospital, which houses former military pensioners (what we would call retirees). They still attend games and have been known to form pregame honor guards for the players to walk through when Chelsea wins the league.

WOMEN'S TEAM: Chelsea FC Women play in the FA Women's Super League, the highest level of women's football. Last season, they won the WSL, the Women's FA Community Shield, the FA Women's League Cup, and were runners-up in the Women's Champions League. They have made it to the quarterfinals of the still ongoing 2020-21 Women's FA Cup. Home games are at Kingsmeadow, which is also the home of AFC Wimbledon (see page 155). Their president is former men's legend John Terry.

HISTORY: Many non-Brits may not realize this, but the Chelsea we know today is a largely modern phenomenon. Chelsea was founded in 1905, in a pub just across Fulham Road that's still there. It's called the Butcher's Hook now, and I suspect it's a fair bit nicer than in those days. Chelsea have played at Stamford Bridge ever since—one of very few clubs in England to still play in the exact original location.

They basically didn't win anything until 1955, though, and that was the second-tier championship. They bagged a few Cups in the late 1960s, but they nearly lost their stadium in the 1980s and were sold in 1982 for £1(!). As recently as the early 1990s, Chelsea was kind of a joke.

They got it together to make the FA Cup final in 1994 and won it in 1997. Then in 2003, Roman Abramovich arrived. The Russian oil billionaire spent $100 million on players and then hired José Mourinho. Since 2004, Chelsea have won five Premier League titles, five FA Cups, three League Cups, two Community Shields, two Champions Leagues (and lost another final to Manchester United), and two Europa Leagues. Chelsea is the only London club to win the Champions League and one of five clubs (and the first British club) to have won all three of Europe's major club competitions.

All of that since 2004! They like to sing "We've Won It All," to which opponents often respond, "You Bought It All."

The club's heroes from those days include Frank Lampard (their all-time top scorer and current manager), Didier Drogba, and Peter Čech (who's also Czech, which always cracks me up). But the statue outside is of Peter Osgood, who played back in the 1960s and early '70s, scoring 105 goals in 289 games. He was on the team that won the FA Cup in 1970, and he scored a goal in every round—the last player ever, for any team, to do so. The next year, they beat Real Madrid to win the UEFA Cup Winners' Cup. He is known as the King of Stamford Bridge, and his ashes are buried under the penalty spot near the Shed End.

Americans, of course, now pay special attention to the Blues since they signed Christian Pulisic, who, in 2020, became the first American to score in an FA Cup Final.

RIVALRIES: Technically, their local rivals would be nearby neighbors Fulham, Brentford, and Queens Park Rangers. In truth, though, none of those clubs has provided real competition for years, and this season only Brentford are in the same league. Chelsea's attention is much more focused on Arsenal, Tottenham, and West Ham, although since they started playing for titles, Manchester United has gotten in there as well. Historically, going back to the '60s and '70s, they don't get along with Leeds United.

SONGS: Perhaps their most famous is a simple, rising and falling chant of "Chelsea" over and over. You'll hear it a lot. There is also one about keeping the blue flag "flying high up in the sky." Another classic is "Carefree," in which they sing, "We don't give a fuck who you may be / We are the famous CFC."

You will also hear, if you listen carefully before each half and after victories, a recorded sing-along called "Blue Is the Color." I don't know that anybody ever sings along except in the States, where a few MLS clubs have adapted it. It was originally released in 1972 for the club's run to the League Cup final, and it's actually the 1972 team singing on the Chelsea recording. In those days all the clubs had a Cup song, but most were terrible and are lost to history.

2020–21 SEASON: 4th in Premier League, Runners-Up FA Cup, Round of 16 League Cup, Champions League Winners

2021–22 SEASON: Premier League (in the top tier since 1989), UEFA Champions League

STADIUM: Stamford Bridge—named for a long-buried bridge over a long-buried creek—has been the home of Chelsea FC since 1905. It has had several incarnations over the years and has looked as it does now since the West Stand was completely redeveloped in 2001.

The end where the away fans sit, along with the traditionally most rowdy Chelsea fans, is the Shed End, so named because in 1933 the old Fulham Road End got a roof built over it and fans took to calling it The Shed. It came down in the early '90s when Chelsea Village, a development that includes two hotels on the site, was built. Part of its wall is still there.

Today the Bridge holds 41,623 but somehow feels smaller to me. In the old terracing days, they once got 82,000 in here for a 1935 game against Arsenal. They have wanted for years to have a bigger home and at one point hoped to purchase the Battersea Power Station, the one whose smokestacks the pig flew between on that Pink Floyd album cover. That fell through, though, and a recent plan would have completely replaced this one with a 60,000-seater. Those plans were shelved in 2018, with no current plans to bring them back.

TOURS: Offered virtually all nonmatch days, a tour costs £30 for adults and £22 for kids. It includes a trip through their rather impressive and trophy-filled museum. They also have a hospitality package that includes a mini tour of the stadium on game days. You can add lunch to these tours for £8.50.

TICKETS: The only way you're getting a ticket from the club is if it's a Cup match against a real nobody or if you buy a membership (requires one per ticket at £30 for last season). With that in hand, you may get one for lesser games, but your best bet is probably the resale section of their website, where season ticket holders can put unused tickets on sale. In all cases, getting two together is hard.

They do have a wide range of hospitality options, many of which I sell as well. One of their buffets is out of this world.

GETTING THERE: Getting to Stamford Bridge is simple. You just take the District line Tube to Fulham Broadway, come out of the station, and turn left. You can also take an Overground train to West Brompton and walk about 15 minutes through a beautiful historic cemetery if it's a day game and you're into that sort of thing.

PUBS: Stamford Bridge is in a very happening neighborhood filled with pubs and restaurants. If you want to check in on the away fans, they won't be allowed into these pubs, but I hear they favor the Courtfield Tavern across from the Earl's Court Tube station.

The Chelsea Pensioner is an old-fashioned place with decent food and good pregame atmosphere. Near the ground, McGettigan's looks a little neon and clubby. Broadway Kitchen and Bar says it's famous for beers and burgers. The Cock looks a bit more traditional with a full menu. Malt House calls itself a sophisticated gastropub. Most of these are off to the right from the station. You might also check out Frankie's at Chelsea Village. And of course the Butcher's Hook is where the club was founded.

GRUB: Aside from all these pubs, the Fulham Broadway station has a food court. Otherwise, you're in London, so I'm sure you can find something!

CRAWLEY TOWN

Crawley Town is a chill, easy way to get some League Two action on the south side of London.

LOCATION: Crawley, West Sussex, about an hour south of London Bridge station by train

CONTACT: crawleytownfc.com, 01293 410000, #TownTeamTogether

NICKNAMES: The Reds

WOMEN'S TEAM: None

HISTORY: Let's take a trip into the world of regional leagues! Crawley Town was founded in 1896 and kicked around leagues like the West Sussex League; the Mid Sussex League; and the Brighton, Hove and District League for decades—all while remaining an amateur club. They turned semipro in 1962 and joined the Southern League—levels 7 and 8 of the pyramid.

Along the way, they won a bunch of Cups whose names I just have to share: Sussex Professional Cup, Gilbert Rice Floodlight Cup, Southern Counties Combination Floodlight Cup, Sussex Senior Cup, and the Sussex Floodlight Cup. The biggest accomplishment was making the third round proper of the FA Cup, drawing Brighton and Hove Albion, which were then in the second tier. Crawley Town lost, 5–0.

Still a part-time team, they made the Conference in 2004. Now known as the National League, that's the highest level under the Football League. In 2005 new owners took them professional, but the team struggled, attendance plunged, and a year later they came within hours of folding. But they survived, and in 2007 they beat relegation by a single point.

New ownership arrived in 2008, and the climb was on. In the 2010–11 FA Cup, they made a dream run to the fifth round proper, beating teams from the Championship and League Two along the way, and they drew Manchester United away. With 9,000 Crawley fans in the stands—undoubtedly the most ever assembled—they lost 1–0 after hitting the crossbar in injury time. They carried that momentum to the Conference championship and their first-ever spot in the Football League.

They actually spent one year in League One, but otherwise they have established themselves as a stable League Two outfit.

RIVALRIES: AFC Wimbledon is supposed to be their rival, but having been to both grounds, I can't imagine it's too intense.

SONGS: Nothing in particular

2020–21 SEASON: 12th in League Two, 4th Round FA Cup, 1st Round League Cup

2021–22 SEASON: League Two (relegated in 2015)

STADIUM: You'll know what level of football you're visiting when you see the club shop and it's the size of a food truck—maybe. Broadfield Stadium, also known as The People's Pension Stadium for sponsorship reasons, is the perfect little League Two ground. It holds 6,134 people, and there are seats on each side and terraces behind each goal.

The away fans will be in the north end, and the rowdy home fans in the south. I suggest being in the south end because you might as well stand with the lads and have a go at the opposing keeper. But I do love a note on the team's website that if you're coming out for the first time, you should call for help finding the best seat—in a 6,000-seat ground!

TOURS: I can't imagine they give tours.

TICKETS: For adults last season, tickets were £18 to stand and £22 to sit. Kids age 10 and under are free!

GETTING THERE: Broadfield is one mile from the Crawley station, so it's a pretty easy half-hour walk. You can also catch bus 10 from Stop A outside the station or take a taxi for a few pounds. The latter could be helpful for getting the cabbie's number to use after the game, though there is a taxi rank at the stadium.

PUBS: The Redz Bar at the stadium is pleasant and welcoming to all ages and both sets of fans. The New Moon is a nice pub less than ten minutes' walk away; it has billiard tables, TVs, and food. Up by the station, The Railway is nice enough. Just north of the station, in the little town center, look for better options at the White Hart and the Brewery Shades.

GRUB: That little downtown area is the place to look for pregame lunch or postgame dinner. If you're in the mood for Caribbean, check out Turtle Bay, which is a chain. Otherwise, it's all the usual options: kebab, Indian, Thai, Italian, etc.

AROUND TOWN: It's a nice enough little town, but honestly, even Wikipedia doesn't list any attractions. I see going to Crawley in three different contexts: as a chill day away from the chaos of London, a stopover on the way to Brighton on the coast, or a landing day if you've arrived at Gatwick Airport, which is on the edge of town.

CRYSTAL PALACE

Not the biggest or one of the best, but one of the most fun clubs to visit, Palace also bring an old-fashioned and local feeling to the Premier League.

LOCATION: The South London neighborhood of Selhurst, about thirty minutes by train from Victoria or London Bridge station

CONTACT: cpfc.co.uk, 0208 768 6000, #CPFC

NICKNAMES: The Eagles. There used to a bald eagle, Kayla, who flew around before games. But she passed away, and I haven't seen anything about replacing her.

WOMEN'S TEAM: Crystal Palace FC Women are in the FA Women's Championship, the second tier of English women's football. They play their home games at Hayes Lane, also the home of Bromley FC.

HISTORY: First of all, yes, there was in fact a Crystal Palace. It's gone now, and it wasn't anywhere near the current location of Crystal Palace FC—which, in turn, is not in the part of South London known as Crystal Palace.

The original palace, which was three times larger than St. Paul's Cathedral and contained the most glass ever used in a building, was built in Hyde Park for an 1851 exhibition. The whole thing was dismantled and rebuilt in 1854 in South London, and the area around it was renamed Crystal Palace. The palace burned down in 1936, but you can still go to the park and see the famous dinosaur statues from the 1850s; they were actually created before much was known about dinosaurs, so some of them are not even accurate.

In the 1890s, a stadium was built next to the palace (a version is still there), and they played FA Cup finals there until 1914. The owners decided they needed more action than that, so they started their own club in 1905: hence Crystal Palace FC, who eventually joined the Football League in 1920 and moved into their current home, Selhurst Park, in 1924.

They didn't make the top flight until 1969. They did some serious yo-yoing during the 1970s, dropping to the third tier and then making it all the way back up before financial troubles brought about another relegation to the second tier in 1981. The next thirty years is a dizzying array of promotions, relegations, near misses, managers, and financial problems.

In 2010 during their second bankruptcy, a group of wealthy fans bought them, and they made it back to the Premier League via the playoffs in 2013. They have been there ever since, even making the FA Cup final in 2016. They lost to Manchester United, but their manager, former player Alan Pardew, made an odd bit of history by dancing a little after Palace scored a goal. Google it.

We should also discuss here a man named Malcolm Allison, who became the Palace manager in 1973. He was a real character known for a fedora, cigars, drinking, chasing women, and making news for all the wrong reasons—like being photographed in the Palace players' hot tub with a porn star. He was a legend; he just wasn't very good at managing, apparently, as he got them relegated twice.

Allison did, however, have a lasting impact beyond the stories. It was he who changed their nickname from Glaziers to Eagles and their colors from claret and blue to the current red and blue.

RIVALRIES: Local neighbors Millwall and Charlton are high on the list of rivals, as are any of the other big London clubs. But the most hated of all is Brighton and Hove Albion, which may seem odd considering Brighton isn't terribly close by. It's all about two managers in the 1970s who didn't like each other, a bunch of tense and high-stakes playoff and Cup meetings, fan-versus-manager throw-downs, and a famous incident when Palace was down at Brighton for a playoff game and somebody took a crap in the visitors' locker room. You know, basic positive human behavior.

Most people call this the M23 derby, but both sets of supporters call it the A23, since that's the road you would actually take to get from Palace to Brighton. I don't know where the M23 thing comes from.

SONGS: The atmosphere at Palace is fantastic. Some Brits I know consider it a bit manufactured, but when the teams come out and the home crowd claps, raises their arms, and sings "Glad All Over," I just get happy. They have a whole routine they do when they score, leading up to a song that starts out "We love you." There's also "Pride of South London" and "Here's to You, Famous Red and Blue."

2020–21 SEASON: 14th in Premier League, 3rd Round FA Cup, 2nd Round League Cup

2021–22 SEASON: Premier League (promoted in 2013)

STADIUM: Selhurst Park is tucked into its neighborhood so tightly that there's actually a grocery store in it. Across every street are houses, and inside is seating for 26,074 people. The Main Stand is actually the smallest and is original, dating to 1924. They plan to replace it and add 8,000 seats to the capacity; this has been approved by the local council but isn't expected to be completed until 2023 at the earliest. Across the way is the larger Wait Stand, where away fans will sit in the north end. Behind that goal is the Whitehorse Lane Stand, where you'll find the family section and much of the hospitality stuff in boxes on the upper level. Behind the other goal is the Holmesdale Road Stand, where the rowdies sit. In fact, in the center of that stand is a section that's unique to English football as far as I can tell in that it literally never ceases to jump, sing, and wave flags.

TOURS: No tours are available now, but they say they're working on it.

TICKETS: A membership is required to buy tickets; the international membership last year was £45 and also got you a discount in the club shop and at some area hotels. Members get access to tickets through the usual channel but can also use the season ticket resale service with a third party called Twickets.

One thing to watch out for is that in the Wait and Main Stands, if you're up high, you won't be able to see the far stand or, probably, the ball if it goes too high in the air. Try to get down low or behind a goal. The Holmesdale is fun!

GETTING THERE: Again, an important reminder: Crystal Palace is not *at* Crystal Palace. That train station is far away. You want Selhurst, Thornton Heath, or Norwood Junction stations. All are serviced by trains from Victoria station and London Bridge (though it's quicker from Victoria). It's about 10 to 15 minutes' walk from each. You can save all the walking by taking a train from Victoria to West Norwood and then hopping bus 468 right to the stadium.

PUBS: Walking over from Selhurst station, you will pass the Clifton Arms, long a Palace pub. The Cherry Tree is right by the Norwood Junction station, and The Albion a block away is a fun Palace pub. By far, most of the pubs (and grub) are along the walk from Thornton Heath. There is a Wetherspoon pub right across from the station, which often lets both sets of fans in. Elsewhere along the route, look for the Prince George at the left turn onto Whitehorse Lane.

GRUB: I just love Doneagles Fish and Chips on Whitehorse Lane along the route from Thornton Heath. And there is some disagreement whether Delly's Caribbean Takeaway (just past the Prince George) or Tasty Jerk (just before the stadium on Whitehorse Lane) is the best Caribbean—a major culinary item in South London. I lean toward Tasty Jerk.

Beyond those, you will see the usual chicken and kebab and sandwich places all along the route, all very crowded.

DULWICH HAMLET

Out in South London, next to a grocery store and behind a car wash, there is a sixth-tier football club that also lies at the complicated intersection of development, tradition, and gentrification.

LOCATION: In East Dulwich, Southwark, London

CONTACT: dulwichhamletfc.co.uk, 02072 748707, #DHFC

NICKNAMES: The Hamlet

WOMEN'S TEAM: In summer 2019, the club decided to get with the program and add a women's team; they merged with a successful local club called AFC Phoenix to form Dulwich Hamlet FC Ladies. They compete in the London and South East Women's Regional Football League at tier 5, with home games also at Champion Hill.

HISTORY: The club was formed in 1893 and spent a hundred years or so in a division now called the Isthmian League, which occupies tiers 7 and 8 of the English football pyramid of leagues. They won that league several times, most recently in 1949, and won a lower division of it in 2013. They are five-time winners of the London Senior Cup, most recently in 2004; that's a competition of the London Football Association. Isthmian league attendances are typically in the hundreds, if that, but The Hamlet set the league record in 2015–16, averaging more than 1,300 per game.

They have played on this site almost continuously since 1912, and their ground, Champion Hill, was first built in 1931. It was actually used in the 1948 Olympics, with South Korea beating Mexico there 5–3. In the 1980s, when the club had financial trouble, they sold some of the land for a Sainsbury's, and the stadium was rebuilt in 1992 to abide by the new safety restrictions.

More financial troubles came along, and The Hamlet were forced out of Champion Hill in March 2018 by the property's owners, Meadow Residential. They played at Imperial Fields, the home of rivals Tooting & Mitcham United, until December of that year.

Ironically, it was while in exile that Dulwich Hamlet finally got themselves promoted out of the Isthmian League. They beat Hendon on penalties in the playoff final to get up to the National League South, tier 6 of the pyramid.

Meanwhile, London is becoming one of the most in-demand, and therefore expensive, places to live in the world. Housing prices are insane, which means there is money to be made in rents, which means that a big piece of property like, oh, a football ground is worth a lot of money to somebody. Hence the ongoing dispute with Meadow Residential.

But what exactly is a football club worth? For most of them, not much, in a financial sense. And certainly not a little club like Dulwich Hamlet. But in emotional and psychological value; in the historical sense; in the keeping of tradition, identity, and a community's sense of itself…well, some things are beyond measure, no?

Dulwich Hamlet have done quite well at attracting new folks into their fold of supporters; in fact, they were named Community Club of the Year by the Football Foundation in 2016. They also have taken on more than a little progressive politics, launching various antidiscrimination and antihomophobia programs; you'll see rainbows all over the ground. Their fans—the hardcore call themselves The Rabble—also engage in a wonderful, and usually long-lost, tradition of switching ends at halftime, so the team is always moving toward their own supporters.

The club focused all their energy, their army of volunteers and supporters mobilized, one of their directors got elected mayor of Dulwich, negotiations with Meadow Residential were held, and on a very happy Boxing Day 2018, The Hamlet came home to Champion Hill.

They were greeted by a capacity crowd of 3,000, and I was there to see it. Old friends were hugging each other, many beers were being bought, and when the PA announcer said, "Welcome home to Champion Hill," a big cheer went up all around the ground. The crowd was just the mix I expected: a combination of young and old, the tattooed twenty- and thirtysomethings, black folks, white folks, Asian folks—the whole South London lot, really, all buying into the club and the non-league football experience. The mayor was even walking around in full robe-and-scarf regalia. And they beat Eastbourne Borough, 2–0.

It was all enough that the two somewhat jaded Arsenal supporters who came with me kept looking around, smiling, and saying, "This is brilliant! We have to come back here."

In 2021, former footballer Peter Crouch, who played at Hamlet on loan from Spurs when he was 17, joined the board. A behind-the-scenes documentary is now in the works.

RIVALRIES: Apparently Tooting & Mitcham United, whose ground they shared briefly in 2018, is a rival. I can't imagine anybody gets too worked up about it. Better known is their friendship with Altona 1893, a Hamburg-based club formed in the same year. They wear each other's colors on occasion and have actually traveled to each ground for friendlies.

SONGS: I didn't notice anything in particular. But I was having a lot of fun.

2020–21 SEASON: League season abandoned; 4th Round Qualifying FA Cup

2021–22 SEASON: National League South (promoted in 2018)

STADIUM: Champion Hill as it exists today dates to 1992, and it has one covered stand on the north side with seating and a bar and all the facilities, plus three terraces. The terrace on the south side is slightly covered and has a stenciled sign on it reading "Toilets Opposite." So everybody calls it the Toilets Opposite Stand. The club shop is in a cargo container, there is usually a jerk chicken cart next to the tea bar, and the whole thing couldn't be more homey if it tried. In 2020, plans for a new stadium on the same site were approved.

One thing of note: at this level of football, you can actually take a beer out of the club bar and to your seats!

TOURS: None

TICKETS: I paid £12 to get in on Boxing Day 2019. I bought ahead on the website, but that was just for the big homecoming day. Also, no one ever checked my ticket!

GETTING THERE: It's just a few minutes from the East Dulwich Rail Station, which is served by Southern Line trains from Victoria (22 minutes, change in Peckham Rye) and London Bridge (15 minutes).

PUBS: The Cherry Tree is right by the station, and it's a nice, clean pub. But you should just go have a pint in the club bar. Support the club, you know!

GRUB: Just behind the station is a "Sardinian/Sicilian" place called Il Mirto with main dishes around £10. Village Tandoori is a five-minute walk south from the station. There are many options about ten minutes away along Lordship Lane. And when I was there, the club had a jerk chicken food cart inside the ground.

AROUND THE GROUND: Dulwich's history goes back a thousand years to Saxon times, and while it has seen a lot of gentrification recently, Dulwich Village is worth a walk around. That's the old commercial district, which still has much of its 18th- and 19th-century charm as well as local shops and places to eat.

FULHAM

Fulham is considered an almost polite, old-fashioned, nonthreatening club, especially for being in a swanky neighborhood and having the ultimate quaint old ground.

LOCATION: In a posh corner of South West London on the banks of the Thames

CONTACT: fulhamfc.com, 0843 208 1234, #FFC

NICKNAMES: The Cottagers (for their ground)

WOMEN'S TEAM: Fulham FC Women play in the London and South East Regional Women's League in tier 5. Games are at Fulham's training ground, Motspur Park, southwest of London near Wimbledon. For more information, contact the club.

HISTORY: Founded as a church boys' team in 1879, Fulham moved into Craven Cottage in 1896. They never made the top division until 1949, and then they bounced up and down through the 1950s and had their glory days in the 1960s. They spent nine of those years in the top flight, led by the great Johnny Haynes, who was on England's 1966 World Cup winners and whose statue is outside the stand named for him.

They lost the 1975 FA Cup final—their only time in the final and their only trip to Wembley until 2018—then they went off the deep end, down to Division Three, and almost out of business in 1987.

They were saved by a very wealthy, eccentric Egyptian named Mohamed Al-Fayed, the owner of Harrods; it was his son who died with Princess Diana. (He's also the one who installed a statue of Michael Jackson at the ground; it's now in the National Football Museum in Manchester.) In 2001 they made the top division (by then the Premier League) for the first time in thirty-three years. They staged a great escape to stay up in 2008, with several Americans involved—foremost among them Brian McBride, for whom a bar in the stadium is named.

Fulham surged to the 2010 final of the Europa League, which they also lost, 2–1 in extra time to Atletico Madrid. American Clint Dempsey was a star on that team and scored one of the club's most famous goals to beat Italian giants Juventus. That turned out to be a high-water mark, as in 2014 Fulham was relegated to the Championship. They went back up in 2017–18 via the playoff, but went right back down in 2019. They spent last year in the Premier League, then were relegated again, and manager Scott Parker left for Bournemouth. Fulham are becoming a yo-yo club.

RIVALRIES: Fulham really hate neighbors Chelsea (who doesn't?), but they have only beaten the Blues nine times in 79 tries, so it isn't much of a rivalry. Still, it's only two miles to Stamford Bridge, and Fulham has a fun song about where to "stick the blue flag." The real bitterness is with Queens Park Rangers, 3.4 miles away, and they are in the same league this season! They've played forty times since 1892, and Fulham have 19 wins to QPR's 14, with seven draws. Brentford are also a rival, but they've played even less, and they are once again in different leagues. Any of these games would be called a West London derby.

SONGS:
- A long, looping chant of "Come…on…you…Whites!"
- A version of "Country Roads" that talks about former owner Al-Fayed taking me back to Craven Cottage by the river
- A taunt at Chelsea: "One team in Fulham, there's only one team in Fulham…"
- Another one for Chelsea: "Stick the Blue Flag Up Your Arse"
- To Volari: "Al-Fayed…oh oh oh oh. He wants to be a Brit. And QPR are shit."
- "We are Fulham, we are Fulham, we are Fulham, FFC! We are Fulham, super Fulham, we are Fulham, fuck Chelsea!"

2020–21 SEASON: 18th in Premier League (relegated), 4th Round FA Cup, Round of 16 League Cup

2021–22 SEASON: The Championship (relegated in 2021)

STADIUM: Craven Cottage is the absolute epitome of an old-fashioned football ground. In fact, the Haynes Stand is a historically protected building and has some of the original wooden seats! It's all impossibly charming and old-fashioned. Best of luck with the restrooms in the Haynes Stand.

The exception is the Riverside Stand, right on the Thames and completely rebuilt for this season. It added about 4,000 seats to bring the capacity to just under 30,000.

The Fulham rowdies, such as they are, sit in the Hammersmith End, and away fans are on the river side of the Putney End. The other side of the Putney End (when Fulham are not in the Premier League) is technically a neutral area, one of the very few in the country where opposing fans can mix; in reality, bigger clubs fill the whole thing, and the whole Putney End becomes enemy territory.

The most famous thing about the ground is the cottage itself, which was built with the Haynes Stand in 1904. The designer forgot to include dressing rooms, so they added the cabin! It still hosts the tiny dressing rooms and manager's office. There are three rows of wood seats on the balcony where the players' wives and girlfriends sit during the game.

TOURS: Tours are offered several days a week for £15 each. Book on the website.

TICKETS: During previous seasons in the Championship, Fulham tickets were a snap; even games against other London teams didn't sell out, and prices were around £30 to £40 for adults. Membership (£30 annually last season) ensures access and gets you £5 off all tickets.

GETTING THERE: The Tube stop you want is Putney Bridge on the District line, about a 15-minute walk away. From there, tend right and walk along Fulham High Street, which turns into Fulham Palace Road. Or go left, through a tunnel, and into Bishop's Park. Yes, you can walk through a park along the River Thames to get to Craven Cottage! However, for some bigger games, the police may only let visiting fans through the park to avoid trouble. They'll probably let a neutral go through if you're nice.

Other options are Hammersmith station on the Piccadilly line or the Putney National Rail station, each about a 20-minute walk. You can also catch a few bus lines down Fulham Palace Road and get off two blocks away.

PUBS: There are pubs all along Fulham High Street between Putney Bridge and the ground. Away fans tend to drink at Eight Bells near the Putney Bridge Tube. The Temperance and the slightly more traditional Golden Lion along Fulham Palace Road seem good choices. A fine option is to walk along the river a few minutes west of the ground on the Thames Path until you reach The Crabtree, a pleasant pub with good food and a fantastic, sprawling outdoor seating area.

GRUB: Food at the ground is pretty standard fare, but the better-than-average pies include Craven Cottage Pie—a traditional meat pie with a crust of mashed potatoes. Otherwise, all the options are along Fulham High Street.

GILLINGHAM

A day out at Gillingham (it's JILL-ing-um) combines third-tier English football with seafaring English history.

LOCATION: Gillingham, Kent, about an hour east from London's St. Pancras Station

CONTACT: gillinghamfootballclub.com, 01634 300000, #Gills

NICKNAMES: Gills, pronounced "jills"

WOMEN'S TEAM: Gillingham gave up their women's team because of the pandemic, but Gillingham Women FC, an independent outfit, play in the Women's National League South at tier 3 of the pyramid. Home games are in nearby Chatham. See facebook.com/GillinghamWFC for more.

HISTORY: If you were to somehow lop off the top two tiers of the English football pyramid, Gillingham would look like a pretty big club.

They've been around since 1893, in the Football League all but a few years since 1920, and continuously in that league since 1958. They have spent fifty-six of those years in the third or fourth tier. It's a good, long run in the league, but they were only in the second tier five years, from 2000 to 2005, finishing as high as eleventh in 2002–03.

Sometimes, the problem with getting up that high is that you make plans to stay there, which is to say you start spending a lot of money on facilities as well as players and their wages. Then when you get relegated, you still have those wages and debts to pay, only now you're selling tickets for the game against Halifax Town instead of the game against West Ham.

So it was that the Gills nearly ran aground and had to sell their stadium in 2008. They bought it back in 2011 and have consolidated since, mainly by selling promising young players. Of course, the thing about selling promising young players is that they go play for somebody else, and you stay in the third or fourth tier!

A few moments from their history bear mentioning:

In the 1980s they bought a player named Tony Cascarino from non-league Crockenhill; instead of money, they paid in track suits and training gear. Cascarino went on to play for Millwall (who paid a nice return of £225,000 for him), Aston Villa, Chelsea, and Celtic. One of his teammates at Gillingham was academy product Steve Bruce, a Manchester United legend and now the manager of Newcastle United.

In 1987 they set a league record by beating Chesterfield, 10–0—a week after beating Southend United, 8–1!

In 1993 it took a win on the last day of the season to stay in the Football League.

In 1999 they were in the Division Two (third-tier) final against Manchester City (haven't they come a long way!) and were up, 2–0, with two minutes left but gave up two goals and lost in a penalty shootout.

They had some good FA Cup runs from 1999 to 2004, making at least the fourth round each year. In the 1999–2000 Cup, they made the quarterfinals, their highest placement ever, but lost, 5–0, at Chelsea in front of 7,000 traveling fans.

They won League Two in 2012–13, only their second professional trophy, having won the same title in 1963–64.

In the 2018–19 FA Cup, they made the fourth round after beating then–Premier League Cardiff City, 1–0, at home on an eighty-second-minute winner. They then lost at Swansea, who no doubt thanked them for knocking out Cardiff.

I should also tell you that their one famous supporter was a man named Brian Moore. You've probably not heard of him, but you've probably heard his voice. He was one of the most famous British announcers of his day. His best-known calls were: "It's all up for grabs now" as Arsenal beat Liverpool on the last day at Anfield to win the title in 1989, and his radio commentary of the winning goal when Aston Villa won the 1982 European Cup, which is now written on the side of a stand at Villa Park. Moore was on the Gillingham board for years, and for twenty years there was a club fanzine called "Brian Moore's Head Looks Uncannily Like the London Planetarium." Apparently that's a line from a song by Half Man Half Biscuit.

RIVALRIES: Millwall and Maidenhead are the closest by geography, but the former is usually above Gills in the league and the latter is two leagues below them in the National League. There is also a rivalry with Swindon Town owing to some testy, high-stakes matches back in the 1980s and '90s. They are in League Two for this season.

SONGS: There is a rocking anthem called "Home of the Shouting Men," but I don't recall hearing it when I was there. Honestly, I was there on a rainy Tuesday night and saw them lose, so I don't recall much singing at all.

2020–21 SEASON: 10th in League One, 2nd Round FA Cup, 3rd Round League Cup

2021–22 SEASON: League One (promoted in 2013)

STADIUM: Priestfield (capacity 11,582) has been their home since the club's founding, but three of the stands were built in the late 1990s. The fourth, the Brian Moore Stand, is an uncovered temporary stand where (trust me) you do not want to sit on a rainy and windy evening. The club originally intended to build a permanent Moore Stand, but now they have shifted to plans for leaving Priestfield entirely. It's an old place with no parking, and they want to maybe get out of the third tier someday.

Home rowdies will be in the Rainham End behind a goal, and away fans either in the Moore or the nearby end of the Gordon Road Stand.

TOURS: None

TICKETS: Last year an adult ticket was £20 to £25.

GETTING THERE: It's half a mile from the train station, so a pretty easy walk. There isn't a bus that will help much.

PUBS: There are a few pubs right in the town center, including the Southern Belle and the slightly more old-fashioned Britannia next door. The designated away-fans pub is the Fleur de Lis, a few minutes away in Gillingham Road. Heading the other way a few minutes from the station, there are two small and very cool microbrew pubs: the Will Adams, and Past and Present. The Cricketers, a few minutes past the ground, is a good option for a sit-down meal.

GRUB: Other than the Cricketers pub, there isn't much near the ground. On the walk from the station, you can swing by the Gillingham Fish Bar, where I had a nice takeaway and talked footy with some visiting Bristol Rovers fans. Peter's Fish and Chips, closer to the station, also gets high marks.

Otherwise, check the next section for suggestions in nearby towns.

AROUND TOWN: Gillingham is, let's say, not known for being glamorous. Or even interesting. But in two nearby towns, there are a few sites worth checking out.

One is Rochester, where a well-preserved castle is worth a visit, as is a nice cathedral. There's a well-known Cathedral Pie shop in town as well. The Tudor Rose is a lovely pub on the River Medway there, and Mrs. Tickit's Pantry is a popular place for afternoon tea. Baggins Book Bazaar on the high street is a local institution.

What I did was stop in Chatham (CHAD-dum) for lunch at the lovely Café Nucleus, which is a hidden gem in a garden just off the otherwise drab high street. And then I went to the historic dockyard there. Dating to the 18th century—King George III's seal is over one gate—this was one of the most important places for the British fleet and is now a museum where you can tour a submarine, a collection of lifeboats, a railway workshop, a 1940s-era destroyer, and a working ropery.

LEYTON ORIENT

This East London club, which is probably bigger than you think, recently shed a toxic owner and climbed back into the Football League after two years outside it.

LOCATION: Leyton, a district in the eastern part of Greater London, on the Central Line less than twenty minutes out from the center

CONTACT: leytonorient.com, 0208 926 1111, #LOFC

NICKNAMES: The O's or Orient

WOMEN'S TEAM: In April 2021, the club cut off its women's team, saying it will start all over. That group, now just called Leyton WFC, is in the Women's National League South East Division One at tier 4.

HISTORY: As with so many football clubs in England, this one started within a cricket club. That was in 1881, and many of the founders were students at what is now called Homerton College; the club and college still play a friendly every season. They had some different names and locations, finally settling in Leyton and as Orient in the 1930s. Through all this time, they never got to even the second tier of the league pyramid.

As you might imagine, there is no real connection between this East London club and anything Oriental. Apparently this came from the fact that, in the club's 19th-century early days, a player had a job at the Orient Shipping Company. I'm not sure how that led to the club's name, but that is what the club historian says—and he wrote twelve books on the subject.

Their peak came in the 1960s and '70s, when they actually made the First Division (now called the Premier League) for the 1962–63 season. They finished last, with only six wins and 21 points from 42 games—but they got there. In fact, they were in the second tier (now the Championship) from 1956 to 1982, but they haven't been back since.

In 1978 they made the FA Cup semifinals, the only time they ever got that far, winning at Norwich and Chelsea along the way; they went out to Arsenal, 3–0, at Stamford Bridge.

One nice bit of history for the club is Laurie Cunningham, who started his career at Orient in 1974 and later became the first black footballer to play for England at the senior level. He later played in Spain but was killed in a car crash in Madrid at age thirty-three. As you walk over to the ground, you'll pass his statue and plaque.

Another historical feature they share with many clubs: financial trouble. Orient were famously sold for £5 in 1995 to promoter Barry Hearn. This is after they went from October 1993 to September 1995 without winning an away game. There is a documentary on YouTube about this called "Club for a Fiver."

More trouble came in 2014, when Hearn sold the club to an Italian, who got them relegated twice in three years and had eleven managers during the same stretch. A British former O's fan bought the club in 2017 (#OurClub!), and when I asked some old-timers about that, it was like I had said, "Remember when your doctor said you were cancer-free?"

Orient were relegated out of League Two—and therefore out of the Football League—in 2017, ending what was London's second-longest run in the league after Fulham. They were in the fifth-tier National League for two seasons but won it in 2018–19, meaning they were back in League Two for last season. They also made the FA Trophy final, which they lost. So it was a magical year, but it ended in tragedy, as their forty-nine-year-old manager, Justin Edinburgh, died of cardiac arrest just days after the 2018–19 season ended.

RIVALRIES: Southend United, some forty-five miles east on the coast, is a main rival but they are not in the same league this season. Dagenham and Redbridge, somewhat closer, are also considered rivals in the East London derby, but they are below Orient in the National League. Besides, I saw that matchup at Orient in 2019 and have to say it didn't feel much like a rivalry. It was New Year's Day, though; maybe everybody was hungover.

Nearby West Ham are also a rival from the old days, but they are now three leagues above the O's.

SONGS: None that I noticed. Again: New Year's Day!

2020–21 SEASON: 11th in League Two, 1st Round FA Cup, 3rd Round League Cup

2021–22 SEASON: League Two (promoted in 2019)

STADIUM: Brisbane Road was essentially rebuilt starting in the 1990s, after the Taylor report required many safety upgrades in the wake of the Hillsborough disaster. That was accomplished by 2006, with some of the money raised by selling the corners of the property for residential flats. This leads to what I believe is a rather unique situation in English football, at least among the sixty-plus grounds I have visited: some of the best seats in the house are people sitting on their private balconies!

Three of the stands are simply named for their location, but the old South Stand is now the Tommy Johnston Stand, named for the club's all-time leading scorer. Away fans will be in the south end of the East Stand, with (from what I could tell) the rowdiest home folks in the Johnston Stand.

One thing for which I cannot find an explanation is why the East Stand's gable reading "Leyton Orient" isn't centered on the pitch.

The whole place is now known as the Breyer Group Stadium, though it will disappoint my American readers to learn that's not the same company as Breyers ice cream. Rather, it's a local roofing outfit.

TOURS: None

TICKETS: The most recent prices we saw for adult tickets were from £18 to £25.

GETTING THERE: Couldn't be easier: Take the Central Line to Leyton, and when you come out of the station, turn right and cross the A12 highway. After a few minutes, cut left through Coronation Gardens, say hello to Laurie Cunningham, and you're there.

PUBS: When you come out of the station, instead of going right for the ground, go left about three blocks to the Leyton Star, a friendly little boozer with burgers, wings, etc. On the way to the ground, you'll pass the bigger and impressive Leyton Technical Pub in the old town hall. The Coach and Horses at Coronation Gardens has reopened since I was there but looks a nice proper pub.

GRUB: In addition to those pubs, along the high road you'll find some chains like Pizza Hut and KFC plus the usual assortment of kebabs, pizza, and a peri peri chicken place called Five Lads. Not sure why American burger joint Five Guys is putting up with that name, but locals told me the place was good.

AROUND THE GROUND: Honestly, unless you're looking for a (barely) affordable place to live in a cool, rapidly gentrifying neighborhood, the football ground is probably the most interesting thing in Leyton. Queen Elizabeth Olympic Park is nearby, with gardens, playgrounds, wetlands, and walking paths.

LUTON TOWN

You know how, when a place gets cool and gentrified, some people say it was a shithole that needed work, but others say it lost its essence and now it's too nice? Let's just say that Luton—both town and club—isn't cool and hasn't gentrified. Yet. And I think it's great exactly like it is.

LOCATION: Luton is thirty minutes north of London St. Pancras.

CONTACT: lutontown.co.uk, 15824 11622, #COYH

NICKNAMES: The Hatters, because in the 17th and 18th centuries the town was famous for making hats, particularly straw hats. It still survives as something of a cottage industry.

WOMEN'S TEAM: Luton Town Ladies are in the Women's National League Division One South East at tier 6. Home games are at Stockwood Park Athletics Centre. See lutontown-ladiesfc.co.uk for more.

HISTORY: If I told you this club was founded in 1885 and has been playing at Kenilworth Road since 1905, and then you walked into the place, you'd probably say, "Yeah, that seems about right." In fact, you would be at the first club in the south of England to go fully professional, in 1891. And no, those seats are not from those days.

Their first glory days were the 1950s, when record goal-scorer Gordon Turner was banging them in and the Hatters were in the First Division. They finished second in 1955 and lost the 1959 FA Cup Final to Nottingham Forest when Turner was out injured. When that team broke up, the Hatters dropped pretty quickly down to the fourth tier.

They climbed slowly back up starting in the 1970s, making the top tier again in the 1980s and beating Arsenal in a 3–2 thriller to win the 1988 League Cup. That year they also made the FA Cup semifinals and were ninth in the league. The next year they made the League Cup Final again but lost to Forest. Some might suggest that their success in these years owed in part to an artificial surface at home (very rare then and now) and the club banning all away fans for a couple of years due to hooliganism.

They climbed to the top tier again in the 2000s, but then a crazy owner left them in administration. Then came the thunderbolt of an FA investigation into illegal payments to players' agents, which resulted in a ten-point deduction one season and thirty the next—the largest amount in the league's history. Although they won the League Trophy in 2009 in front of 40,000 Hatters supporters at Wembley, they dropped out of the Football League days later and spent the next five seasons in what is now the National League.

I am sure that a Luton Town fan reading the previous paragraph would wish to add layers to this story, and we can all probably agree that, say, Manchester City might not have been docked forty points for similar infractions. I don't know the whole story and didn't ask my neighbors at the game. But I did see a sign at the ground that read, "Established 1885, Betrayed by the FA 2008." So let's assume there's some deeply held bitterness about all this.

Anyway, they got back to League Two in 2014, then successive promotions in 2018 and 2019 landed them in the Championship, where they have remained.

RIVALRIES: Watford, and here is where things get exciting. The two teams faced off twice in the Championship in the 2020-21 season (the first time in 14 years), resulting in a win for each club. Sadly, due to the pandemic, both matches were played without spectators. Historically, the Beds-Herts derby is a most bitter affair, in which Luton have the upper hand with 54 wins to 37 in 119 meetings since 1900. There was crowd trouble with this one as recently as a 2002 League Cup tie, and a former Watford resident told me that the whole town shut down whenever the Hatters were in for a game. So I absolutely want to see this one ASAP, but will have to wait, as Watford were promoted to the Premier League in 2021.

QPR also get angry stares, as does Millwall, if only for the time their fans tore up Kenilworth Road in a 1985 riot. Google that one sometime.

SONGS: As they have risen in recent years, they have taken to singing "Fuck the FA, we're on our way back." There are other variations on this regarding the FA and thirty points, and who knows what they sing about Watford!

2020–21 SEASON: 12th in the Championship, 4th Round FA Cup; 3rd Round League Cup

2021–22 SEASON: The Championship (promoted in 2019)

STADIUM: There was a time when the builders of football grounds and the owners of clubs simply didn't give a damn about supporters. Fans were fenced in like animals, made to stand on concrete terraces, given almost nothing for toilets, fed garbage, and otherwise neglected—at best.

And then in the 1990s the Powers That Be made the clubs clean up their act, mainly by banning alcohol in the viewing area and making the top clubs replace terraces with seats.

At Luton and other places, that directive arrived more like "put in seats," which Luton did in its 1922(!) Main Stand, apparently in the most minimalist way possible. They put a long metal rack on each level of the terrace, hit every yard sale on Bedfordshire for any spare slab of plastic they could locate, then pinned it onto the metal racks. Voilà—seating! They even have backs in the multicolored upper tier.

They haven't spent money on the place because they've said for years they were going to replace it. So there are posts everywhere, obstructed views galore, chipped paint, and water dripping. It's awesome. And I am 100 percent not being sarcastic. I hate the modern, clean, plastic grounds with executive boxes and seats far from the pitch. Going to "the Kenny" is both a trip back in time and a commitment to the experience. I sat in the corner behind a floodlight tower!

Away fans enter between two flats, the club shop is a shipping container, you have to walk down dark alleys to get around the place, and it's all right next to a giant motorway. Honestly, go to Kenilworth Road before they replace it, as planned, with something nicer, maybe, in town. And then for fun, ask any other club's supporters you meet if they've been there.

If you actually want an unobstructed view, go for the Kenilworth Road End; that's got the rowdy home fans and only two posts. If you want the full old-school experience, go for the lower Main Stand or the home terrace.

TOURS: I chuckle at the very thought.

TICKETS: The last prices we saw were £30 for adults.

GETTING THERE: It's an easy 20-minute walk from the Luton Station. There isn't a bus line that helps, either.

PUBS: There's nothing at or near the ground. Right outside the station is the George II, a Greene King outlet. The Bricklayers Arms is a nice, chill choice on a quiet street behind the station. The Brewery Tap, just on the edge of the city center, has good food, a big beer selection, and lovely outdoor seating. The local Wetherspoon is the giant White House in a mall with a movie theater and bowling alley. The Bear Club is a live music venue focused on jazz and blues.

GRUB: Again, everything is in the center. Aside from the pubs above, check out the "Indian tapas," which I guess just means Indian small plates, at Papa J's. Monna Lisa is a rated Italian place near the station. The Engine calls itself an American diner as well as a "shisha shack and hookah bar," and it has a giant menu and outdoor seating on Astroturf, so I don't know what's going on there.

There are a few good options in the old-fashioned Luton Indoor Market as well: Thai, curries, Mongolian, and more.

AROUND TOWN: Here's a fun game: Say "Luton" to any English person. I can almost guarantee they will say "shithole." It's like a call-and-response thing. I'm sure there are rough parts, and I imagine it was all "rough" not long ago. But it's twenty-five miles from London, it has an airport with cheap flights to Europe, and the early signs of gentrification are already in place. Luton is about to boom.

Meanwhile, there are some semi-interesting things to do around town. Over in the Hat District, which is coming back as a creative center, the Hat Factory hosts art shows and dance events, and it has a café. If you're really into hats, make an appointment online with Philip Wright for a tour and fitting.

Elsewhere, Vinyl Revelations for records and Ahh Geek Out for comics hint at the early hipster stage of what is to come.

There's also a big carnival in town on the last Saturday in May.

And that's all I've got on Luton. It's about Kenilworth Road, honestly.

MILLWALL

Millwall's supporters proudly claim the mantle of "Last of the Real Clubs." What I think they really mean is "vulgar" clubs. And there's truth to it: no place can rock, or disturb, or entertain like Millwall at a big game.

LOCATION: Bermondsey, one stop out of London Bridge station in South East London

CONTACT: millwallfc.co.uk, 020 7232 1222, #Millwall

NICKNAMES: The Lions

WOMEN'S TEAM: The Millwall Lionesses were founded in 1971 and in the 1980s became the first women's team to be associated with a professional men's club. But in 2019, they announced a split with Millwall FC and changed their name to London City Lionesses. That club now competes in the second-tier FA Women's Championship. Check the londoncitylionesses.com for the latest on them. Meanwhile, Millwall FC started a new women's team called the Millwall Lionesses, who play in the fifth-tier Eastern Region Women's Football League. See millwall-lionesses.com for more on them.

HISTORY: That the club was founded by workers at a factory in the Isle of Dogs area sets the tone for all of Millwall's utterly unglamorous story. The specific area was called Millwall, and they kept the name even after bouncing around to a few grounds and eventually leaving for New Cross. That was The Old Den, a truly intimidating and feared place they inhabited from 1910 until 1993. Such was the atmosphere in the 1960s that Millwall set the then-league record with fifty-nine home games unbeaten—keeping thirty-five clean sheets and only conceding thirty-three goals during that run.

Meanwhile, the Lions have been promoted eleven times and relegated ten times, mostly between the second and third tiers. They have only been in the top flight for two seasons, from 1988 to 1990. They got into financial trouble when they hit the third tier in the mid-1990s and have not made it back to the top level since. They've also never won a major trophy.

What they did lead the country in, at least according to popular media, was hooliganism. There are movies and books all about this, especially the rivalry with West Ham United both on and off the pitch. Obviously hooliganism was, back in the '70s and '80s, a widespread problem, but for some reason Millwall's reputation has never shaken it. Perhaps that's because it has held on a bit; in one famous episode, the Lions made the 2013 FA Cup semifinals, which they lost. The game was marred by a fair number of Millwall fans fighting each other in the stands. Not a big deal, but it just had to be Millwall.

(For an example of what it can be like at The Den when another London club is the opponent, see "When Ollie Came Back to The Den" on page 32.)

These days the games at Millwall are perfectly safe, but *hostile* is not a word wasted on the atmosphere. Nor would *bleak* be inappropriate for the surroundings. It's truly remarkable to me the difference one gets in a single train stop from London Bridge. And developers have noticed: Millwall has been under threat for some time now to lose its ground because that part of London is prime for infill and gentrification. That there are thousands of people screaming and cursing in a drab stadium surrounded by an industrial wasteland makes me happy; it amounts to a giant middle finger from the world of proper football to the forces of "progress."

One other story has to be told here. During a 2017 terrorist attack at London Bridge, three knife-wielding men ran into a restaurant and started screaming and attacking people. One man, who said later he'd had "four or five pints—nothing major," stood up, yelled, "Fuck you—I'm Millwall," and went right at them with his bare fists. He was stabbed multiple times but gave dozens of people the chance to escape before the terrorists took off with the dude chasing them down the street. Everybody agreed: if you're in a fight, you'll take a Millwall guy.

RIVALRIES: Any London club is less than welcome, with particular venom reserved for Crystal Palace and Charlton, both also from south of the river. But there's a special level of hatred for West Ham United. This goes back to the East End days at the end of the 19th century, when the clubs were formed by dockworkers at rival companies. There was a mini riot and pitch invasion at this match as recently as 2009. Millwall also dislikes Leeds United quite a bit (the feeling is mutual), which is mainly about hooliganism from the bad old days that actually flared up once or twice in the last ten years.

SONGS: There are two traditional songs at the beginning of games. One is the last part of "Hey Jude," with "Millwall" replacing "Hey Jude." The other is a classic, country-and-western sing-along called "Let 'Em Come" that was written specifically for the club. It has great lyrics about eating jellied eels and drinking glasses of beer. At the end everybody holds up their arms and belts out "Let 'em all…come down…to The Den!" If they win, you'll hear "Rockin' All Over the World" after the game.

But the defining song of Millwall is one of the great, goofy songs in all of football:

No one likes us, no one likes us!
No one likes us, we don't care.
We are Millwall, super Millwall.
We are Millwall, from The Den.

2020–21 SEASON: 11th in the Championship, 4th Round FA Cup, 3rd Round League Cup

2021–22 SEASON: The Championship (promoted in 2017)

STADIUM: The Den holds 20,146 in four separate stands. One is the Dockers Stand, which is named for dockworkers, not a clothing brand. The Cold Blow Lane Stand behind a goal honors the location of The Old Den. The North Stand behind the other goal is for visiting supporters, and the Barry Kitchener Stand is named for the club's longest-serving player. The best place to sit is on either side close to the away fans.

TOURS: Behind-the-scenes tours of The Den cost £17 for adults. Check millwallfc.co.uk for more details.

TICKETS: The last prices we saw for an adult ticket ranged from £23 to £30, kids under 16 were £10 to £13. Only the derby games will sell out.

GETTING THERE: The quickest way is to take the train from London Bridge to South Bermondsey. It's about a 5-minute walk from there. However, for more food and drink options (see below), take the Overground to Surrey Quays or the Underground to Canada Water. Or go nuts and take the London river bus to Greenland, which is at Surrey Quays.

PUBS: The "official" Millwall pub is called the Blue Anchor; it's on Southwark Park Road, to the right from South Bermondsey station about fifteen minutes. Right across from the Surrey Quays station is the Surrey Docks, a Wetherspoon outlet with an outdoor seating area. It will be packed, as will the smaller and more old-school Whelan's Free House nearby. Over by New Cross station, the Five Bells has been a traditional Millwall place for years.

GRUB: I recommend the Surrey Quays station for a simple reason: one of the better fish and chips places I have found in London is near there. It's called Express Fish Bar and will be mobbed before the game. It's essentially all takeaway, so make sure you get a fork (I once failed to—big mess) and just munch it up on your way to The Den.

There is also the Millwall Café at the stadium serving decent food in a fun atmosphere.

AROUND THE GROUND: I won't attempt a travel guide to London, but I do think the Borough Market at London Bridge is fantastic. Plenty of amazing food in there. The Old Oak Pub is classic as well. And if you want to pay £25 and up to visit the top of The Shard with a million other people, it's near London Bridge.

OXFORD UNITED

In the City of Dreaming Spires lie beautiful buildings, famous colleges, amazing history, and a little football club recently on the up.

LOCATION: One hour west of Paddington station in London

CONTACT: oufc.co.uk, 01865 337500, #OUFC

NICKNAMES: The U's or the Yellows—same as Cambridge United, oddly

WOMEN'S TEAM: Oxford United Women are in the Women's National League South, the third tier, with home games at the Oxford City FC ground. Check the club's website for the latest.

HISTORY: Oxford United's history follows a generally familiar course among smaller English clubs: ancient founding, early glory, obscurity, more recent glory, decline, and resurrection. In their case, the founding was in 1893, the early glory was in leagues you've never heard of, and the recent glory was in the 1980s under a manager named Maurice Evans.

They made the top flight in 1986. They barely stayed up, but they won the league Cup, which was then known as the Milk Cup, and is now known as the EFL Cup or Carabao Cup. Let's just move on. The point is, 1986 was by all accounts the high-water mark.

Also of note from that Milk Cup win: Evans, the manager, let his winner's medal be collected by the club's seventy-two-year-old physio (trainer). Proper gentleman move, that.

As money became more important in the league, the U's became less so, and they almost went away in the late 1990s. In fact, they almost merged with Reading FC, but the fans of both clubs revolted. They came back from the edge thanks mainly to their chairman Firoz Kassam, although they dropped out of the Football League in 2006.

They got back up in 2010, playing the Conference (now National League) Playoff final at Wembley in front of a game-record attendance of 42,000—of which 35,000 were Oxford fans.

In the 2015–16 season, they finished second in League Two, which earned them promotion to League One. They also lost the final of the League Trophy, 3–2, to Barnsley at Wembley that season.

After getting back to the third tier, they finished midtable three years running and lost another League Trophy final. Then, in 2019, they beat two Premier League teams on the way to the League Cup quarterfinals. They finished fourth in the league and made the playoff final, which they lost to rivals Wycombe Wanderers. They weren't as successful in the Cups in 2020–21 but did finish sixth in the league.

RIVALRIES: Swindon Town is the most disliked; they are just thirty miles away, and the two clubs have met more than 50 times since 1962. Reading, a similar distance away, is also a rival, as are Wycombe Wanderers. There is an Oxford City (where the United women play), but they are in the National League South, the sixth tier, and the two haven't had a competitive match since the 1950s.

SONGS: "*Yel*-lows, *Yel*-lows" and a long, rolling "Cooome on you Uuuuu's!"

2020–21 SEASON: 6th in League One, 1st Round FA Cup, 2nd Round League Cup

2021–22 SEASON: League One (promoted in 2016)

STADIUM: The Kassam, named for the influential former chairman, is an odd place really. It's in Oxford Science Park, which is really just a business campus. The stadium has only three sides, with the open end revealing a bowling alley and a Frankie and Benny's restaurant. Basically, that's a sign that your ground is new and has little character.

Outside there's a statue of a bull ox, owing to the town's name (oxen crossing a ford). Inside, there is a pub of sorts called the Reception Area, but you can, in fact, get a beer there. The club shop, when I was there, was just a table set up in the corner.

The main noisemakers sit in the East Stand—the bottom of the U, appropriately—underneath banners about the Spirit of '86. The away fans will be in the North Stand, toward the opening. I would recommend the Lower South Stand for the view of the action and away fans or the east end to be amongst the singers.

TOURS: No tours are available at this stadium.

TICKETS: 2020–21 prices ranged from £20-28 for adults. If they sell out one game, I'd be amazed, unless they get a Premier League biggie at home in a Cup.

GETTING THERE: It's a weird place to get to as well. From the train station, take bus 5 (Blackbird Leys) for 35 minutes to Sandy Lane, and then walk another 15 minutes.

Alternatively, take bus 1 (also Blackbird Leys!) to Queens Lane, then bus 3A (Littlemore) for 20 minutes to the stadium. Or you know what? Take a cab. It's almost 5 miles and should be about £15. Get the taxi's number for after the game.

PUBS: There are only a couple of pubs anywhere near the ground. The Blackbird is about fifteen minutes' walk and has a large outdoor area. The Catherine Wheel, on the route of bus 5, feels like it's almost out in the country. And The George, also on that bus route, looks like a friendly local.

But this being Oxford, there are some amazing pubs around town. Drink and eat in one of these:

- The Kings Arms has been there since 1607!
- The Eagle and Child is where J. R. R. Tolkien used to hang out with C. S. Lewis. They let mortals in as well.
- The Lamb and Flag, across Gloucester Green, is owned by St. Johns College and has been there since 1613.
- There is another pub, named something like Land Inn, which is the oldest pub in town. It is where Bill Clinton allegedly didn't inhale, where the future Australian prime minister set a world drinking record, and whose location and precise name, by local tradition, I will not share. It's fun to find it on your own.

GRUB: Again, there's nothing by the ground except that Frankie and Benny's. Eat in town; there are a few options in The Covered Market.

AROUND TOWN: Touring the non-football Oxford is both easy and pleasant, and you don't need me to explain it. Just take a train about an hour from Paddington, and you'll be there. I'll point out a few things you might want to look for, though.

The Hop-On Hop-Off bus is quite good, especially if you catch one with an actual tour guide on it. Get a ticket and board at the station. Otherwise, it's the usual earphone business. I had nice walks through Christchurch Meadow, down to the Thames, and through various side streets.

The many colleges in town are often closed, but they have hours in the afternoon when they might be open. They're all basically set up like monasteries, with a central courtyard or garden, and they range from a few dozen students in attendance to several hundred.

You can take Harry Potter tours to see sites from the films, but honestly I couldn't care less unless I get to meet Emma Watson. Research this on your own.

I took a £20 walking tour from Visit Oxford Tours and enjoyed it, mostly as a way to pick a local's brain for two hours.

I also took a £20 Thames boat tour from Oxford River Cruises, which was nice for a little peaceful break and because the river is pleasant. It lasted about an hour.

The Covered Market in an 18th-century building, open daily, is really cool and not to be confused with the every-Wednesday outdoor market, which is kind of lame. In The Covered Market, look for the cake shop, my version of heaven.

QUEENS PARK RANGERS

For the London soccer tourist, a game at QPR is a great option: not as sketchy as Millwall, not as posh as Fulham, not as hard to get into as the Premier League clubs, and in a cool part of town.

LOCATION: Shepherd's Bush in West London

CONTACT: qpr.co.uk, 020 8743 0262, #QPR

NICKNAMES: QPR, the Rs, the Hoops (for their shirts)

WOMEN'S TEAM: Queens Park Rangers FC Women play home games at Heston Sports Ground in the London suburb of Hounslow. They are in the Women's National League Division 1 South East, tier 4.

HISTORY: Rangers have been around since the 1880s and played at Loftus Road since 1920, but they never made it to the top (then First) division until the '60s. They expanded the ground then, and they memorably won the League Cup from Division Three in 1967. The final was 3–2 over West Brom at Wembley, after QPR trailed 2–0 at halftime, with the winner scored by Lazarus. I just had to get that in.

That's the only major trophy they've ever won, though they would like you to know it's more than Fulham and Brentford have between them.

The next year, QPR were relegated; then they made it back up in 1972. The main thing they were known for was being the first team, in 1981, to put in artificial surface, which in the UK is called a plastic pitch (they took it out after five years). That season, they made the FA Cup final but lost to Spurs in a replay. Then they went back down to the Championship for fifteen years. They made it up for two years, got relegated again, and then....

One thing you'll need to know about QPR is Zamora's goal. For the fans, that's all you have to say. But if not, let's review. In May 2014, the final spot for the Premier League came down to the Championship playoff final between QPR and Derby County at Wembley Stadium in front of 80,000-plus fans. Bobby Zamora won it, 1–0, late in the game, for QPR. It's an amazing video to see (and hear!) on the club's YouTube channel.

Of course, being QPR, they finished last and got relegated back to the Championship the next year. They've been there ever since.

RIVALRIES: Their most bitter foe is Fulham, just three miles away. Brentford is also high on the hated list; any game between two of those three is a West London derby and should be seen if possible. QPR also hate Chelsea, but they don't play often, and it hasn't been competitive between them for years.

SONGS: Aside from the usual assortment, their traditional theme is a very cool drum-and-horn thing called "Papa's Got a Brand New Pigbag." It's by an early '80s post-punk/funk rock/dance-punk band called Pigbag. It sounds like something an impossibly cool marching band might play. QPR fans sing a version of it as well, throwing in "Hoops!" along the way. By the way, Middlesbrough claims they had this song first. I take no position in the matter.

2020–21 SEASON: 9th in the Championship, 3rd Round FA Cup, 1st Round League Cup

2021–22 SEASON: The Championship (relegated in 2015)

STADIUM: Loftus Road, known as the Kiyan Prince Foundation Stadium since 2019 (in honor of the former QPR youth team member Kiyan Prince who was fatally stabbed in 2006), will probably seem absolutely tiny when you walk in. It holds 18,439 people in a two-tiered rectangle packed so close to the pitch that I'm convinced you could throw beer from the back row and hit a player. It may have been done, in fact. Watch during the pregame warm-ups as players take shots and miss the goal; some spectator is gonna get killed someday.

Another reason it feels so cramped is that, unlike many smaller stadiums in England, there are no gaps between stands in the corners. You really feel like you're right on top of things here. Also, if you're more than about five-foot-eight, you may feel like you're sitting on top of the person in front of you. And all I can say for the restrooms is good luck, and I hope you're not claustrophobic like I am.

The away fans will be in the upper tier of the School End behind a goal. The rowdiest QPR fans, at least by reputation, sit in blocks Q, P, and R—no, really—of the Ellerslie Road Stand, as well as behind another goal in the Loftus Road Stand. They just call that one The Loft. The biggest stand is the South Africa Road Stand along the side opposite the Ellerslie; it has the dressing rooms and VIP boxes, etc.

There have been on-and-off plans for years to build a new stadium, which honestly is highly needed. Currently those plans are off, mainly as QPR is stuck in the Championship.

TOURS: Tours are given a couple of days per week as well as on game days and cost £15 for adults.

TICKETS: As long as they are in the Championship, tickets are not that hard to come by. If it's a derby, or if they are having a good season, it could be tough just because it is a small place. If they draw a Premier League club in a Cup, it might be hard as well—but you'll want to be there. The most recent prices we saw were from £25 to £34. If you can't get them from the club, I usually have good seats available.

GETTING THERE: The quickest trip is to aim for the White City Underground station on the Central line or Wood Lane on the Hammersmith and City line. From either of those stations, turn right onto Wood Lane, walk up to South Africa Road, and turn left. You can't miss it from there. It's about five minutes' walk from White City and seven from Wood Lane.

I recommend taking a London Overground train or Tube to Shepherd's Bush, which is about a 15-minute walk away. Shepherd's Bush is a cool area, and the walk along Uxbridge Road takes you past restaurants, pubs, and the quite cool Shepherd's Bush Market. Westfield London Shopping Centre, Europe's largest mall, is also right there.

PUBS: The traditional fan's favorite is the Queen's Tavern right by the ground; it used to be called the Springbok in keeping with the area's South Africa theme. It will of course be "heaving" but has good atmosphere; you'll need a home-section match ticket to get in.

Elsewhere along Uxbridge Road, look for the small and traditional White Horse, which hangs QPR stuff before games but also, oddly, has a bit of a shrine to Newcastle United's Alan Shearer. Across the road is the spacious Queen Adelaide with a big outdoor area. The Crown and Sceptre, a few minutes' walk away on Melina Road, is a nice local with a strong QPR bent. All of these will require a match ticket to get in.

GRUB: Again, all the action here is along Uxbridge Road—or in the Westfield Mall. Along the road, look for Tai Buffet with Thai, Chinese, and vegetarian options; Haranna Lebanese; Burgista Bros for gourmet burgers; Ayam Zaman for Syrian; or Nando's for peri peri chicken. You can grab a falafel in the market or just do what I did, which was dive into some place where I was the only white guy and wound up eating…well, something really good. My find was the Banaadiri Restaurant. No idea what I ate.

AROUND THE GROUND: All of this is only about a half hour by Tube from Hyde Park, and even less from Kensington Palace, the Natural History Museum, and the Victoria and Albert Museum—if these things matter to you.

READING

A fun day out from London or a good arrival-day trip from Heathrow, Reading is a pleasant town with a happening downtown and a nice stadium.

LOCATION: Thirty minutes west by train from Paddington station in London or about forty-five minutes by bus from Heathrow Airport

CONTACT: readingfc.co.uk, 0118 968 1100, #ReadingFC

NICKNAMES: The Royals, because they are in the Royal County of Berkshire. Until the 1970s they were called the Biscuitmen because a famous biscuit (cookie) company was founded there. Sadly, they changed their nickname when the company moved away. I would definitely buy a Biscuitmen shirt.

WOMEN'S TEAM: Reading FC Women are in the top tier of women's football, the Women's Super League. Home games are at Madejski Stadium, which they share with the men's team.

HISTORY: Here is a club that, from 1920 to the mid-1980s, spent all but a handful of seasons—and those were in the late '20s—in the third tier. So the whole idea of Reading being a thing in English soccer is relatively new. In fact, they never made the top division until 2006, some 135 years after their founding.

Their promotion season, 2005–06, is one they sing about often. They lost only twice in forty-six games, scored ninety-nine goals, and set the record for the division with 106 points. When I saw them a few years back, they were playing Leicester City, who had just confirmed their own promotion to the Premier League. Reading were staying in the Championship, so naturally the Leicester people spent the afternoon singing "Going Up, Staying Down" to the tune of "Yellow Submarine." Reading's response was "We have the record, 106!"

Reading finished eighth that first year up, then did the yo-yo thing and changed divisions five times in six seasons. They have been in the Championship since 2013, but in 2017 they made the playoff final, where they lost to Huddersfield Town in a penalty shootout. The next two years, after being so close to the Premier League, they sank to twentieth in the Championship both times, but since then have had better results.

One game in their history bears mention, though they won't want to remember it. In 2012 they played Arsenal in the League Cup and led, 4–0, after thirty-seven minutes. Arsenal stormed back, forced extra time, and scored three more in the extra thirty minutes to win it, 7–5. Thus did Reading become the first team in either Cup to score five goals and lose.

RIVALRIES: They used to have a thing with nearby Aldershot Town, but that club went out of business, and the current phoenix version of that team is down in the National League, three levels below the Royals. Reading has had to settle for disliking Swindon Town, Wycombe Wanderers, and Oxford, the latter in part because of a bizarre plan the two sets of owners hatched in the early 1980s to merge those two clubs. I get the sense both Oxford and Swindon care more about each other than Reading.

SONGS: They seem fond of "Sweet Caroline," and they have a funny one that says:

> We're not Real Madrid
> We're not Barcelona
> We are Reading FC
> Madejski is our owner.

2020–21 SEASON: 7th in the Championship, 3rd Round FA Cup, 2nd Round League Cup

2021–22 SEASON: The Championship (relegated in 2013)

STADIUM: Madejski Stadium, Reading's home since 1998, is named for a former owner, a local businessman who got them to the top division and largely paid for the construction. I'll let Wikipedia speak on what it's like: "It is an all-seater bowl stadium with a capacity of 24,161 and is located close to the M4 motorway. It is built on the site of a former household waste dump and is surrounded by methane vents."

So it's not exactly romantic, but it's not all that bad. It actually has good views of the action, and you sit quite close to the pitch. Outside one end is a nice big grassy area where the away fans lounge around pregame, and the area is clean if not exciting. I had a funny conversation with a fan who was a longtime season ticket holder. I asked him if he missed the old stadium. He said he did, then added that it was a horrible dump that smelled like stale beer and urine. This place is nice, he allowed; it just lacks character.

Away fans sit in the south end.

TOURS: Tours are offered some Sundays for £12 and must be booked ahead.

TICKETS: Tickets range from £23 to £29 and, unless they draw somebody big in a Cup, can be bought on the day.

GETTING THERE: It's three miles out from the train station, but there is a bus called the Football Express that runs to the stadium for £4 round trip. To find it, head right when you leave the station and walk across a big new courtyard to a turnaround where the buses line up.

PUBS: As you might have guessed, there is nothing out by the stadium, so have a pint in town. There's a pub called the Three Guineas that has been designated for away fans right at the station. The nearby Greyfriar gets good marks from the beer gurus, and The Gateway is an Irish pub with sports on TV.

Over by the river, where you ought to go for a stroll anyway, look for Bel and the Dragon and the Fisherman's Cottage, both within twenty walking minutes of the station.

GRUB: The food action in town is all along Castle Street and in the pedestrian zone, also along the redeveloped waterfront. There are some chains in there, but Handmade Burger Co. has good burgers and a nice view.

AROUND TOWN: After cruising the downtown and riverfront, if you want some peace and quiet, you can walk along the Kennet and Avon Canal admiring barges and boats and swans. You can also walk the Thames Path from near the station through King's Meadow or as far as you'd like. And there's a Museum of English Rural Life at the university.

The Reading Museum has some 7,000 items related to that biscuit company, Huntley and Palmers. Their factory in Reading was the largest biscuit factory in the world in the 19th century (this makes me even sadder that it's gone!). The Abbey Quarter is an area of ruins related to the Reading Abbey, a major site in medieval times and the burial site of King Henry I.

Stevenage is one of several clubs that perfectly fit the bill if you want to get just out of London for the day and see some proper small-club family football.

LOCATION: Stevenage is a northern suburb of London.

CONTACT: stevenagefc.com, 01438 223223, #StevenageFC

NICKNAMES: The Boro

WOMEN'S TEAM: Stevenage FC Women play in the Women's National League Division 1 South East, tier 4 of the pyramid, with games at The County Ground in Letchworth, Hertfordshire. See the club website for more.

HISTORY: First, there was Stevenage Town, which formed in 1889 and lasted until 1969, when it went broke. It was replaced by Stevenage Athletic, which went bust in 1976. Then came the current club, Stevenage Borough FC, which almost died again in 2009 but was saved—and dropped *Borough* from its name. So we are talking about a club on the fringes.

They toiled around in the lower reaches of the English Football Pyramid until the mid-1990s, then made the Conference and stayed there until 2010. During the 1997–98 season, they drew Newcastle at home in the FA Cup. They held the then-mighty Magpies, who actually played Alan Shearer, to a 1–1 draw, then lost the replay at St. James' Park, 2–1, on a controversial Shearer goal that many say didn't cross the line.

Since then, they have bounced back and forth between League One and League Two, with a highlight being 2011–12, when they made the round of sixteen in the FA Cup, held Tottenham at home, and lost a replay at White Hart Lane.

In 2019, they almost made the playoffs to get into League One, but the next season the bottom fell out. They finished twenty-fourth and last in the final table, but when Macclesfield

Town got a huge points penalty for financial shenanigans and Bury went out of business, Stevenage were spared relegation. They were fourteenth in League Two last season.

RIVALRIES: Luton Town, now a couple of leagues above them in the Championship, and Barnet, now a league below them in the National League.

SONGS: Nothing in particular. When I saw them win a game, they did a fun back-and-forth Tetris dance.

2020–21 SEASON: 14th in League Two, 3rd Round FA Cup, 1st Round League Cup

2021–22 SEASON: League Two (relegated in 2014)

STADIUM: Their home since 1980 is called The Lamex, possibly my least-favorite stadium name; that's a sponsorship thing, of course, and its real name is the far superior Broadhall Way. The capacity last year was 7,800, with just under half of those being seats. But last season they debuted a new North Stand, funded in part by £500,000 raised from 200 supporters. Last we saw, the visitors were in the South Stand, the family section was in the North, the hospitality and bar in the South, and the rowdies on the East Terrace. Go stand with the lads and do it right.

It's across a major road from a shopping center and a Burger King. It's also next to a piece of forest you can see on a map, but that's more of a reclamation project than anything especially charming. Still, it's a modern and cozy little ground with several things I like about these lower-league clubs: many people outside greeting each other by name, a ticket office worker happy to welcome an American and encourage him to "tell your friends back home we need the support," a handwritten list of upcoming games, a "wall of fame" with no one you've ever heard of, and a sparse club bar filled with fans of both clubs happily knocking back a few pints and comparing notes on their seasons.

Tottenham also uses the ground for some youth games.

TOURS: I can't imagine a tour has ever been requested!

TICKETS: Tickets cost around £20 for adults and are easy to get.

GETTING THERE: Stevenage station is 25 minutes on the train from London's King's Cross. The club runs a shuttle bus from the bus and train stations that costs just £1 return; otherwise it's about a 30-minute walk. The nearest bus stop is about 10 minutes away, so a taxi is a good call, especially if you pop over to the high street for food and drink before.

PUBS: There is a small, family-friendly club at the ground. There are several pubs on the high street in town, including a Wetherspoon pub called the Standing Order. The Marquis of Lorne offers traditional cask ales, and I had a lovely meal and visit at The Chequers, which also has outdoor seating.

GRUB: It's the usual stuff at the ground; hit one of the high street pubs or Misya for some decent Turkish.

AROUND TOWN: Ask any local: nothing happens here! It's just a bedroom community for London, and the only thing you're going to be here for is the game and a pregame pint. Walking in from the station, though, after you cross a motorway, you will be greeted by a mural featuring a surprising number of people who have some connection to the place. Walk about fifteen minutes left to the high street, get something to eat and drink, and then catch a cab to the game.

TOTTENHAM HOTSPUR

Tottenham Hotspur are a club with a proud and trophy-filled history, a large following, a shiny new stadium, and a reputation for just screwing things up.

LOCATION: The North London neighborhood of Tottenham

CONTACT: tottenhamhotspur.com, 0344 499 5000, #THFC

NICKNAMES: Spurs or (far less often) the Lilywhites. Please don't say "the" Spurs or Tottenham Hotspurs. It's Tottenham (TOTT-num) or Spurs.

WOMEN'S TEAM: Tottenham Hotspur FC Women are in the Women's Super League. Home games are at The Hive, home ground of Barnet FC.

HISTORY: Sometimes I try to compare English soccer clubs to American teams for perspective, and with Spurs, I always come up with the Dallas Cowboys. They were kings of the world a few decades ago, remain very popular today, are famous for wearing white at home, and have an amazing stadium, but they have won just one League Cup in the last twenty years, and their fans are always kind of frustrated.

They were founded in Tottenham, a North London neighborhood, in 1882 and took their nickname from Sir Henry Percy, nicknamed Harry Hotspur, who lived around there. Harry, a character in Shakespeare's *Henry IV*, was also said to be fond of fighting cocks, so in 1910 a player made a nine-foot statue of a cockerel. It stood on top of their old stadium, White Hart Lane, from then on and now adorns the new place.

Spurs, along with Manchester United, were the only club to win trophies in each decade from the 1950s through 2010. Their glory days were the early 1960s, when they became the first club to win the League and FA Cups ("doing the double") in the same year in the 20th century. That was 1960–61. They won the FA Cup again in 1962, then the UEFA Cup (now the Europa League) in 1962, becoming the first English club to win a European trophy.

Their last trophy was the 2008 League Cup, but their last League title was 1961, and their last FA Cup was 1991. For many years since then, they have failed to get it done, and they finished behind Arsenal in the league for decades until 2016–17. Gunners fans enjoyed taunting them with shirts and stickers reading "Mind the Gap." Arsenal fans also created an annual holiday, St. Totteringham's Day—the day when it's confirmed Spurs will finish behind Arsenal again. In fact, when you have things going your way and it falls apart for some reason, that's said to be very "Spursy."

At the moment, both Spurs and their bitter rivals are suffering. Tottenham, after making the 2019 Champions League Final, are toiling this season in the new Europa Conference League, a rung below the Europa League. They might comfort themselves knowing Arsenal aren't in Europe at all.

An interesting tidbit of history is that for years Spurs were the favored club of Jews in London. This was originally because there were many Jews in their neighborhood; in the 1930s, it was estimated about one-third of their supporters were Jewish. (Opposing fans used to taunt them during Saturday games with chants of "Does Your Rabbi Know You're Here?") You will still hear chants of "Yid Army" and "Yiddo" that date from the 1970s and '80s when Tottenham supporters turned this insult back on their tormentors. But this is becoming somewhat controversial, and many folks are suggesting "the Y-word" should go away.

Another cultural note: thanks to the presence of forward Son Heung-min, there are hundreds of flag-waving and camera-toting South Koreans at every Spurs home game. One of the great and strange pleasures of English football is the postgame atmosphere in which everybody leaves except the waves of Koreans who descend to the lower rows to get a selfie and, they hope, an up-close view of their hero.

RIVALRIES: Arsenal, whom they have played 203 times in the North London derby, are the huge rival. The rivalry started when Arsenal moved to North London after Spurs were already well established there, then got voted into the Football League ahead of them. They also hate any other London club, Chelsea in particular

SONGS: The biggest is "When the Spurs Go Marching In." You might also hear "Glory Glory Tottenham Hotspur" and "Being a Yid." Their three biggest stars have their own songs as well. Their song for the homegrown star is "He's One of Our Own."

2020–21 SEASON: 7th in Premier League, 5th Round FA Cup, Runners-up League Cup, Round of 16 UEFA Europa League

2021–22 SEASON: Premier League (top flight since 1978), UEFA Europa Conference League

STADIUM: Spurs now have a new, 62,850-seat, $1 billion Tottenham Hotspur Stadium. It was late, it was over budget, and Spurs had to endure a longer than planned exile at Wembley. But it was worth it, as the place is simply astonishing. There is no way it will live up to White Hart Lane for atmosphere; that was easily the loudest stadium I have ever visited. But that one only had 36,000 seats, and Spurs needed to grow. The new one, still waiting on a sponsor name, is right next to where the old one was.

The main interior feature is the 17,500-seat, single-tier South Stand, where they seat the loud Spurs folks; there are also bars between the rows for (they hope) the eventual "safe standing" experience. Behind that is a five-story glass enclosure with a food court and a large public space. There is also a microbrewery, completely insane hospitality options with heated seats and USB ports, and a climbing wall on the outside of the stadium. But the notable thing is that they are making a big push for NFL games, and that means having two pitches. Seriously. While the artificial NFL surface is in use, the grass soccer pitch divides into pieces and slides underground into a controlled growing environment.

The entire complex, by the way, is cashless.

TOURS: For a self-guided tour with a "multimedia" device it costs £26.25 for adults. They also have a "Dare Walk"—the club's motto is "To Dare Is to Do"—that includes a walk outside the upper levels of the stadium and onto a glass walkway some 150 feet above the pitch, where you can visit the legendary golden cockerel that was on top of the old stadium for decades.

Book all of that (well ahead) at experience.tottenhamhotspur.com.

TICKETS: Even with this new stadium, tickets are tough. Like most clubs, Spurs have a membership and loyalty scheme, and like most big clubs, a membership is virtually required for each ticket you want, and even with one, you will probably have to deal with the members' resale area. Adult memberships start at £48. Check their website for the latest.

GETTING THERE: All of the transit in the immediate area was swept up in the stadium redevelopment, but this much didn't change: the closest rail station is White Hart Lane on the Overground line, just a couple of minutes away. Get there from Liverpool Street Station. The club was recently trying to change White Hart Lane Station to Tottenham Hotspur Station, and I think it's not a coincidence that there is an Arsenal Station near their biggest rivals' ground. The closest Tube station is Seven Sisters on the Piccadilly line. From there it's a half-hour walk, so it's better to grab a bus (route 149, 259, 279, or 349) for 11 minutes.

PUBS: If you can get into The Bricklayers on the high road, that's the place to be. It is a classic supporters pub. Just a little north is Coach and Horses, another Spurs pub but with more outdoor seating and, if the weather is nice, grilled meat on the menu. Right across the street from the stadium is the No. 8 Hostel, formerly the Bell and Hare, with another beer garden. Strangely, its address is No. 17 White Hart Lane. There's a pretty good beer selection inside the stadium, including from the local Beavertown Brewery.

GRUB: As of last season, the promised redevelopment of the area hadn't really kicked in yet, and the pandemic set it all back again, so the food options in the immediate area were lots of jerk chicken and pizza and kebab places all up and down the high road. None of them stood out in particular.

WATFORD

Watford are becoming something of a yo-yo club, bouncing between the Championship and (for this season) Premier League. Still, as a game day, they are an easy and fun way to catch some footy while you're in London.

LOCATION: Watford, Hertfordshire, essentially a northern suburb of London, fifteen miles from the center by train

CONTACT: watfordfc.com, 01923 496000, #WatfordFC

NICKNAMES: The Hornets and occasionally the Golden Boys or Yellow Army

WOMEN'S TEAM: Watford FC Women compete in the Women's Championship, the second tier. Home games are at the ground of semipro team Kings Langley FC about ten miles north of Watford FC.

HISTORY: We can kind of skip ahead here. Watford was formed in 1881, joined the Football League in 1921, and basically spent the next sixty years in the third tier. It was in 1976 that their modern history started—with a rather unusual source.

A certain Reginald Kenneth Dwight grew up in the area. He stood on the Watford FC terraces and then made a bit of money in the entertainment business after changing his name to Elton John. He bought his favorite club in 1976—who gets to do that?—and said he was taking them to the top. They were in the Fourth Division at the time.

He hired Graham Taylor as manager, and off they went. They crushed the Fourth Division in Taylor's first year and, by 1982, were all the way up in the First. Incredibly, that season they finished second behind Liverpool, thus qualifying for the UEFA Cup (today's Champions League). So in seven years, they went from playing Hartlepool and Northampton Town to losing to Sparta Prague in the third round of Europe!

They lost the 1984 FA Cup final to Everton, but of course this couldn't last. Taylor left for Aston Villa in 1987, and Watford was relegated the next season. They were back in the third tier within ten years. Taylor came back in the late '90s, secured two straight promotions to the new Premier League, then retired for good in 2001. They would pop up a couple of times in the Premier League over the next several seasons. Sir Elton sold the club in 2002 but remains its honorary life president.

They got back in the Premier League in 2015, and lost the final of the 2018–19 FA Cup, but one story along the way has to be told. In the 2013 Championship playoffs, they drew Leicester City in the semifinals. Leicester won the first leg at home, 1–0. At the very end of the second leg at Watford, the Hornets were up, 2–1, with extra time looming. Leicester drew a penalty. Make it and go to the final at Wembley. But the Watford keeper saved it, then saved the rebound shot, and then Watford sprinted down the other way. Troy Deeney blasted in a ninety-seventh-minute winner and leaped into the wildly celebrating crowd. They lost the final to Crystal Palace, but still. It's one of the more amazing soccer videos you'll ever see.

They were relegated to the Championship in 2020 after finishing nineteenth. But they bounced right back up for this season after finishing second to Norwich City.

RIVALRIES: Nearby Luton Town are the biggest rival; they finally played again for the first time in 14 years. In their two Championship fixtures during the 2020-21 season, each club got a win.

SONGS: Back in the 1960s, Watford adopted the theme song to a BBC show called *Z-Cars*, kind of a drum-and-fife number. (In England they say "ZED-cars.") That's random enough; apparently, it was the manager's favorite show. What makes it odder is that Everton uses it as well. They will also do a call-and-response to spell out Watford.

2020–21 SEASON: 2nd in the Championship (promoted), 3rd Round FA Cup, 3rd Round League Cup

2021–22 SEASON: Premier League (promoted in 2021)

STADIUM: Their home since 1922, Vicarage Road—may it ever remain so named—is surprisingly pleasant and cozy for a Premier League ground; its capacity is 21,997. The oldest part of it was built in the 1980s, and it's all had work done recently to make it nice all around. My beer guru Andrew says their selection is well above average.

Along one side is the Graham Taylor Stand, and on the other the Sir Elton John Stand. Along the top of the latter is written a long quote from "Your Song." When they dedicated it to him in 2014, he famously said that not only did he never think he'd have a stand named for him, "I never thought I would sit in a stand." The home rowdies will be in the Rookery Stand behind a goal, and the away fans in the other end's Vicarage Road Stand.

TOURS: No tours are available at this stadium.

TICKETS: When they were previously in the top tier, prices went from £36 to £42, and tickets were hard to get in such a small place. A membership would certainly help, and it also gets you into an online exchange for season ticket holders releasing their tickets. We also sell a lovely hospitality package there.

GETTING THERE: From Euston station in London, there are three ways to get to Vicarage Road:

- Take the Tube to Watford, which is the slowest way.
- Take London Overground service from Euston to Watford High Street, which is the closest station to the ground. But this ride is about 40 minutes.
- The best way to do it is to take the 16-minute West Midlands Trains service (not the Overground, which has more stops and takes longer) from Euston to Watford Junction. You can even use your Oyster card to get there. Watford Junction is a big suburban train station that is about a 20-minute walk, passing lots of food along the way, from the ground. The first bit of walking directions can be odd on Google Maps, so I'll save you some trouble: take the middle of the three streets in front of you, past the Holiday Inn onto Clarendon Road.

PUBS: The closest is The Oddfellows pub in Fearnley Street, an Irish-themed place that had a barbecue going when I went past. In the town center are three big chain pubs, including an Aussie-themed Walkabout, an O'Neills and a Wetherspoon pub called the Moon Under Water.

GRUB: Also on the walk from the station, you will come across the fun New Watford Market with lots of food options; it's open Tuesday through Saturday until 5:30 p.m. There is a Five Guys, which will be packed. I also had a nice meal once at Taste of Lahore near Watford High Street station.

WEMBLEY STADIUM

Obviously this is not a club, and this year not even a club's temporary home. But you might want to catch a Cup, playoff, or international game there, or just go out for a tour. It's an incredible place.

LOCATION: Northwest of Greater London about thirty minutes from the center by train

CONTACT: wembleystadium.com, 0800 169 2007, #Wembley

NICKNAMES: None, really. It's just the national stadium. But the word *Wembley* means a lot more than the stadium anyway. Read on to see why.

HISTORY: The idea of a national stadium is slightly confusing to us Americans. Almost every country in the world has one except us. We are, of course, just too big for such a thing, and we're used to big games moving around anyway. Imagine having the Super Bowl in Dallas every year just because it's in the middle of the country.

In England, the final of damn near everything in men's football is at Wembley Stadium: Cups, League playoffs, all of it. Even the FA Cup semifinals are there now. It's for this reason that "going to Wembley" signifies "playing for silverware," and why, whenever a club confirms they are headed there, their fans start singing:

Que sera sera,
Whatever will be will be.
We're going to Wemb-a-lee!
Que sera sera.

It's also where the men's national team plays most of its home games. (The women's FA Cup final has been there since 2015; otherwise, the women, including the national team, move their games around.) Wembley has hosted Champions League finals, 2012 Olympic gold medal games, concerts, and NFL games. In 2021 it also hosted the semis and final of the UEFA European Championships.

By the way, Wembley is an actual place that people live in. The stadium is named for the place, but the way people talk about it, you would think that the stadium is the entire place.

This is the second Wembley Stadium. The first stadium, built on the same spot in 1923 for an exhibition, was originally called the Empire Stadium and held 127,000 people, mostly on terraces. Four days after it opened, they had the FA Cup final there, but they didn't bother to sell tickets. It's estimated that between 240,000 and 300,000 people showed up, and they poured onto the field, threatening the game itself. Enter legendary Police Constable George Scorey and his horse, Billie. The horse was actually grey but looks white in the old films. They (with some help) pushed the crowd back, and Bolton Wanderers beat West Ham United, 2–0. The bridge outside the stadium is still called the White Horse Bridge.

That stadium, which also hosted Live Aid in 1985, just got too old and dumpy, so it came down in 2002. To the consternation of many, so did its iconic twin towers. The debris wound up under a mound in a park called Northala Fields, so you can still climb the old Wembley there if you'd like.

All the finals moved to Cardiff for a few years while the new intergalactic spaceship of a stadium was built. It opened in 2007 and holds 90,000 for football (Adele drew 98,000 for a concert). There are three rings of seats; the one in the center is called Club Wembley and is backed by a concourse that wraps around most of the stadium, with bars, restaurants, shops, and even a champagne bar. In the lower level, the sideline seats that are always empty early in the second half are the Bobby Moore Club, named for the hero of the 1966 World Cup winners whose statue also stands outside overlooking everything like a Greek god. You have to be about as rich as a god to sit there.

For league and Cup games, each club is assigned to one end of the stadium and gets 25,000 to 40,000 tickets. The remaining seats are in the club areas, where you are not allowed to wear team shirts, cheer too much, or engage in "persistent standing." If one team is from London and the other from up north, the police actually steer them to separate train stations, each one closest to their end of the stadium. This is in part for convenience and also for keeping the loonies away from each other. It only takes a few, you know.

Just a few random facts before we move on. The stadium has 166 executive suites in addition to all the club stuff. The arch over the top actually holds up much of the roof. It's 1,033 feet long and is the longest unsupported roof structure in the world. The crossbar that played a major and controversial role in the 1966 World Cup Final (look it up) is in the lobby; you can see it on the tour. Wembley has 2,618 toilets—the most of any venue in the world. It has thirty-five miles of power cables, 120,000 cubic yards of concrete, and 25,000 tons of steel. I am pretty sure it can fly and communicate with other planets. All of this cost £798 million to build.

Aside from Bobby Moore, there is also a statue of five rugby players. I could not tell you a single thing about any one of them.

If you want to win a trivia contest sometime, the first competitive game there was won by Stevenage Borough (now FC), 3–2 over Kidderminster Harriers in the FA Trophy final of 2007.

TOURS: The Wembley tour is, for me, totally worth a trip out there. Tours are offered almost every day that there isn't a game on. An adult ticket is £22 and kids under 16 are £15. There are also VIP options. The tour lasts about an hour and fifteen minutes, and it's pretty much a standard tour: in the box seats, hospitality areas, dressing rooms, and media room, then through the player tunnel to the touchline. It's just all a lot bigger than usual. And there's a royal box, which you still can't sit in, lowly commoner. You will need to book tours ahead at bookings.wembleytours.com.

There is also a small café and a museum about England winning the 1966 World Cup. In fact, there is a *lot* about England winning the 1966 World Cup. It's kind of the only thing they ever did, other than invent the game.

GETTING THERE: Wembley has several access points from London's transit system. The closest Underground stop is Wembley Park, about a 10-minute walk away. This is on the Jubilee and Metropolitan lines; note that the latter has fewer stops. A bit farther away is the Wembley Central station, which has both Underground (Bakerloo line) and rail services.

Traditionally, Wembley Park is the way to go, as you come out of the ground with thousands of other people and walk Olympic Way up to the stadium.

But I'm here to tell you that the best way is to go to Marylebone station in London and take Chiltern Railways one stop to the Wembley Stadium station. You're on the train 9 minutes, and from there it's less than 10 minutes' walking.

Whichever way you go, plan to get there early, and assume that it will be three levels of nightmare getting out of there after the game.

Also note that, thanks to NFL fans bringing who knows what to games, there is now a strict bag policy at Wembley. Basically, try not to bring one. A purse is fine, but anything bigger than 11 x 8 x 8 inches has to be stored nearby for £5.

PUBS: If you're in Club World (which is where most of the hospitality stuff is), you'll have myriad options on the concourse. The traditional pub for pregame, though, is The Green Man on Dagmar Avenue. It's about a fifteen-minute walk from the stadium and has a sprawling outdoor seating area that will be insane before games. Sometimes it's designated for one team's fans, but you can possibly talk your way in, unless you're wearing the other team's shirt. Also popular is The Torch on Bridge Road, sort of behind Wembley Park station.

If you're starting out from Marylebone as I recommend, there is a sports-themed pub in that station and two other pubs—The Globe plus the more traditional Allsop Arms—within a block.

GRUB: The amazing blog *Londonist* has an entire post about where to eat (and drink) in Wembley, whose population they say is two-thirds Asian. Go over to Londonist.com and search "eat drink Wembley."

If you're starting at Marylebone, hit up Firebrand Pizza next door to The Globe pub. It's legit Italian.

For a little taste of my fun adventure at Wembley, check out "Invasion of the Tartan Army" on page 162.

WEST HAM UNITED

West Ham has been a bit of a zombie club of late: a big, traditional club wandering and a bit lifeless after moving from their old home to one that inspires ambivalence. But they're off to Europe for this season!

LOCATION: London Stadium in the Queen Elizabeth Olympic Park, in the city's East End

CONTACT: whufc.com, 0333 030 0174, #COYI

NICKNAMES: The Irons or the Hammers, both because of their industrial roots

WOMEN'S TEAM: West Ham United Women compete in the Women's Super League, tier 1 of the pyramid. Home games are at Dagenham & Redbridge Stadium.

HISTORY: Americans can imagine that the Green Bay Packers dominated in the old days—as they did. But then they never had Brett Favre and Aaron Rodgers or became good again, and then they moved out of Lambeau Field to some shiny, new, boring stadium next to a mall in the suburbs. Here's hoping this season's Europa League adventure will breathe some life into them.

The club was founded by 1895 (the actual date is vague) by workers at the Thames Ironworks. They had some good years in the 1920s and '30s, but they were a power in the late 1950s and '60s. West Ham won the league in 1958, the FA Cup in 1964, lost the final in 1966, and won the (now) Europa League in 1965. When England won the World Cup in 1966 at Wembley, three star players—captain Bobby Moore, Martin Peters (who scored in the final), and Geoff Hurst (who scored the only World Cup final hat trick in history) were all West Ham players who came up through their youth system. West Ham fans like to claim—sometimes in song—that their club won the World Cup.

They won the FA Cup in 1975 and again in 1980; that was their last major trophy and also the last time a club not in the top division lifted that one. Since 1978, they have switched between the top two divisions eleven times. They won the Championship playoff in 2012 and are now in the Premier League, where last year they finished sixth, good enough for their first European spot since 2016.

The biggest thing to happen in their recent history was leaving their traditional stadium, the Boleyn Ground, aka Upton Park. They played there from 1904 to 2016, but since it held only 35,000 people and the club wanted to grow, they moved to London Stadium after a long argument with the City of London. The Boleyn was one of the great old stadiums in the country, truly intimidating and loud, and without question something was lost in the move. You might even hear fans singing "We Should Have Stayed at the Boleyn."

RIVALRIES: Obviously they don't care for the other London clubs, especially Chelsea and Tottenham; a shared history of hooliganism doesn't help. There is an odd rivalry with Sheffield United because of a controversy over a player signing in 2007 that helped West Ham stay up and send the Blades down.

But it's the rivalry with Millwall that is strictly personal. Both clubs go back to industrial companies in the East End, so we're talking about factory workers from the same neighborhood going at it. (You might hear it called the Dockers derby. They don't mean clothing.) They have played ninety-nine times in 118 years, with Millwall leading in wins, 38–34. They haven't played since 2012, but the last three times they hooked up, there was fairly widespread fan trouble. I so wish they were in the same league!

SONGS: West Ham sings one of the most famous, and frankly oddest, songs in all of football, "I'm Forever Blowing Bubbles." Let's just take a look at the lyrics and imagine that they are supposed to inspire the team to victory:

> I'm forever blowing bubbles
> Way up in the air
> They fly so high
> They reach the sky
> And like my dreams, they fade and die.
>
> Fortune's always hiding
> I've looked everywhere.
> I'm forever blowing bubbles,
> Pretty bubbles in the air.
> United! United! United!

The PA system (which Brits like to call the Tannoy) plays the 1975 FA Cup version with the crowd taking over on "Fortune." All of this happens with machines cranking out bubbles all over the stadium. So where did it come from? It's a bit convoluted; it's an old show tune that arrived at West Ham through a soap commercial, a local schoolboy who tried out with the club, and his creative headmaster.

2020–21 SEASON: 6th in Premier League, 5th Round FA Cup, 4th Round League Cup

2021–22 SEASON: Premier League (promoted in 2012)

STADIUM: This whole area used to be London Docklands, the biggest port in the world. Then it was the scene of the 2012 Olympics. Now it is Queen Elizabeth Olympic Park, known by the locals as Betty Park. It's one of the largest urban parks in London and has restored wetlands and plenty of open space, as well as some of the Olympic venues. London Stadium was one of those; it held 80,000 for track and field but was reduced for its current use.

It is beautiful, large, clean, impressive, and rather unpopular. Some of this is because it isn't Upton Park, but it's also a rather sterile place surrounded by concrete and construction with a mall nearby and a bizarro tower next to it. The stadium holds 57,000 in a two-tiered circle; one of the objections is that the stands are so far back from the pitch. Away fans will be in the southwest corner, usually in both tiers, which due to stadium goofiness have a pretty large gap between them.

TOURS: There are several tour options here: basic guided or self-guided tours are £19, guided match-day tours are £30, a VIP match-day tour with a couple of perks is £45, and a tour led by a "legend" that only true Hammers will recognize is £40.

TICKETS: West Ham isn't one of the big six, but they are in London, so tickets can be tough if they're doing well or playing a big opponent. Getting a membership (around £40, depending on the type) will help and will get you into a ticket exchange where season ticket holders release unused tickets. Those prices can get up to £80, but compare that to the illegal secondary market and you'll be happy. Some of the hospitality packages are affordable as well.

GETTING THERE: There are three train stations for getting there, the main one being Stratford—but not Shakespeare's Stratford. This station is on the London Overground, Tube (Jubilee and Central lines), and Docklands Light Railway. It's also next to a big mall called Westfield. By the way, many Brits pronounce *mall* as in "malware."

You can also use Stratford International station on the other side of Westfield and served by trains from St. Pancras station, or Hackney Wick, a smaller station on the other side of the stadium. If you're arriving early and it's more convenient for you, use Hackney Wick. But don't try to leave that way. It's tiny, it will be crowded, and the trains arriving from Stratford will already be jammed.

To leave, you will probably head for Stratford and be herded along like cattle, since this is how most people leave. To keep people from rushing in all at once, they occasionally stop the flow with big red stop signs then let them go with big green go signs. All very efficient. Expect cattle noises from the crowd.

PUBS: There is notoriously little right around the stadium. Near Stratford station, there are a couple of pubs called The Goldengrove (a Wetherspoon) and The Goose. Also popular, I am told, with fans before the game is a Wetherspoon pub called Hamilton Hall near Liverpool Street station, where you can catch an Overground for Stratford.

Close to Hackney Wick, there is a brewery and pizzeria called CRATE next door to a cool pub with outdoor seating called Howling Hops. Walking away from the stadium a short way from Hackney Wick gets you to Mason and Company, which has craft beers and Italian food.

GRUB: Aside from those mentioned above, Westfield Mall has a bunch of the usual options. Right next to the tower and stadium is a place called The Last Drop that has beer and food; being so close, it will of course be mobbed.

Don't forget you can always eat and drink elsewhere. You're in London, after all.

AROUND TOWN: You will certainly notice the Orbit Tower, a crazy-looking 376-foot structure right next to the stadium. It is officially both a piece of art and a tourist attraction added for the Olympics by then-mayor (and now prime minister) Boris Johnson. (One nickname for the Orbit is "Boris's Johnson.") It is also a ride and an observation tower. For £11.50, you can go to the top and look around, and then you can either take the lift back down, walk down the steps, rappel down (which the Brits call abseiling), or take the world's longest tunnel slide inside the structure. You'll have to tell me how any of those are!

The park is worth a walk around as well. There are wetlands and arenas, and signs will point you to the spot where the medal platforms stood. Otherwise, unlike their old ground, this area doesn't offer much to the non-soccer tourist. If you're curious about the old scene, go to Upton Park on the Tube, check out Queen's Market (and see if the One Pound Fish guy is around), and get something from the Arabic world to eat.

WIMBLEDON

League One football in a quiet and lovely part of Greater London—and Wimbledon has an absolutely uplifting story to boot.

LOCATION: Kingston upon Thames, a half hour southwest from London's Waterloo station

CONTACT: afcwimbledon.co.uk, 020 8547 3528, #AFCW

NICKNAMES: The Dons or the Wombles, the latter after fictional characters in a series of children's novels set in Wimbledon Common. There is, in fact, a Womble walking awound the gwound.

WOMEN'S TEAM: AFC Wimbledon Ladies play in Women's National League Division One South East, tier 4 of the pyramid. Home games are in nearby Carshalton; see afcwimbledonladies.co.uk for more.

HISTORY: So this is a little complicated—far more so than I have space for here. There once was a club named Wimbledon FC that existed from 1889 until 2004 and played their games at a ground called Plough Lane in Wimbledon. They rose through the ranks, made the Football League in 1977, and then remarkably made the top division. They were founder members of the Premier League in 1992, won the FA Cup in 1988, and got relegated in 2000.

Then financial troubles came, and the owners decided to move the team. Americans read this and say, "Yeah, no big deal." But to the English it was…well, there aren't really words for it. Moving a team had never happened before and hasn't since. I asked English people about it, and they actually looked nauseated. But move they did to Milton Keynes, itself a "new town," and they changed their named to MK Dons. The league and FA opposed it, but some independent commission approved it—because money—and then banned anyone from appealing their decision and strongly suggested that nobody try to resurrect the Wimbledon club.

Thousands of Wimbledon supporters and fans all over the country basically told them all to fuck off. And then they did something great: they started their own damn club! A few of them met at The Fox and Grapes Pub on Wimbledon Common, where the original club used to change for games. They selected a manager and designed uniforms based on the original. They had tryouts and picked a team from the 230 guys who showed up. They entered the Combined Counties Football League Premier Division; that would be tier 9 of the pyramid, where attendance averages about fifty. Wimbledon averaged more than 3,000. The fans own seventy-five percent of AFC Wimbledon.

At once, they started kicking ass and taking names. The first year, 2002–03, they won their last eleven games and finished third. The next year they won their first twenty-one (that's thirty-two in a row!), then finished the season as unbeaten champions with forty-two wins and four draws. They moved up a level to the Isthmian League First Division and led that wire to wire. Along the way they went unbeaten for seventy-eight straight games (February 2003 to December 2004), a new record for any level of football in the UK. One player, Kevin Cooper, scored sixty-six goals in the 2003–04 season.

Three years later came another promotion, and they won that league in the first year. In May 2011 at Manchester City's stadium, they beat Luton Town in a playoff to make the Football League. That would be five promotions in nine years, making them the only Football League team that was established in this century. They made League One in 2016 and have stayed there since—barely. The last four seasons, they have finished eighteenth, nineteenth or twentieth. In 2018–19 they memorably beat West Ham at home 4–2 to make the 5th Round of the FA Cup.

Meanwhile—and this was the best part—MK Dons got relegated to League Two for a season in 2018. AFC Wimbledon was then ahead of their cursed zombie former selves.

And now for the final cherry: this year they are playing in a new Plough Lane; the Wombles have finally come home.

RIVALRIES: MK Dons, obviously, are a rival. I have heard it referred to as The Derby That Shouldn't Exist. They have played eleven times, with the total wins by MK Dons 7, and by Wimbledon 2. They also have rivalries with relative neighbors Crawley Town and Sutton United, but they have left both behind while climbing the pyramid. Millwall and Charlton get some mention as rivals as well.

SONGS: They have quite a few about MK Dons (whom they disparagingly call the Franchise) and about wanting to go back to Plough Lane, including one set to the tune of "Show Me the Way to Go Home."

2020–21 SEASON: 19th in League One, 2nd Round FA Cup, 1st Round League Cup

2021–22 SEASON: League One (promoted in 2016)

STADIUM: This season, Wimbledon have a whole new stadium back on their ancestral home of Plough Lane in the actual district of Wimbledon. Construction started on that in 2019, and for a while last season they were playing at QPR's Loftus Road. The new Plough Lane seats 9,215 with the ability to expand to 20,000.

TOURS: No word yet on tours of the new stadium.

TICKETS: Last year, adult tickets cost £22 or £30.

GETTING THERE: The two closest rail stations are Earlsfield, on the South Western Railway about 12 minutes out from Waterloo, and Haydons Road, on the Thameslink service around 30 minutes from Blackfriars. Each station is around a 15-minute walk from the ground.

PUBS: I suppose you could swing by The Fox and Grapes and see the place where all this started, but it's not very close to either stadium. It's on Wimbledon Common, a sprawling bunch of parks a little over a mile from Wimbledon station.

There are two good options near the new ground: The Corner Pin and a craft brewery called By the Horns. Clearly, more research is required!

GRUB: Again, I haven't been there, but there seem to be more options beyond the north side of the ground, coming from the station.

AROUND THE GROUND: With all this talk of Wimbledon—yes, it's that Wimbledon. You can take tours of the All England Lawn Tennis and Croquet Club for £25. Take a taxi from the Wimbledon Park Tube; see wimbledon.com for details.

WYCOMBE WANDERERS

Poor Wycombe finally made the Championship for the first time, then their fans couldn't see them because of the pandemic. They were relegated on the last day last season but are still a fun day out.

LOCATION: High Wycombe, about thirty-five minutes west of London's Marylebone Station. "High" in the UK, by the way, is like saying "Main" in the US, so there's no Low Wycombe. There is a West Wycombe, but let's move on.

CONTACT: wycombewanderers.co.uk, 01494 441118, #Chairboys

NICKNAMES: The Blues or the Chairboys, because High Wycombe has been known since the 16th century as a center for furniture manufacturing, especially chairs. Their particular claim to fame is the Windsor chair. There's even a Chair Making Museum in town, if you're interested.

WOMEN'S TEAM: Wycombe Wanderers Women (aka the Chairgirls) compete in the Southern Region Women's Football League Premier Division, tier 5 of the pyramid. Home games are in the Flackwell Heath area of town.

HISTORY: This is where Wanderers become such a cool story. Their founding was like virtually everyone else's—as an amateur club in the 1880s. In their case, it was furniture workers getting together for games. But here's the thing: as the wave of professionalism swept over the country soon after (the Netflix series The English Game covers a bit of this), Wanderers stayed amateur, all the way into the 1970s.

They spent much of the 20th century in the Isthmian League, a regional outfit at tiers 7 and 8 of the pyramid. Their biggest accomplishment was winning the FA Amateur Cup in 1931. They also won the Isthmian five times, and in 1974 they made the FA Cup Third Round—as an amateur team—where they held first-division Middlesbrough at home before losing the away replay, 1–0.

So up to that point they were a very successful amateur team. They went pro in the 1970s and won the Isthmian League a few more times, but they kept turning down promotions to higher leagues. They simply couldn't afford the travel.

Then in 1990 it all changed when they moved to their current home, Adams Park, because the old one just wasn't up to par. Among other issues, the pitch sloped about 10 percent.

They also hired a young Martin O'Neill as manager. In 1991 they won the FA Trophy, and in 1993 they did the double of Conference (now National League) champs and FA Trophy again. O'Neill turned down Nottingham Forest to stay another year and, in 1994, led Wanderers to the Football League for the first time in their hundred-plus-year history.

O'Neill got them promoted again the next year, to what is now called League One, before leaving for Norwich and then many other top clubs, as well as the Irish National Team. But Wanderers stayed in the Football League, bouncing around between League One and League Two.

At the start of the 2019-20 season, though, things were dire. They had only nine players under contract in the summer of 2019. That's when a New Orleans attorney named Rob Couhig, who had previously owned a minor league baseball team, was looking to get into English soccer and found Wanderers.

I don't mean to paint him as the savior, but isn't this what you want from an owner? It comes from a story in the *New Orleans Times-Picayune*:

> Couhig made his pitch. He'd open his checkbook to acquire competitive players. He'd improve the food, beverages, and live entertainment at the stadium. He'd make it easier for people to buy tickets and find parking.

Leave it to a guy from New Orleans to understand what the people want. And it worked. When the season was called for the pandemic, the league adjusted the table to a points-per-game basis, which got Wanderers to third place and the playoffs. They rolled Fleetwood Town, 6–3, in the semifinals and beat Oxford United, 2–1, in the final at Wembley. For the first time ever, they made it to the second tier. The promotion to the Championship did not last long, as the Wanderers were relegated back to League One after finishing in 22nd place during the 2020-21 season. Unfortunately, they finished just one point behind Derby County and safety.

After the game, Adebayo Akinfenwa—the thirty-eight-year-old forward who stands six feet one, weighs 224 pounds, and goes by the nickname "Beast Mode"—gave a remarkable interview. Four years before, he had helped Wimbledon get promoted in his last game for them. So he was out of a job for that interview, and he asked clubs to look into him. Wanderers did. This time he invited (successfully, it turns out) Jurgen Klopp of Liverpool to hit him up (just socially this time) on WhatsApp! This is something you have to Google to believe.

Akinfenwa is almost worth the price of admission on his own. Just the sight of him is something to behold, but the dude can play, and it's obvious he is beloved as a teammate and club ambassador.

RIVALRIES: Apparently there is some heat with local teams Oxford, Reading, and Luton Town.

SONGS: Nothing special I noticed

2020–21 SEASON: 22nd in the Championship, 4th Round FA Cup, 1st Round League Cup

2021–22 SEASON: League One (relegated in 2021)

STADIUM: I could show you pictures of Adams Park (capacity 9,448) that make it look as if it's surrounded by trees and fields. And it is—on three sides. On the fourth side is the industrial estate you'll probably spend fifteen minutes walking through to get there. Bit of an odd place in that regard, but a nice one once you're there.

Just over half the seats are in the main Frank Adams Stand on the south side. Adams was a former player who actually purchased their previous home, Loakes Park (1895 to 1990), and then gave it to the club. Owning their stadium helps these small clubs immensely. The Adams Stand is two tiers, so if you want a high view of the action (and trees), sit in the upper Adams.

The other three sides are more like a lower-league place, with single tiers of about 1,200 seats in each. The home rowdies will be in the west BMI Healthcare stand, which is also the only one with terracing. So if standing with the lads is your aim, go west! Away fans will be behind the other goal in the east Lords Builders Merchants stand.

The old gates from Loakes Park are just outside.

TOURS: None

TICKETS: In their previous seasons in League One, they never sold out, and adult tickets are £20 to £28.

GETTING THERE: If you're walking from High Wycombe Station, plan for an hour. You can knock about 30 minutes off that by taking the 32 bus from Stop S just outside the train station. This gets you to the industrial estate, at which point everyone will get off the bus and start walking. Follow the colors. I paid £8 for a taxi to the same spot. There are also "football special" buses from the station; ask there for details.

PUBS: There are three at the ground, which is nice because there's nothing else within that fifteen-minute walk. Right at the base of the hill is the Hour Glass, which has a big space out back. All these let in both sets of fans during previous seasons.

Down in town, there's a Wetherspoon called The Falcon, an O'Neills, and a cool traditional pub called The Antelope, among others.

GRUB: They have a proper little barbecue, Chairboys Village, right at the ground, so if the weather's nice, that's an option. There is also food in the stadium pubs, but nothing special. You'll find all the usual chains down by the station and on High Street.

AROUND TOWN: Even longtime supporters told me there's little to do around town for a tourist. There is the aforementioned chair museum, on the very slim chance that appeals to you. The main attraction in town is the Hellfire Caves. Apparently, in the 18th century, old chalk mines were dug out further and became the meeting place of some kind of high-society men's club for who knows what kind of debauchery. They claim Benjamin Franklin once visited as well. I didn't make it there, but it looks a little freaky, with statues here and there and a voice narrating through speakers. Look for it online for more info.

Hughenden Manor, on the north side of town, is a National Trust Victorian-era home with a cafe and 1,500 acres of walkable scenery; get there via the 300 bus from Oxford Street in town. West Wycombe Park and Estate is a similar place on the west side of town; take bus 40 from the High Wycombe Bus Station for about thirty minutes to the Swan Inn Pub.

I've got this theory that one of the main reasons for the existence of soccer—indeed, sports in general—is so that grown men can go out in public, get drunk, act like children, vent their anger, sing, and scream a bunch of obscenities. Sometimes it really seems like that's what the whole thing is about.

I thought about this after seeing a World Cup qualifier between England and Scotland. I was sure it would be a big deal; it's not as if there's no history between the two. And with the World Cup on the line and Wembley as the stage, the stakes could hardly have been bigger. Also, London at Christmastime is something truly special.

But I was still not ready for what I saw upon emerging from the Covent Garden station: a Christmas wonderland with lights and Santas and shoppers and musicians. And men in kilts. Drinking and singing men in kilts. And garbage.

In reading the history of this matchup, one often encounters the phrase "a Tartan Army invasion of London." And from the looks of things on the road between the Nags Head and the White Lion on James Street, an invasion was indeed on. We had noise, we had blue face paint, we had feathered hats, we had Scottish flags, and we had songs in such a fine Scottish brogue that even when listening back to a video, I couldn't tell you what they were singing.

I was far from being the only tourist in the area recording the scene. It had rather the feel of a human zoo. "Honey, look, it's drinking time, and they're starting to sing. Oh dear, that one fell down." And they were making a horrific mess. And perhaps leering a bit too much at the tourist ladies, even if some of the former wanted their pictures taken with members of the Army.

I saw on Twitter that there was even more of it going on in Trafalgar Square. So, off I went. And my goodness, it was a scene. This time there were no gawking tourists; I think they were scared to go into it. I dared to, but on a couple of occasions I thought my camera might be requisitioned, and at least one empty beer can was kicked my way.

On the train to Wembley, I wound up trapped in a car with half a dozen of them. At first, again, it was kind of funny, seeing the commuters so shocked. One song, in particular, caused heads to shake in bewilderment; it's to the tune of a traditional Scottish folk song:

> Oooo, I know a lassie,
> A bonny, bonny lassie
> She's as tight as the paper on the wall.
> Legs like a spider,
> I'd love to fuckin' ride her.
> She's Mary fae Maryhill.

Barbarians from the north take over central London.

When it's combined with gyrating hips, swirling tongues, and hands banging on the roof of the car, it does make an impression.

Off to our right were a few very British gentlemen—what-what and cheerio and tweed and all that—and they thought the boys were charming. Then one of them started to sing along, encouraged in such by the leader of the Tartan Platoon, who was dancing and hopping all over the car. Eventually the oldster was belting it out, as if to say, "Brilliant, boys! I know a lassie as well!" I'm still not sure if it was funny, pathetic, or both.

Our local Army unit, upon arrival at Wembley Park, blended into the larger march—which I have to say appeared all Scottish. This was before England made the 2018 World Cup semifinals, and back then it was damn hard to find a fan base more down on their team, more discouraged, more spiteful toward their own than those of English soccer. They invented the game in the 19th century, won one World Cup in 1966 at the old Wembley, and since then have only made a few semifinals and one final—Euro 2020, which they lost at home. And yet somehow everyone convinces themselves that England should be world-class at this.

Scotland is under no such illusions, at least when sober. And their passion for the event, if not the game, can't be overstated. They may lose on the pitch, but they will be heard!

Ah, right. The game. Well, the stadium is magnificent, a true palace, all gleaming and seemingly the size of some movie-set spaceship. It even has TV screens telling you where your favorite snacks are available. Now that's thinkin'!

The scene inside was magnificent: the Tartan Army loud and proud, the English fans doing their best to drown out the visitors' anthem. England belted out a proper "God Save the Queen," highlighted by a neighbor of ours yelling "*your* queen" at the Scots. Old grudges die hard.

And then the game started—the game being frankly the least interesting part of the night. England won, 3–0, on three headers. It was an overrated and not too interesting England taking care of business against a poor Scotland, the latter being on their way out and the former on their way to (or so we assumed) another embarrassment in Russia in two years. It's like when Nottingham Forest play Aston Villa and you say to yourself, "This game used to mean something."

The English did have a fun song set to The Monkees' "Daydream Believer":

Cheer up, Gordon Strachan,
Oh, what can it mean
To a fat Scottish bastard
With a shit football team!

Indeed, most of the excitement was in the stands—and most of it was hatred. A few Scottish fans managed to get into our section and decided for some reason to wear their colors, which inflamed local passions. Wave after wave of "Fuck off" and "Wankers" rolled at them, with one of them being removed by the stewards for having the audacity to say something back. Chests were bowed, noses tapped together, and escort out was made, to the usual soundtrack of English cheerios.

The game made the Scots go silent, and though they enjoyed themselves, I can't say the English fans set a really high standard. They care, sure, and they're happy to win, but I wouldn't go so far as to call them happy.

Not so for the Scots, the game be damned.

THE EAST

HULL CITY

Out on the east coast of England, in a historic and friendly fishing town, is a beautiful new stadium which is home to a somewhat troubled club.

LOCATION: Hull (officially Kingston upon Hull), two and a half hours northeast from King's Cross in London, two hours from Manchester

CONTACT: hullcitytigers.com, 01482 504600, #HCAFC

NICKNAMES: The Tigers, because of their black-and-gold striped uniforms

WOMEN'S TEAM: The club doesn't have a women's team, but there is an independent Hull City Ladies in town. They are in the third-tier Women's National League North, and home games are at Haworth Park in Hull. See hullcityladies.com for more.

HISTORY: I hate to overstate things, but one could say with some degree of accuracy that the first ninety years or so of Hull City's history lacked major events. They were formed in 1904, made the FA Cup semifinals in 1930, and otherwise kicked around from the second to the fourth tier without making much news.

Financial trouble—such a common story for clubs like this—came in the 1980s when Hull were in the fourth tier. After a couple of changes in ownership, in 2000 they were briefly locked out of their own ground. Things stabilized, and in 2002 they moved into their shiny new KCOM Stadium, then earned consecutive promotions up to the Championship. After yet another change in ownership, Hull won the 2008 Championship playoff final at Wembley to finally, after 104 years, make the top tier.

Thus began their yo-yo days. Four relegations and three promotions in 12 years have left them probably a bit dazed and demoralized. They finished twenty-fourth and last in the Championship in 2019-20, losing 16 of their final 20 games. But last year they won League One, so they're back up! They have done well in Cups: they made the FA Cup final in 2014 and scored two early goals against Arsenal, but the Gunners came back to win it late. They made the fifth round of both Cups in 2015–16 and the League Cup semis the next year, losing 3–2 on aggregate to Manchester United.

They have not had good luck when it comes to ownership. Hull, sadly, must be added to a list of clubs (Blackpool, Charlton, Leeds) whose supporters have recently gone to war against their own clubs' owners. In Hull's case, that would be Assem Allam, who bought the club in 2010. In 2013 he announced that he was going to change the club's official name from Hull City AFC to Hull City Tigers for marketing reasons. (He said, among other wacky things, that if he owned Manchester City, he would change their name to Manchester Hunter.)

The supporters flipped out, but in response to one opposition group, City Till We Die, Allam said they "can die as soon as they want." The FA rejected his name change plan, and he said he wouldn't be attending any more games. The club also didn't buy a single new player after being promoted to the Premier League in 2016. Needless to say, they went back down the following season. Attendance dropped by some twenty percent, and when I was there in 2019, the loudest song was "We Want Allam Out."

At least now they're back up in the Championship and can have fans back in the stadium, for better or worse.

RIVALRIES: Leeds United, another Yorkshire club, are the biggest rivals. And yes, Hull is in Yorkshire, specifically, the East Riding of Yorkshire. What a name! Hull City doesn't care for Sheffield United either. They share a Humber derby, named for a local river, with Scunthorpe and Grimsby Town, but they are rarely in the same league.

SONGS: They'll do "Can't Help Falling in Love," and if they're really on top, they'll sing "You're Getting Mauled by the Tigers." There's a "She'll Be Wearing Black and Amber When She Comes," and "City Till I Die" has taken on greater significance of late.

2020–21 SEASON: 1st in League One (promoted), 2nd Round FA Cup, 3rd Round League Cup

2021–22 SEASON: The Championship (promoted in 2021)

STADIUM: Clean, modern, comfortable, and usually half empty, the KCOM Stadium holds 25,400 people in the usual perfect rectangle of the modern football stadium. It is surrounded by a park, it's visible from miles away, and in fact it has won awards for its design.

It opened in 2002 as the KC Stadium, but the sponsoring cable and internet company changed its name to KCOM in 2016. Away fans will be in the northeast corner, rowdy home folk in the south end. For night games they put on a light show with rock music and lots of screaming several minutes before the game.

TOURS: Members-only tours are offered about once a month for £5. Book way ahead if you're interested.

TICKETS: The most recent prices we saw were from £12 to £30 and tickets are easy to get.

GETTING THERE: It's a 20-minute walk from the train station which, by the way, is called Hull Paragon Interchange. Numerous bus lines make the trip from the Carr Lane stop outside the station, 63, 66, and 151 among them.

PUBS: The closest is the Boot Room, whose bigger sign says Parkers. Hull fans also like to drink in the pubs closer to the old ground, Boothferry Park, which is just a few minutes away down Anlaby Road: the Three Tuns, the Silver Cod, Malt Shovel, and Brownies.

Hull being a former major fishing port, there are some proper old pubs in the old center: The Bonny Boat, The Punch Hotel, The Empress, and The Sailmakers Arms are all worth a visit.

GRUB: These Yorkshire folk are awfully proud of their traditional delicacies—Yorkshire pudding being the most famous example. In Sheffield they eat (and sing about) chip butties, and here it's the Hull pattie, which might sound like pâté in the local accent. This is a bunch of mashed potatoes with salt, pepper, sage, and perhaps onion—all of it, naturally, battered and fried. They are traditionally sprinkled with something called American Chip Spice, a paprika-based seasoned salt which was invented in Hull in the 1970s and is only available in the UK.

If you notice a pattern in these Yorkshire treats, you're right: they don't exactly scream flavor or originality. Still, the nice "pattie slappers" (an actual term) at Bob Carver's downtown claim a secret recipe dating to 1888, so go and see what you think. You can even go crazy and slap it into a roll, which they call a breadcake, for a pattie butty! Every chippy in town serves patties, and East Park Chippy was recommended to me. No doubt citizens would fight over who has the best if they weren't all so incredibly nice.

The traditional place for a full English breakfast is Thieving Harry's, which will sound like "Theevinarries" when the locals say it.

AROUND TOWN: Hull has a beautiful downtown area that was built up when it boomed in Victorian times. You'll want to stroll through the Old Town and Museum Quarter, which includes the Maritime Museum, the Streetlife Museum, and the *Arctic Corsair*, a deep-sea trawler converted to a museum. The Deep is a massive aquarium with forty sharks and 3,500 fish. If you happen to visit in September, keep an eye out for the Hull Folk and Maritime Festival, when lots of old ships come in and people sing and dance shanties all over.

NORWICH CITY

Norwich City, back in the Premier League this season, is a tradition-rich club with an old-school stadium in a beautiful and historic city just a couple of hours from London. Just to be clear, it's pronounced NOR-itch.

LOCATION: Norwich, Norfolk, two hours east of Liverpool Street station in London

CONTACT: canaries.co.uk, 01603 721902, #NCFC

NICKNAMES: The Canaries, due to a history of breeding the birds in the area

WOMEN'S TEAM: Norwich City Women FC, who are not affiliated with the men's club, play in the FA Women's National League Division 1 South East, tier 4 of the pyramid. Home games are at The Nest in Horsford.

HISTORY: Norwich City was founded in 1902 and struggled mostly in the third and fourth tiers until the late 1950s. During the 1958–59 FA Cup, they made the semifinals as a Third Division side, beating Tottenham and Manchester United along the way. The next season they made the Second Division and finished fourth, and then the year after that they won the League Cup, beating Rochdale 4–0 in a two-legged final.

Aside from one season, they have been in the second or first tier ever since. They made the first tier in the early 1970s, when they also lost two League Cup finals at Wembley. They won the League Cup again in 1985, beating Sunderland in the final, 1–0. (Read more about that interesting final in the Sunderland entry on page 342.) They would have made it into a European competition based on that, but all English clubs had been banned for hooliganism.

The peak came in the early 1990s when they were founder members of the Premier League and finished third the first season. That got them into the UEFA Cup (now Europa League), where they became the first British team to win at Bayern Munich before bowing out in the third round. In the 1994–95 season, they won only one of their last twenty league games and got relegated again. They even spent a year in League One (tier 3) as recently as 2009.

But they gained two straight promotions, getting back to the Premier League in 2011. They spent a few years up but went back down in 2016. Thus they are a bit of a yo-yo club of late, but they are credited with running a tight financial ship. When they went up to the Premier League two seasons ago, they didn't go crazy and buy a bunch of players. So when they went back down, they kept the team and manager together, won the Championship last season, and they're back up again.

Their majority shareholder is a super famous TV cook who is also the author of several cooking and religious books. Such is the fame of Delia Smith in the UK that she has caused runs on various products, such as minced beef, just by mentioning them on TV; this is known as the "Delia Effect." She also gained attention in 2005 when, at halftime of a home game with Manchester City, she went on the pitch, grabbed the microphone from the on-field host, and went on a tear. "A message for the best football supporters in the world: we need a twelfth man here. Where are you? Where are you? Let's be 'avin' you! Come on!" It's even crazier than it sounds—and is, of course, on YouTube.

RIVALRIES: Norwich shares the East Anglian derby with Ipswich Town, to whose fans I would like to apologize here for not having them in the book. I just haven't made it to Portman Road yet, but I will soon!

The two sets of supporters have a genuine hatred for each other, which I have witnessed in person. Being British, they also have a sense of humor about the whole thing. It's a heavily agricultural area, leading to their calling the rivalry the Old Farm derby and the Combine Clasico.

It's Norfolk vs. Suffolk, each club being the only one in its county. Oddly enough, the distance of forty miles between Norwich and Ipswich is thought to contribute to the hatred. Nobody seems to know anybody who supports the other club, which apparently makes it easier to chant "scum" and worse at them in public. It's also a close rivalry (forty-seven wins for City, forty-five for Town), and since neither of them ever wins any silverware, beating each other seems to be all they have.

Sadly, with Ipswich down in League One, the two rivals don't seem likely to meet up anytime soon. Come on, Cup draw!

SONGS: Norwich have what is thought to be the oldest football song still in use in the world. It's so old, it's not even really a song; it's a throwback to the days of sis-boom-bah and all that. It's called "On the Ball City," and they start every game with it after the announcer counts down from three. It goes like this:

Kick it off, throw it in, have a little scrimmage,
Keep it low, a splendid rush, bravo, win or die;
On the ball, City, never mind the danger,
Steady on, now's your chance,
Hurrah! We've scored a goal.
City! City! City!

2020–21 SEASON: 1st in the Championship (promoted), 4th Round FA Cup, 1st Round League Cup

2021–22 SEASON: Premier League (promoted in 2021)

STADIUM: Carrow Road is another of my favorites: in town, old but comfortable, cozy, and loud. It's also really, really green and yellow. It holds 27,244 and was built in 1935, and of course there's been a lot of work done since. Today there are four separate stands with infill at the corners that make it feel nearly closed in.

It also has great banter between home and away fans, as the most passionate City fans sit in the Barclay End behind a goal and the away fans are just across the corner in the near end of the South Stand, which is actually named for a former club chairman named Sir Arthur South.

TOURS: Tours are offered a few times a week for £10 each.

TICKETS: Tickets ranged from £20 to £50 when Norwich were in the Championship, so expect them to be more than that this year—and tough to get. The high end of the range is for tickets in some lounges in the City Stand, which is where I sat for the derby; it's highly recommended. You get a good seat and access to a little bar space with free non-boozy drinks.

GETTING THERE: It's just a 10-minute walk from the train station, and a lovely one at that. Along the way you will pass plenty of places to eat and drink.

PUBS: Right across the river from the station is a great little pub called The Compleat Angler. Farther down that road, which leads to the center, is the Prince of Wales. Walking to the game, if you take the path along the river on Wherry Road, you'll pass the Queen of Iceni and then a Wetherspoon. All this and more is in a new development called the Riverside. Back near the station, look for the Coach and Horses with TV, real ale, and good food.

Down in the center, there are all sorts of options, including The Bell Hotel, The Belgian Monk (with Belgian beers and a cool patio), The Mash Tun and Gin Palace (the gin bar is upstairs), St. Andrews Brew House (good food), and—out behind the cathedral, near the river—The Adam and Eve, a 17th-century building on a site known to have had a pub since 1429.

Norwich is a good place for the beer lover.

GRUB: The Riverside has lots of places to eat, the pubs listed above serve food, and the Norwich Market in the center has nearly two hundred stalls…but none of that matters to me. In the many years I have spent researching this book, the very best fish and chips I had—indeed, the best I can even imagine—came from the ninety-year-old Grosvenor Fish Bar in the medieval quarter. I could have bounced a pound coin off the crust, and the fish fell apart in a pile of steamy goodness upon first contact. They fry just about everything that walks, crawls, or swims, and they deliver to a pub across the street. You're welcome.

AROUND TOWN: Norwich is one of the lesser-known gems I have come across in my English travels. It's an easy train ride from London but just long enough that you'll want to spend the night. (If you do, may I recommend Marlborough House near the station.) From medieval days all the way up to the Industrial Revolution, Norwich was second only to London. Even the tradition of raising canaries goes back to the 15th century.

You want to wander around the old city center to check out all the shops and pubs and little walkways. The Market, one of the largest in Europe, is right in the center near The Forum, an amazing glass structure that houses the library and also collections relating to the US 2nd Air Division, which was based here for decades. Make your way to the Norwich Cathedral, begun in the 11th century, have a pint at the Adam and Eve, and then follow along the river and look for Elm Hill, an intact medieval street so charming they use it in movies.

One final, random fact: Norwich was the original home of Colman's Mustard. Sadly, their little shop and museum in town closed in 2017, and in 2019 the production plant was moved to Burton-upon-Trent.

BOURNEMOUTH

The Premier League run of this "little club that could" ended in 2020, but seeing a game in Bournemouth still means visiting a posh and lovely seaside town for a game in a tiny stadium. Maybe you can get tickets now, too.

LOCATION: In Dorset on the South Coast of England, about two hours from Waterloo station in London

CONTACT: afcb.co.uk, 0344 576 1910, #AFCB

NICKNAMES: The Cherries, for their shirts, or Boscombe, for their former home and name

WOMEN'S TEAM: AFC Bournemouth Women are in the Southern Region Women's Football League Premier Division at level 5 of the pyramid. Home games are at the Verwood Town FC ground, a little north of town.

HISTORY: If you just started paying attention to the Premier League in the last few years, you might have noticed Bournemouth and thought, *Where's that?* and *Gosh, that's a small stadium.* What you would be missing is that this little club came from almost nowhere to get into the top division in 2015, thus becoming a model for small clubs with big ambitions.

They started as Boscombe FC around 1900 and moved into the current location in 1910. They made the Football League in 1923 and eventually settled in as a Third Division team. In fact, they hold the record for most time spent in that division. They changed their name to AFC Bournemouth in 1971, and in the 1980s a manager named Harry Redknapp took them to their first lofty heights: a win over the defending champions Manchester United in the FA Cup in 1984. Then Bournemouth went up to the second tier in 1987.

Almost inevitably, financial troubles came, and Redknapp left. So did his replacement, Tony Pulis. By the end of the '80s, they were back in the third tier. A few years later, they were in free fall. They struggled in the fourth tier, were continuously on the verge of bankruptcy, and were docked points by the league for not managing their finances correctly.

In the 2008–09 season they were at the bottom of League Two, ten points from safety and under the youngest manager in league history, thirty-one-year-old former player Eddie Howe. They stayed in the Football League that year with a 2–1 win over Grimsby Town on the last day; Steve Fletcher scored a goal in that game with ten minutes to go. Finances were so grim, they were passing cans around the ground, and everybody agreed that Fletcher's goal had saved their very existence.

Howe turned out to be a wonderful manager, and a wealthy owner came in. The combination got them to the third tier in Howe's first season. He then left for Burnley, and Bournemouth's progress stalled. But in 2012 Howe returned and got them to the Championship that season. Just two seasons later, they won the Championship and made the top flight for the first time. They finished as high as ninth in 2016–17 before the magic ran out; they were relegated in 2020 after finishing eighteenth, and the next day Howe resigned. One fears now for the finances and fortunes of a club that flew so close to the sun, especially after more than a season without fans.

RIVALRIES: I asked a steward about rivalries when I saw a game there, and he said they used to have rivals in the area, but they'd left them all behind. Then he added, "Honestly, we're just living the dream, punching way above our weight, and we don't have a problem with anybody!" You would think that fellow South Coast clubs like Southampton and Brighton would qualify, but apparently not.

SONGS: They like to sing "Keep the Red Flag Flying High from Dean Court to Wembley." They also do a cool old-fashioned tribute to their former selves with a simple "Boscombe—Back of the Net!"

2020–21 SEASON: 6th in the Championship, Quarterfinals FA Cup, 3rd Round League Cup

2021–22 SEASON: The Championship (relegated in 2020)

STADIUM: The Vitality Stadium, named after a sponsorship deal with an insurance company, was called Dean Court until Bournemouth made the Premier League. It is tiny—like, 11,360 seats tiny. There are at least ten high school football stadiums in Texas bigger than that. I mention high school football because that's almost what the place feels like. The new stadium was thrown together in 2001 in a matter of months, and when the club made the Championship in 2013, they built a temporary stand in one end. It's still there.

The away fans will be in the south end of the East Stand, so if you have any choice in the matter, sit in the south part of the West Stand or east part of the South Stand to be close to them. Also, be in your seats early, as they put on a somewhat goofy light show before the games.

TOURS: No tours are available at this stadium.

TICKETS: Because the stadium is so small, this was probably the toughest ticket in the Premier League when they were up there. And since last year no one could go, it's hard to say what the situation will be with Bournemouth in the Championship. I'm as curious as you are!

GETTING THERE: The main rail station in town is about a 30-minute walk or, when I was there, a £10 cab ride. You can also take the P2 or P3 Yellow Bus for six stops to Queens Park Hotel. It's a five-minute walk from there. Or just get a cab and make sure you have their number for postgame, especially if you're staying closer to the center of town.

PUBS: There is one at the stadium, but the best option around is the Queens Park Hotel on Holdenhurst Road; you'll pass it if you walk to the stadium. Along that same walk, you'll also pass the smaller and hipper Firkin Shed.

GRUB: There is really nothing around the ground at all; eat in town before you head out. As a posh resort town, it's got some pretty good options.

AROUND TOWN: Bournemouth the city was founded fairly recently, by British standards, as a resort town catering to the upper classes. As such, it's not really on the foreign tourist route, but it is a lovely place to spend some time. It's only a couple hundred years old and remains largely upscale and peaceful today, with a long sandy beach, a nice pier, beautiful gardens, stately homes, and access to a wild stretch of coast called the Jurassic Coast.

It's in Dorset, which is of note because it's the only part of England where people pronounce the letter *r*. So when somebody from Dorset says "Dorset," you know they're from Dorset. Sort of like when a person from Minnesota says "Minnesota."

Take the Hop-On Hop-Off tour bus along the coast to the village of Poole, which is touristy but in a kind of old-fashioned way: the waterfront has pubs and chippies and ice-cream places, and tour boats leaving for harbor cruises. I got a combo bus/boat ticket so I could ride out to the village of Swanage. Along the way, we saw fabulous chalk cliffs, which I thought were only in Dover.

Swanage is a nice little village on its own, with the hundred-mile-long South West Coast Path passing through and a little downtown with shops and places to eat. Follow the Coast Path up an obvious grassy slope near the harbor for a wonderful view.

BRIGHTON AND HOVE ALBION

Brighton and Hove Albion is a club gearing up for its fifth top-flight season in a row after not being there for more than three decades before. It's one of the best short football trips outside London as well: great town, lovely area, terrific new stadium.

LOCATION: Brighton (Hove is the town next door) is one hour south of Victoria station in London.

CONTACT: brightonandhovealbion.com, 0844 327 1901, #BHAFC

NICKNAMES: The Seagulls. *Albion*, by the way, is based on an ancient word for "Britain"; two other league clubs use it: Burton and West Bromwich.

WOMEN'S TEAM: Brighton and Hove Albion Women's FC play in the Women's Super League, level 1 of the pyramid. Home games are at Broadfield Stadium in Crawley, also the home of Crawley Town FC.

HISTORY: Brighton was founded in 1901 and bounced around the lower leagues until 1979, when they made the top division for the first time, staying there for four years. In 1983 they made the FA Cup final and drew with Manchester United, 2–2—a game that is most famous for a moment when Gordon Smith had a shot to win it in extra time but was denied by the United keeper. The moment lives on because it was a heartbreaker, and because the announcer famously said, "And Smith must score!" right before he didn't.

United won the replay, 4–0, and Brighton were relegated, proving that soccer is utterly cruel.

By the mid-1990s, they were in real trouble, sitting at the bottom of the lowest division of the Football League. They were in such bad financial shape they had to sell their stadium. In the last game of the 1996–97 season, they needed at least a draw at Hereford to even stay in the league. At halftime they trailed 1–0. Enter the hero, Robbie Reinelt, who scored a last-minute goal to keep Brighton up and send Hereford down. Again, the game is cruel.

From there, Brighton began a long rebuilding process, but not before having to play two seasons at Gillingham FC's stadium seventy-five miles away. They then spent twelve years at a local stadium about the size of some amateur club grounds. In the mid-2000s, to get out of financial trouble, the board had to pitch in £7 million, with another £2.5 million raised from, among other things, re-recording a hit song called "Tom Hark" by the Piranhas. You might think you don't know this tune, but Google it. You will certainly know the melody if you've been to a few games in England. The Brighton version is called "We Want Falmer," referring to the new stadium. Another thing they did to raise money: nude Christmas cards with the players. I'm serious.

They then spent ten years in the second tier, barely missing promotion in 2015–16, but they made it up for the 2017–18 season and are still there, meaning a lot more people will know about an exciting club to go see in a wonderful coastal town near London.

RIVALRIES: Crystal Palace are their rivals, which is odd, because they are forty-five miles apart—a long way in English soccer. So why do they hate each other? It goes back to the 1970s, when their two managers carried on an old rivalry from when they were teammates at Tottenham. In one season they played each other five times, including a double FA Cup replay that was settled, by all accounts, by a terrible referee decision. This, in turn, led to a Palace fan throwing coffee on the Brighton manager, who threw some words and hand signals back. You get the idea. It's been tribal ever since.

SONGS: Their anthem, the one they play when the teams come out, is an old marching tune called "Sussex by the Sea." Not everybody gets into it, which the club is trying to rectify. Here are some of the lyrics:

> Good ol' Sussex by the sea,
> Good ol' Sussex by the sea,
> Oh, we're going up to win the Cup,
> For Sussex by the sea.

2020–21 SEASON: 16th in Premier League, 5th Round FA Cup, 4th Round League Cup

2021–22 SEASON: Premier League (promoted in 2017)

STADIUM: The fancy new American Express Community Stadium, with 30,750 seats, is five miles from the Brighton center in the suburb of Falmer. They have played there since 2011. Back then it had 22,000 seats, but it's been expanded a few times. It has a somewhat unique and modern design that puts almost all the seats on the sides, and it gets high marks for being one of the better new stadiums around.

Away fans will be in the southeast corner behind a goal, home rowdies in the opposite north end.

TOURS: Tours are offered Monday, Friday, and Sunday. You can book a private tour on another day if there are four or more in your group. Adults are £15. Lunch is available on the Sunday tours for £15 to £20.

TICKETS: The last prices we saw for adult tickets ranged from £30 to £45. They can be tough for the bigger opponents, but a membership (£30) will help. It also gets you access to a season ticket resale area on the website.

GETTING THERE: You'll want to take a train to The Amex, and it's simple. From the main station in Brighton, take a train bound for Lewes and Seaford; the third stop is Falmer, right next to the stadium. Everybody on the train will get off there. Leaving is a bit tedious since everybody wants to get on that train, so find a pub to hang out in.

PUBS: The Swan Inn on Middle Street is the only option close to the stadium, so it will be mobbed and you will need to show a home-section ticket to get in. But there are plenty of pubs right outside the Brighton station: the Evening Star, The Prince Albert, the Queen's Head, and the Railway Bell are all good choices. Down by the beach look for the Victory Inn. Over by the Pavilion (see below), look for the cavernous and cool Ye Olde King and Queen.

GRUB: As is so often the case with these new places, there's nothing by the stadium, so eat in town. There are all sorts of things in The Lanes (see below). Down at the beach, look for seafood at the Tempest Inn and the Regency; both have patios if by some miracle the weather is decent. I had a great lunch at The New Club, also down by the water.

AROUND TOWN: Brighton is a fantastic place to visit, and as it's just an hour from Central London, it's a terrific day trip for a game. It is very much an old-school coastal town, with its Victorian trappings and seriously modern and hip vibes. Among the things to see:

- The Brighton Palace Pier, which opened in 1899, has an arcade, food, and even a roller coaster out at the end.
- The famous and very weird Royal Pavilion was built as a seaside retreat for the royalty in the 18th century. It will have an outdoor skating rink in winter.
- The Lanes is a web of narrow streets filled with artisan shops and cafés and cool art. Included in here is the bizarro chocolate paradise called Choccywoccydoodah. It's choco-delic, man!

- The British Airways i360 is a glass ball of an observation tower that rises 531 feet above the beach.
- The nearby historic town of Lewes (pronounced like "Lewis") works well as a starting point before the game, as getting from there to the stadium involves fewer people. There you can find many historic buildings, charming old streets, an 11th-century castle, Harvey's Brewery, and—if it happens to be the fifth of November—the biggest Bonfire Night celebration in the country. It's pretty much Mardi Gras in flames.
- There is also a football club in Lewes, Lewes FC, which plays at tier 8 of the pyramid and, since their founding in 1885, in a ground called The Dripping Pan. I just had to get that in.

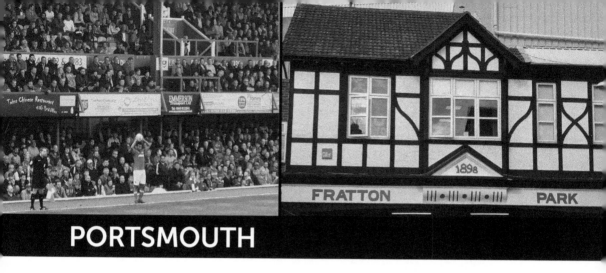

PORTSMOUTH

If you want to go back in time, inside and outside a football ground, especially if you have any interest in naval war history, get yourself down to Portsmouth and catch a game at Fratton Park.

LOCATION: On the south coast, about ninety minutes from London's Waterloo station

CONTACT: portsmouthfc.co.uk, 023 9273 1204, #Pompey

NICKNAMES: Pompey, pronounced POM-pee. There are two basic theories on this: that it comes from "Po'm P," an abbreviation for Portsmouth Point in ships' logs, and that it comes from the HMS *Pompee*, an infamous prison ship moored in the harbor for years. Either way, it predates the club.

WOMEN'S TEAM: Portsmouth Women play in the Women's National League South, tier 3 of the pyramid. Home games are at the ground of Baffins Milton Rovers FC, in the eastern part of the city.

HISTORY: Portsmouth was founded in the 19th century, had glory days in the early 20th century and early 21st, almost went out of business and was saved, and now they are building back up. If that sounds familiar, it's pretty much the story of half of English clubs.

This club was founded in 1898 by a pub owner and some friends. There is a blue plaque at 12 High Street in Old Portsmouth that commemorates the founding. For the ground, they picked a piece of land near Fratton station, and they have played on that spot ever since.

The founders hoped they might get a rivalry going with already existing clubs in Brighton and Southampton. They were right on one count. In fact, in their first home game they beat Southampton 2–0, and if I know Portsmouth at all, they've been singing about that result ever since.

They climbed up through the leagues, reaching the First Division in the late 1920s and losing FA Cup finals in 1928 and 1934 before finally winning it in 1939. They won the league in 1949 and 1950, hung around the top through the decade, and got relegated in 1959. In less than thirty years, they were in the Fourth Division and bankrupt, after which they had a long period of mediocrity and instability until the early 2000s.

Legendary manager Harry Redknapp arrived in 2002 and took them to the championship of Division One (which we now call the Championship; it's confusing), and then they spent eight years in the Premier League. Redknapp left for archrivals Southampton, causing many fans to hate him forever, but then he came back, and they were divided on whether to hate or love him. It's complicated.

The two memorable events in this stretch were winning the FA Cup in 2008 (winning at Man U along the way) and the last day of the 2004–05 season. That's when Portsmouth lost at West Bromwich Albion, which meant that West Brom stayed up and Southampton went down, leading to both West Brom and Portsmouth fans partying on the pitch at The Hawthorns.

Financial woes led to another relegation in 2010. In 2012 the Pompey Supporters Trust bought the team, which was then down in League Two. They made League One in 2017, and that summer the Supporters Trust sold the club to a member of the Eisner family of entertainment fame.

They made the League One playoffs in 2019 and 2020, and in 2019 they made the League Trophy final, where they and Sunderland combined to break the attendance record for that competition with 85,021 at Wembley. Pompey won it on penalty kicks. They made the final again for 2020, but lost to Salford City, again on penalty kicks.

RIVALRIES: To say that Southampton are rivals would be like saying the ocean is rather damp. I'll give you just one example: When I saw Pompey play Fleetwood Town, the fans constantly booed a Town player, which I assumed was for something I missed during the game. Then it occurred to me that he might have once played for Southampton, which in Portsmouth makes you scum forevermore. Neither was the case. I saw later on Twitter that they were taunting him because he grew up as a Southampton fan and had tweeted that Fratton Park is a shithole.

Really, it's an obsession with these folks. They haven't been in the same league for years, but if they run into each other in a Cup, I will suspend my usual advice and tell you to stay as far away from that derby match as you possibly can.

By most standards, Bournemouth and Brighton would appear to be nearby, but Portsmouth fans assure me they don't give a crap about either club.

SONGS: Portsmouth has one of the most famous songs—a chant, really—in all of English football. It might also be the oldest, but I suspect the folks in Norwich would disagree.

It seems that back in the day a local club called Royal Artillery FC played their games close enough to the guild hall that its bells could be heard and in fact alerted the referees to passing time. The fans would sing to the tune of the bells, telling the ref to blow full time. When Royal Artillery FC met its demise, many fans transferred their allegiance—and the chimes song—to Portsmouth FC. If you have a grandfather clock, you will know the tune when you hear it: "Play up, Pompey! / Pompey, play up!" It seems to come from the entire crowd naturally and spontaneously, like when the team earns a corner, and 20,000 fans suddenly and all at once belt it out. It's extraordinary and profoundly simple.

By the way, the Southampton fans sing to the same tune: "Fuck off, Pompey! / Pompey, fuck off!"

They also play a folksy tune called "Portsmouth" when the teams come out, and everybody claps along. That goes back to their FA Cup run in 2008.

2020–21 SEASON: 8th in League One, 3rd Round FA Cup, 2nd Round League Cup

2021–22 SEASON: League One (promoted in 2017)

STADIUM: I love me an old football ground, and Fratton Park is one of the greats in that regard. It's the only home the team has ever had, and the two side stands date from 1925 and 1935. Everything about the South Stand in particular just screams old school, especially the (mock, but who cares) Tudor facade that houses a ticket office and an entrance. It was designed by famous architect Archibald Leitch, whom you can read more about on page 356.

The ultras are in the west end, the 1997 Fratton Stand, which has a design of a former player Jimmy Dickinson on its seats. He holds the club record with 764 appearances from 1946 to 1965. That's the second most by one player for one club in history. The away fans will be in the other end, the Milton, on the north side by the police command center.

They have been saying for years that they want and need a new stadium, so please, get to Fratton Park before they go and build whatever boring atrocity they are almost certain to replace it with.

TOURS: Tours are available on the mornings of home games for groups only; call to book ahead.

TICKETS: Tickets cost £26 for adults, and they rarely sell out.

GETTING THERE: From the main rail station in town, which is called Portsmouth and Southsea, you have three options. You can walk half an hour, take bus 1, or take a train to Fratton and walk 10 minutes from there. The bus, which you catch at Stop M near the station, involves the least walking and takes the same amount of time.

PUBS: There are historic pubs in Old Portsmouth, but the ones most associated with the football club are Good Companions and the Shepherds Crook, both fairly near the ground. The former has become a designated away-fans pub, and the latter is closer to the ground, with a large outdoor area (just in case it isn't raining).

On Milton Road, close to the ground, look for the Milton Arms and the Brewers Arms. Also, I am told that at the football-themed Newcome Arms, you might come across the legendary John Anthony Portsmouth Football Club Westwood, perhaps the most famous football supporter in England. And yes, that is his legal name. In the normal world, he runs a bookshop in town; in the football world, he can be seen wearing a massive stovepipe hat over a curly blue wig, blowing a bugle, and ringing a bell to the Pompey tunes from his spot in the Fratton Stand. He has sixty Portsmouth tattoos, "PFC" on his teeth, and the club crest on his head. He is simply a legend.

GRUB: There is only fast food around the ground, so eat in town. I thought Deep Blue on the South Parade Pier had good fish and chips. There are plenty of options in the Gunwharf Quays area, as well as in Southsea just north of its common.

AROUND TOWN: Portsmouth has a naval history that goes back to Roman times. It was the main port of the British Empire and was considered the most fortified port in the world in the 19th century. It was a major point of embarkation for the D-Day invasion, and it is still considered the home of the Royal Navy as well as some two-thirds of its fleet.

As such, many of the sites around town are related to all that:

- The Mary Rose Museum displays a 16th-century sunken warship that was found in 1971 and raised nearly intact in 1982—one of the most famous such raisings in history. There are thousands of artifacts, intense research, and even skeletons of some crewmembers.
- The HMS *Victory* was Lord Nelson's flagship and in fact is still a commissioned vessel of the Royal Navy. You can take a tour of this massive ship, including the precise spot where Nelson died at Trafalgar.
- Both of the above are in the Historic Dockyards, along with the submarine museum, the 1860 HMS *Warrior*, harbor tours, the Royal Navy museum, and an explosives museum. If you're into this stuff, it's heaven in Portsmouth.
- The D-Day Museum also includes the 272-foot-long *Overlord Embroidery*.
- The Royal Armouries is another military museum—one that occasionally shoots live cannons.
- Spinnaker Tower, built to look like a sail, is a 560-foot observation tower in Portsmouth Harbour. There are many options to visit, but the basic trip up is about £13 for an adult.

- Gunwharf Quays is a recently redeveloped area of shops and cafés.
- Old Portsmouth is where you'll find the cathedral, pubs that date to the 17th century, and the town's small fishing fleet.

SOUTHAMPTON

A solid Premier League club for years now, Southampton are also famous for developing—then selling—young players. They're in a major port city that makes a nice day or overnight trip from London.

LOCATION: On the South Coast, about ninety minutes south from London's Waterloo station

CONTACT: southamptonfc.com, 0845 688 9448, #SaintsFC

NICKNAMES: The Saints, because they were originally formed as a church team

WOMEN'S TEAM: This is a little confusing, but the club "withdrew their support" for the women in 2005 after the men's team was relegated out of the Premier League. Lame. Now the club has started up a new one called Southampton FC Women, who play in the FA Women's National League Southern Premier at tier 3; home games are at Testwood Park in Totton. The website is southamptonfc.com/women.

Meanwhile, one of the more successful women's clubs in the country is in town—confusingly called Southampton Women's FC. Never affiliated with the men's club, they were formed in 1970 and have won the FA Women's Cup eight times, second only to Arsenal. See southamptonwomensfc.co.uk for more on this team.

HISTORY: The club formed in 1885 as a church team, earning them the nickname Saints, and they played in the old Southern League until World War I. In 1920 they made the Football League and have been there ever since. In 1922–23 they did something mildly interesting: they won fourteen, lost fourteen, and drew fourteen, for forty-two points from forty-two games. They also scored and conceded the exact same amount of goals. Guess where they finished in the table.

They first made the top flight in 1966 and spent eight years there, finishing as high as seventh, making some minor European competitions, and going out in the early rounds.

They got their only FA Cup win in 1976 while in the Second Division, when they beat Manchester United, who had just finished third in the First Division. It's considered one of the bigger Cup final upsets.

They made it back up in the late 1970s and spent twenty-seven years there, during which they made the UEFA Cup (now Europa League) a few times but didn't get anywhere, and once finished as high as second in the league. In the late 1980s, their academy produced two of the great natural scorers of all time: Matt Le Tissier (born on an island in the English Channel) and Alan Shearer. The latter was sold to Blackburn in 1992 for a national record (read more about him in the Newcastle United chapter), but Le Tissier stuck around for his whole career, through 2002, scoring 161 goals in 443 games. He converted forty-seven of his forty-eight penalty kicks and scored the last goal at their old stadium, a late winner in a 3–2 triumph over Arsenal. During all that time, the Saints stayed up but never finished higher than seventh.

In 2005 they were relegated, and financial troubles came along. By 2009 they were in League One, but new ownership arrived. They won the League Trophy while down there and got back to the Championship in 2011 and then to the Premier League in 2012. In the summer of 2014, they got something of a reputation by selling many of their best players: Rickie Lambert and Adam Lallana to Liverpool; Calum Chambers to Arsenal; and Luke Shaw to Manchester United. Their manager, Mauricio Pochettino, also left for Spurs. In the next few years, they would also sell Sadio Mané and Virgil van Dijk to Liverpool. Gareth Bale came through their youth system as well. During that time they had two top-ten finishes in the Premier League and made (and lost) an FA Cup semifinal and a League Cup final.

I guess if you keep selling all your best players, trouble eventually comes along. For two seasons they barely stayed up, stumbling to seventeenth and sixteenth in the league, but the last two years consolidated at eleventh and fifteenth.

RIVALRIES: They share the South Coast derby with Portsmouth, and it's one of the more bitter rivalries around. They have played 140 times since 1899, most recently a 4–0 Southampton win at Portsmouth in 2019's League Cup.

SONGS: As one might imagine, the main one is "When the Saints Go Marching In."

2020–21 SEASON: 15th in Premier League, Semifinals FA Cup, 2nd Round League Cup

2021–22 SEASON: Premier League (promoted in 2012)

STADIUM: St. Mary's Stadium, which replaced the 15,000-seat Dell in 2001, holds 32,505 in perhaps the perfect statement of the modern, rectangular stadium. It's surrounded by industrial sites and is hardly in the most romantic location, but inside it's perfectly nice and spacious. The away fans will be in the north end.

The statue outside is of Ted Bates, known as "Mr. Southampton" after he played and managed there, served on the board, and was president. The statue itself has an interesting story. This is a replacement of the first one, which lasted exactly one week amid protests that its arms were too short and it looked more like the chairman of Portsmouth.

TOURS: Tours are available on nonmatch days for £15 and on match days for £10. Book well ahead for match-day tours.

TICKETS: Last year tickets ranged from £39 to £46 for adults and could be hard to get. Get a membership or call the club. They also have some really nice and affordable hospitality options, a couple of which I sell.

GETTING THERE: There is usually a shuttle bus from the main train station (call the club or ask at the station to confirm), which is nice because it's a half-hour walk. You can cut that time in half by grabbing bus 18 from the Civic Center and then walking from the Britannia Road stop. It should be less than £10 in a cab.

PUBS: The main action near the ground is along St. Mary's Street, just west of the stadium. There, you'll find the Kingsland Tavern and The Joiners packed with home fans. Same for The Chapel Arms on the other side of the stadium, on Marine Parade. In town there are some neat older options like The London Hotel on very cool Oxford Street and the Flying Dutchman nearby. There is a Wetherspoon pub called the Standing Order on the high street, closer to the station, and my buddy and I had a nice postgame hangout at the Duke of Wellington in a restored 15th-century building on Bugle Street in the medieval quarter.

GRUB: There's nothing out by the stadium, so eat in town. Most of your options will be along the high street, including a decent Indian buffet at Coriander and an old-school Greek diner called George's on St. Michael's Street.

AROUND TOWN: Southampton has been a big port for years and is now mainly associated with the cruise industry. White Star Line (of *Titanic* fame) was here, and now Cunard is. It has also been something of a spa town since the 18th century. Its history goes back to Roman days, and like many port cities, it was heavily bombed during World War II.

The high street is also known as the Queen's Mile and leads down to the waterfront; this begins maybe a ten-minute walk from the station. There are still some of the medieval walls around and a small quarter of medieval buildings around the Tudor House and Garden.

If you're into the *Titanic* at all, this is where it made its last stop, and there's a great section of the SeaCity Museum all about it. Hundreds of locals were hired on as ship staff and died in the disaster. Southampton is also the home port of the *Queen Mary II*, a massive cruise ship that might be down at the docks; if so, go and have a look at it.

WEST COUNTRY AND WALES

BRISTOL CITY

Seeing a game at Bristol City FC is like arriving at the intersection of small-town, community football and the modern age—all in a very cool town.

LOCATION: Bristol, just under two hours southwest of London's Paddington station

CONTACT: bcfc.co.uk, 0117 963 0600, #BristolCity

NICKNAMES: The Robins

WOMEN'S TEAM: Bristol City Women, aka the Robins, play in the Women's Championship, the second tier, with home games at Twerton park in Bath. Check the club's website for details.

HISTORY: Sometimes, you sit down to research the history of a football club, and you just don't find a lot. That's the case with City, which was formed in the 1890s. They've spent a total of nine years since in the top flight, made and lost the 1909 FA Cup final, and won the League Trophy a few times. Since 1980, they have been mostly in tiers 2 and 3 of the pyramid. I know a Bristol City fan, and when I ran all this past him, he thought for a moment and then said, "Yeah, I guess we're not too interesting, are we?"

Like many clubs, they hit financial troubles. For them it came in the early 1980s and coincided with a drop to the third tier. In fact, they had three straight relegations from 1980 to 1982—one of only three English clubs to suffer such a fate.

They made the second tier again in the early '90s, with a major highlight from those years being a third-round FA Cup win over Liverpool at Anfield. But soon they dropped back into the third tier, losing in the playoffs a couple of times. Then they made the Championship (tier 2) for six years but went back down in 2013. The word *yo-yo* comes to mind.

They wiped out League One in the 2014–15 season, gaining ninety-nine points, winning the league, and beating Walsall 8–2 on the last day to cap it all off. They have been in the Championship since. In 2017–18, they made the League Cup semifinals, knocking out Manchester United at home in the quarters. They lost to Man City in the semis.

For three years, they finished in the upper reaches of the Championship, but last year they slumped to nineteenth This feels to me like a city that deserves Premier League football.

RIVALRIES: Bristol Rovers are the main rival, but they haven't been in the same league since 2001. The two have only met four times since then, all in minor trophy competitions.

Lately the bigger rivalry has been with Cardiff City, who are now in the Championship as well. This is called the Severnside derby, for the river that both cities are on. With Cardiff in Wales, this is one of the few "international" derbies.

SONGS: The teams come out to "One for the Bristol City," which continues:

> Two for the boys in red,
> Three for the fans down Ashton Gate.
> We'll follow till we're dead, me boy,
> Follow till we're dead!

It's not very good, but they also don't play it for very long.

2020–21 SEASON: 19th in the Championship, 5th Round FA Cup, 3rd Round League Cup

2021–22 SEASON: The Championship (promoted in 2015)

STADIUM: Ashton Gate—I'm really glad it doesn't have a sponsorship name—is a beautiful and modern stadium that holds 27,000 people and still feels like an old ground. They have been there since 1904, but the oldest current stand dates to 1970. The main stand, the Lansdown, opened in 2016 and has solar panels on the roof. It was part of a massive redevelopment of the whole area that makes it all feel very modern and cool, with better food options than most stadiums.

Away fans will be in the Atyeo Stand, named for former player John Atyeo, who played 645 times for the club and is the top scorer, with 351. His statue is outside. The rowdy home fans will be in the opposite end, although when I visited there was some pretty good banter between the away fans and the near end of the Dolman Stand.

TOURS: No tours are available at this stadium.

TICKETS: The last prices I saw for adult tickets were £21 to £36, and nothing sold out.

GETTING THERE: It's a 45-minute walk from the main Temple Meads station, although a nice one along the River Avon. You can cut that walk in half by taking a train to Parson Street, or you can walk from Temple Meads Station to Redcliff Hill and take Bus 24. A cab will be around £10.

PUBS: Along Ashton Road near the stadium, look for The Coopers Arms and The Rising Sun. The Robins, a bit farther away, is a sports bar but less interesting. Bristol Beer Factory has a tap room nearby with better options than atmosphere. All will probably require a home-section ticket to get in.

GRUB: There are some good places on North Street near the ground, in a neighborhood called Southville. Go figure. The area is clearly gentrifying, and in fact since I was there, a local pub has turned into a tapas bar called El Rincon. Thali has good Indian food, Fishminster good fish and chips, and both the Burger Joint and Pizza Workshop offer high-end artisanal versions of those classics.

Otherwise, look for pubs and grub in the center, especially along the restored harbor.

AROUND TOWN: For a bit more on what to see and do in town, check the next listing on Bristol Rovers.

BRISTOL ROVERS

Bristol Rovers are a friendly little club in a goofy stadium in a very cool city.

LOCATION: Bristol, just under two hours southwest of London's Paddington station

CONTACT: bristolrovers.co.uk, 0117 9096648, #BRFC

NICKNAMES: You might think it's Rovers, but that's part of their actual name. No, they are The Gas because their old stadium was near a gasworks that had quite the odor. Bristol City fans made fun of them for it, but being English, they took the insult as a matter of pride and carried on. So you get to hear "gasheads" yell, "Come on, The Gas!" They are also called the Pirates, and that's the character you'll see walking around the ground.

WOMEN'S TEAM: The current version of Bristol Rovers Women's FC was formed in 2019. They won their first league title in 2021. The Gas Girls will play in the Northern Division of the South West Regional Women's Football League, tier six, for the 2021-22 season, with home games at Lockleaze Sports Centre. See bristolroverswomensfc.com for more.

HISTORY: The club was founded in 1883, joined the Football League in 1920, and has never made the top flight of English football. The best they ever did was finish sixth in the Second Division twice in the 1950s. Those were basically the glory years; they also twice made the quarters of the FA Cup in that decade, the furthest they've ever gotten. They haven't even been in the second tier (now called the Championship) since the early 1990s.

In 2002 playing in the fourth tier, they won an FA Cup game away to Derby County, which was then in the Premier League—the first time anybody had done that from the fourth tier. In 2008 they made the FA Cup quarterfinals again, getting a home game with West Bromwich Albion. Bristol Rovers lost, but they set the stadium attendance record at 12,011.

They bottomed out in 2014, getting relegated out of the Football League for the first time. They bounced back in style, earning promotion to League Two after one. The very next year, they made League One with an injury-time winner at home on the last day. If you want to endear yourself to a local, ask them about that goal; it was by Lee Brown, and you should check it out on YouTube. Alas, they were relegated again in 2021.

RIVALRIES: Bristol City are rivals, of course, but they rarely play. They haven't been in the same league since 2001, and since then they have played just four times, in the minor League Trophy.

They hate their West Country neighbors like Swindon Town, Plymouth Argyle, Exeter City, and Yeovil Town. They also don't like nearby Cardiff, but they hardly ever play them either.

SONGS: Their anthem is "Goodnight, Irene." Apparently this started in the 1950s, when they sang it to taunt Plymouth Argyle fans who were leaving early because they were getting whipped. It stuck and is still their signature today. It's really something to hear a bunch of English people singing a mournful song by a Louisianan named Lead Belly that mentions suicide, supposedly to inspire their team. But they give it a proper go.

2020–21 SEASON: 24th in League One (relegated), 3rd Round FA Cup, 1st Round League Cup

2021–22 SEASON: League Two (relegated in 2021)

STADIUM: Rovers play in the 12,300-seat Memorial Stadium, an odd place that was originally built for rugby. One stand doesn't stretch the length of the field, another is only partially covered, and another is narrow but quite tall. It's near a road with lots of shops and has a super friendly vibe. Another oddity: this piece of land was originally called Buffalo Bill's Field because Bill played there in 1891.

TOURS: No tours are available at this stadium.

TICKETS: Tickets range from £16 to £26, with the rare option of putting down cash at the turnstile!

GETTING THERE: It's a bit far from the center—a little over three miles from the main train station, Temple Meads. The closest station to it is still a half-hour walk. So take a cab or bus 73, which goes right along Gloucester Road.

PUBS: There is one at the stadium, but there are better ones along Gloucester Road. The Wellington was hopping when I visited. Also in the area are two pubs listed in the CAMRA *Good Beer Guide*: The Annexe Inn on Seymour Road and The Drapers Arms on Gloucester.

GRUB: I found a decent chippy on Gloucester called Bishopston Fish Bar. There are plenty of other places to check out along that road, including one I liked called Atomic Burger.

AROUND TOWN: I live in Portland, Oregon, home of bearded hipsters and artisan this and sustainable that, and the first Bristolian I ever met (that's actually what they're called) told me that Bristol is the Portland of England. Within minutes of arrival, I saw a guy playing bagpipes in front of a food cart selling pickles, and I knew he was right. Bristol is young and hip and becoming a hot city. It's said to be nearly as expensive as London.

It's a pretty easy day trip from London, but is also only twelve miles from Bath, where many tourists go. In town, I suggest you take a boat tour of the historic harbor; I enjoyed Bristol Packet Boat Trips. Also check out the beautiful and historic train station, walk around the downtown, walk up to (and across) the amazing Clifton suspension bridge, and go up Cabot Tower in Brandon Hill Nature Park.

You may have also heard of Banksy, a famous and anonymous street artist. Bristol is where Banksy started, and the visitor center down at Harbourside can give you a map for a self-guided walking tour of some of the famous works around town. In fact, street art remains a big thing in Bristol, which gives artists free rein to create in designated places. Check out Stokes Croft Road, Nelson Street, and the Dean Lane skate park for examples.

CARDIFF CITY

Cardiff City, in a beautiful and historic city, has one of the most passionate fan bases in the country and a truly insane rivalry that is on again for this season.

LOCATION: Cardiff, South Wales, about two hours west of London's Paddington station by train

CONTACT: cardiffcityfc.co.uk, 0845 365 1115, #CardiffCity

NICKNAMES: The Bluebirds

WOMEN'S TEAM: Cardiff City Women play in the Welsh Premier Women's Football League, with games at the Cardiff International Sports Campus very near the stadium. But a bigger local team, Cardiff City Ladies, which used to be affiliated with the men's club, is in the Women's National League South at tier 3 of the English system. Their games are at the CCB Centre in a town with an incredibly Welsh name, Ystrad Mynach.

HISTORY: Cardiff City was founded in 1899 as a way to keep cricketers in shape during the winter, a common story among football clubs. They made the Football League in 1920 and had a good run there, making the First Division in 1921 and twice finishing runner-up in the league, once by a goal average of .024 per game. They played in two FA Cup finals, winning it in 1927; a statue of that team's captain, Fred Keenor, is outside the stadium.

They dropped quickly after that, nearly going out of the league in the 1930s, and they became essentially a lower-league team for decades. They spent a few unimpressive years in the First Division, but as recently as the 1990s they were down in the Fourth Division. Since they kept winning the Welsh Cup, they qualified for various second-tier European competitions, and they made the semifinals of the UEFA Cup Winners' Cup in the 1960s. Eventually forced to make a choice, they abandoned the Welsh Cup for the FA Cup in 1995.

It was in 2000 that another familiar theme came along: foreign investment. A Lebanese owner pumped in lots of money, got Cardiff City to the second tier and into an FA Cup final (they lost), but left them with terrible debt. He sold to a group from Malaysia led by an apparently interesting character named Vincent Tan. He decided that after 114 years playing in blue, Cardiff City—the Bluebirds, remember—should play in red. He said this was to increase their international marketing appeal. The fans revolted, but Tan owns the club. It took three years and, he said, some advice from his mother to change them back to blue.

Cardiff made the Premier League in 2013, but they were relegated the next season. Starting in 2016, they rebuilt under manager Neil Warnock and finished second in the Championship in 2017–18, beating out Fulham for the automatic promotion spot by two points. They lasted one year in the Premier League and have been in the Championship ever since, which is good news for us neutrals because…

RIVALRIES: Cardiff aren't fond of either of the Bristol clubs (which is called the Severnside derby, for the local river) or nearby Newport County, but they rarely play the latter. However, the South Wales derby with Swansea is one of the most intense rivalries around—and they are back together in the Championship!

There have been some notable events in this one. In 1988 Cardiff won away at Swansea, and a group of their fans was chased into the sea after the game. In 1993 Swansea fans at Cardiff tore out and threw chairs at their hosts, who then invaded the pitch. This resulted in the derby being the first fixture in British history to have away fans banned for several years. All told, Cardiff have forty-four wins and Swansea thirty-seven, with twenty-eight draws.

SONGS: There's one called "I'll Be There" that's an ode to the coal mining days. As near as I can tell, the only part they sing is "With my little pick and shovel, I'll be there." They sing "You Are My Cardiff" to the tune of "You Are My Sunshine." They also have more than one about Swansea, including one about people there eating rats.

2020–21 SEASON: 8th in the Championship, 3rd Round FA Cup, 1st Round League Cup

2021–22 SEASON: The Championship (relegated in 2019)

STADIUM: Cardiff City Stadium replaced Ninian Park as the club's home in 2009. It holds 33,280 and is yet another example of a not-too-inspiring new stadium. However, Cardiff City fans can make a lot of noise, and when I saw them play Nottingham Forest in the Championship a few years ago, it was rocking pretty well.

The away fans will be in the corner between the Ninian and Grange Stands, so if you want a good view of them, sit on that side of the Grandstand. The loudest Cardiff fans will be in the opposite end in the Canton Stand.

TOURS: You have to request a tour on the club website.

TICKETS: In prior years in the Championship, tickets were easy to get and ran from £18 to £32. A membership (£20) will probably guarantee access to all but the derby.

GETTING THERE: The closest train station is Ninian Park, which is five minutes away. Trains run there every half hour from Cardiff Central; it's four minutes and £2 on a train bound for Radyr. You can also walk from Cardiff Central in about 25 minutes or take bus 95. After the game, the club runs a free coach to Cardiff Central; look for it in the circle near the statue of Fred Keenor, or just ask a steward.

PUBS: There is not much good out by the stadium unless you are walking out from the center. In that case, look for The Ivor Davies and The Canton Cross Vaults, both along Cowbridge Road near Leckwith Road, which is where you turn south for the stadium. There is one uninteresting pub at the stadium, The Sand Martin, but they only serve drinks if you are sitting down and having a meal.

In town, there are some great options. I saw huge crowds of Bluebirds at the old-fashioned Queens Vaults, the more modern O'Neill's, the Old Market Tavern, and in particular at The Borough. All those are right along the high street.

GRUB: Again, it's all about eating in town. Check out some of the arcades (basically covered shopping streets) in town for good options, and pop into the Cardiff Market, open since 1891, for, if nothing else, some traditional Welsh cakes. If you go out to the Bay (see below) there are more options out there.

AROUND TOWN: Cardiff Castle is the main attraction in town and just a few minutes' walk from the station. It was built in the 11th century on Roman ruins, and in the 17th century it became the home of a series of marquesses, which is something like a duke. There are self-guided tours of the grounds as well as guided tours of the home and clock tower.

The National Museum of Art is highly rated and includes the largest collection of Impressionist works outside of France. The Doctor Who Experience closed, if that means anything to you; they film the show here, and the city is trying to get a new one open. Cardiff Bay, once one of the great coal-exporting ports in the world, has been redeveloped with restaurants and bars; a boat tour out there is recommended and can be booked on the spot. And all of this is connected by the usual Hop-On Hop-Off bus, which you can pick up at the castle.

Also, check online for specialty tours to book ahead, like a Cardifferent Historic Pub Tour, a Castle Connoisseur Tour, and various food tours. Check as well to see if Street Food Circus is on. It moves around the city during nice weather.

CHELTENHAM TOWN

Kind of a "while you're out there" way to add some football to a Cotswolds visit.

LOCATION: Cheltenham is two hours west of London's Paddington Station.

CONTACT: ctfc.com, 01242 573558, #CTFC

NICKNAMES: The Robins

WOMEN'S TEAM: Cheltenham Town Ladies, unfortunately called the Robinesses, are in the FA Women's National League South West Division, tier 4. See ctlfc.com for more.

HISTORY: The club was formed in the 1880s and spent fifty years in regional leagues before turning pro in the 1930s and spending the next fifty years in the Southern League. They made the fifth tier (now National League) in the 1980s and then, under manager Steve Cotterill, made the Football League in 1999. In 1998 they won the FA Trophy and had their best-ever result (round 3) in the FA Cup. Cotterill eventually left for a half a dozen other clubs, most recently Shrewsbury Town.

Over the next ten years, Town popped up as high as League One a couple of times. To give you an idea of their stature in the game, among the accomplishments they most brag about is when they did the double over Leeds United during the 2007–08 League One season. Other than one season in the National League (when they were champions), they were in League Two until winning promotion to League One last season.

All of this is to say, they're a tiny club. So let's take some time here to talk about the town instead. It's officially called Cheltenham Spa, and everyone calls it a Regency spa town. The Regency period started around the later part of King George III's reign, when he went nuts and was replaced by his son, who ruled as the prince regent. After Crazy George's son and grandson had ruled, they were replaced by Queen Victoria, who was queen for, like, 148 years. So the Regency era was, say, 1795 to 1837, when she took the throne.

As for spa, that's because of mineral springs discovered in the area in 1716. A retired mariner named (amazingly) Henry Skillicorne saw the commercial benefit of the springs and had the good sense to marry the owner's daughter. He started to build things up, and when George III and his family visited in 1788, it was game on.

By the 1830s a whole new town had essentially been built, and horse racing had also become popular. The Cheltenham Festival was established around 1860; this is the number two annual event in the type of racing where horses jump over stuff. (I might as well get this out of the way: I despise horse racing for more reasons than I wish to go into here, so I also know very little about it.) There are still many other cultural festivals throughout the Cheltenham calendar, the biggest of which is the Cheltenham Gold Cup, which usually coincides with St. Patrick's Day and is, to hear a local describe it, a virtual Irish invasion of the town and the biggest drinking throwdown in the world.

All of this lies about two hours west of London's Paddington Station and at the foot of the Cotswolds, which you can think of as England's Tuscany—a land of rolling hills, sheep, and old stone villages packed with charm. The 102-mile Cotswold Way, a walking path through the whole area, starts twenty miles from Cheltenham in Chipping Camden and passes through the Cheltenham area, most notably a couple of miles away at Leckhampton Hill.

RIVALRIES: These days it's mainly about Forest Green Rovers, some twenty miles away in Nailsworth. But even they are in a different league. In older times it would have been local neighbors Gloucester City and Hereford, now three leagues below them in the pyramid.

SONGS: None that I noticed. A few years back the team recorded one called "Cotswold Pride" for an FA Trophy run, but everybody seems to act like that never happened.

2020–21 SEASON: 1st in League Two (promoted), 4th Round FA Cup, 2nd Round League Cup

2021–22 SEASON: League One (promoted in 2021)

STADIUM: Their ground is called Whaddon Road—officially the fantastic Jonny-Rocks Stadium, named for a local limo service—and holds 7,066, most of it seating but with a couple of terraces. The main stand is the Jelf Stand, where you find the ticket office, bar, and club shop. The away fans will be just to the right of this stand, in the all-seated Hazelwoods Stand.

TOURS: None

TICKETS: Last we saw it was £16 to stand and £21 to sit.

GETTING THERE: It's about two miles from the station, so a taxi may be the best bet. I walked it in just over an hour, adding a swing through Pittville Park on the way (see Around Town).

PUBS: I asked the steward in the car park where to get a pint, and he suggested the bar in the club. I said I wanted a proper pub, and he said the Sudeley Arms. It was closed, so I can't report on it, but it looked a standard local pub and has since reopened.

The Kemble Brewery Inn was recommended for real ales and looked a cool place. Elsewhere in town the Cheltenham Motor Club was recently the CAMRA (beer gurus) Pub of the Year. In the center, the Old Courthouse is a beautiful pub in a two-hundred-year-old building, and the Whittle Taps had a nice feel and big menu.

GRUB: The Old Courthouse and Whittle Taps are an option, but I had a lovely meal at Bill's right in the center. There are also outlets of all the big chains around town, including Prezzo, Turtle Bay, and Wagamama.

AROUND TOWN: I just used a £1.50 walking map I got from the tourist information place in the center, which is about a twenty-minute walk from the station (or take Bus D). Although the town is "only" about 250 years old, there are some nice buildings and parks to check out, particularly Pittville Park, which is lined with beautiful old homes. In the park, look for the 1830 Pump Room, a 1903 café, and a super charming boathouse where (outside of winter) you can rent paddleboats or just have some ice cream.

FOREST GREEN ROVERS

Known mainly for their status as a green and vegan club—no, really—Rovers also offer a great way to combine small-town football with a visit to the heart of the Cotswolds.

LOCATION: Nailsworth, a village in the Cotswolds about two transit hours west of London's Paddington station

CONTACT: forestgreenroversfc.com, 01453 834860, #FGRFC

NICKNAMES: The Green Devils

WOMEN'S TEAM: The FGR Women play at the same stadium (imagine that!) in the South West Regional Premier League at tier 6 of the pyramid; check the website for fixtures.

HISTORY: The club was founded by a local minister in 1889 and kicked around a bunch of tiny leagues like the Stroud and District and the North Gloucestershire for decades, playing teams with names like Braintree and Tow Law Town. In 1975 they got up to the Hellenic League Premier Division, a southern league at level 9 of the pyramid, and found success there. In 1982 they won the FA Vase by beating a team actually called Rainworth Miners Welfare, 3–0, and then they played in the tier 7 Southern League for seven seasons. They made the tier 6 Conference in 1998.

All of this is to say that Rovers were one of countless little clubs toiling away out in the villages of England—until Dale Vince became their chairman in 2010. He had been a "New Age traveler," which seems to be like a Deadhead without the Grateful Dead. At one point he was living in a windmill-powered van on a hilltop! He started a company called Ecotricity, doing alternative clean energy, and has turned Rovers into a kind of sustainability demonstration project. The players (and fans at the stadium) are on a vegan diet; the pitch is organic; the lawn mower is solar-powered, unmanned, and runs on GPS; the lights are solar; the address is on Another Way; grass clippings go to local farmers; and the team now wears a striking neon-green kit.

Vince also put money in with all that peace and love, and Rovers kept playing their way up through the leagues. After the 2016–17 season, they made the playoffs of tier 5 and won the final at Wembley, 3–1 over Tranmere Rovers. Thus did Nailsworth, population 7,746, become the smallest town ever to host a Football League club. As you might expect, the team struggled, but they stayed up (by one point) in 2017–18—and hey, at least all the ground-hoppers and the "do the 92" crowd got to try samosas and go for a walk in the Cotswolds!

They actually finished fifth in League Two in 2018–19 and made the playoffs, where they again faced Tranmere Rovers—but this time they lost in the semifinals. They made it to the league semifinals again in 2021, but lost to Newport County on aggregate.

RIVALRIES: Anybody from nearby is a rival (Swindon Town and Cheltenham Town), but they have come so far that they've left all their traditional rivals behind.

SONGS: "Not Bad for a Village Club."

2020–21 SEASON: 6th in League Two, 1st Round FA Cup, 1st Round League Cup

2021–22 SEASON: League Two (promoted in 2017)

STADIUM: The New Lawn sits on top of a hill on the edge of Nailsworth—a hill which, to hear your average beer-laden British football fan tell it, roughly approximates Mount Everest. It is very much a League Two ground, with 5,032 capacity that includes 2,000 seats. The long away terrace on one side has no roof, which leads home fans to sing, "It's gonna rain in a minute." Apparently the club is considering a partial roof and some seats for their guests, and eventually a whole new ground out by the expressway.

TOURS: No tours are scheduled, but it's worth a call.

TICKETS: Tickets cost around £25 for adults and are super easy to get.

GETTING THERE: Unless you rent a car, you'll need at least one train and a bus to get there from London. From London Paddington, you need to get to Stroud (which could involve changing in Swindon or Gloucester), then take bus 63 from the Merrywalks shopping center about an hour to Nailsworth. No trains go there. The ground is on top of a fairly steep hill on the edge of town; just ask around or follow the colors.

PUBS: The club has one at the ground called The Green Man. It's clean, comfortable, friendly, and serves real ale from a local brewery. The George in town is also a nice option; just remember you have to climb the mountain to get to the game, so go easy on the pints.

GRUB: There's vegan at the game, of course; the samosas were excellent—hot and fresh. There are "burgers" made with something called Quorn; let me know how they are. (I do wish to point out that visiting fans often sing "You can stick your veggie burgers up your arse.") Otherwise, Nailsworth is a bit of a tourist town, so there are options. I had a fine meal at Wild Garlic, which also has nice B&B rooms upstairs. Balti Nailsworth looked tasty. Walkers is a traditional chippy on Bath Road.

AROUND TOWN: If you know anything about the Cotswolds, you don't need me to tell you how lovely they are—I mean, assuming you like old villages with stone cottages perched on hilltops and surrounded by sheep pastures and brooks and patches of forest. The Cotswolds are pretty much England's Tuscany. You want to check out the Egypt Mill Hotel, an amazing restored 16th-century mill on the creek. (Rooms are in the £100 to £150 range, some with a dinner allowance.)

I took a lovely walk up through the hills to Minchinhampton Common, where cows roamed a golf course, then over to Minchinhampton itself, where I found a fantastic coffee shop serving local bread and dairy products. The Cotswold Way, a famous 107-mile hiking trail, is not far away and worth doing a section; I went eight miles from Painswick to Kings Stanley using buses to get there and back.

SWANSEA CITY

One of three Welsh teams in the English football system, Swansea rose from near oblivion in 2003 to become the model of a scrappy little club hanging on in the Premier League—until 2018.

LOCATION: Swansea, South Wales, about three hours west of Paddington station in London

CONTACT: swanseacity.com, 01792 616400, #Swans

NICKNAMES: The Swans

WOMEN'S TEAM: Swansea City Ladies play in the top-tier Welsh Premier Women's Football League. Home games are at Llandarcy Academy of Sport in nearby Neath.

HISTORY: Swansea Town was founded in 1912 and changed its name to City in 1969. They bounced around among the lower leagues for sixty-plus years before catching fire in the late 1970s with three promotions in four seasons. This put them in the top tier for the first time in 1981, when they finished sixth—still their highest finish. Incredibly, they turned right around with two straight relegations and went bankrupt in 1985!

By 2001 they were in League Two, the lowest level of the Football League. Their finances were disastrous, managers were coming and going, and an Australian group of owners bought the club and got rid of all the best players. Dark times. They avoided relegation out of the league only by winning on the last day of the season in 2003.

The short version of what happened then is that the supporters—ordinary citizens of Swansea, the ones who live and die with the club—rallied to the cause and purchased a 20 percent share of the team. Incredibly, ten years later in 2011, they found themselves in the Championship playoff final at Wembley—which they won, 4–2, over Reading. From the brink of extinction to the Premier League in ten years!

A wonderful film was made about this called *Jack to a King*. (Jack is a local nickname that comes from the Welsh word for "seamen" as well as a legendary dog named Swansea Jack who saved twenty-seven people from drowning in the 1930s. There's a monument to him in town.) That film is on YouTube in a kind of limited format, but it's also available elsewhere.

The Swans were a midtable Premier League team for the next five years, and they won the League Cup in 2013. But the energy started running out in the 2016–17 season, when they slipped to fifteenth, and in 2017–18 the dream ended, for now, with relegation to the Championship.

RIVALRIES: Cardiff City is their rival in the South Wales derby, which is so intense that for several years away fans were banned outright. I saw Swansea play Burnley at home once, and I swear their fans spent half the game singing songs about Cardiff. They have lesser rivalries with Bristol City as well as Bristol Rovers and Newport County, though the latter two are currently in different divisions.

SONGS: They have one that confused me for a while, until I realized the last line was in Welsh. It's called "Hymns and Arias," and it goes:

> And we were singing
> Hymns and arias
> Land of my fathers
> *Ar hyd y nos.*

That last line means "all through the night." There is another good one that starts out "Swansea o Swansea" and goes on about standing on the north bank (of the old ground) until the day I die. They also occasionally crank out, "England is full of shit," and they'll chant, "You Jack bastard," at somebody, which means they like them.

2020–21 SEASON: 4th in the Championship (lost playoff final), 5th Round FA Cup, 1st Round League Cup.

2021–22 SEASON: The Championship (relegated in 2018)

STADIUM: Liberty Stadium, their home since 2005, is another of the new, symmetrical, and not terribly interesting stadiums, but it's one of the louder ones I've been to. It's also not out on the edge of town, which means a game there still feels pretty old-school. It holds just over 21,000, so it's cozy as well.

Away fans will be in the middle of the North Stand and the most vocal Swansea folks in the nearest end of the East Stand. So try to sit in that corner somewhere if you have a choice.

TOURS: Tours are only offered to groups once a month, so check the club website well ahead if interested.

TICKETS: The last prices I saw were for around £30, and only the derby sold out.

GETTING THERE: It's a couple of miles from the main rail station, so a taxi (around £7) or city bus would be best. Buses 4, 34, 50, and 51 all go there from the High Street station.

PUBS: There are two options right at the stadium, both modern and clean and heinously crowded: the Harvester pub and Frankie and Benny's chain restaurant. Not too far away is The Plough and Harrow on Llangyfelach Road; good luck pronouncing that one!

In town, look along entertaining Wind Street—pronounced like "wind a clock"—for the No Sign Bar and the Bank Statement.

GRUB: Aside from the Frankie and Benny's, near the stadium you'll find a decent chippy called Rossi's, as well as Azad Tandoori and Pizzeria Vesuvio—and even a Pizza Hut and KFC if you're feeling homesick.

Better options are in town. I had a fine meal one night at the Belle Vue Bistro (three courses, mineral water and coffee for £27) and a surprisingly good Chinese meal at Gigi Gao's Favourite Authentic Chinese restaurant for about 13 quid.

Traditional Welsh foods include rarebit (basically cheese sauce on toast), laverbread (made from boiled and pureed seaweed!), Welsh cakes, and Glamorgan sausage, made with cheese, leeks, and breadcrumbs. Look for those in the Swansea Market.

AROUND TOWN: The central city is worth a walk around; go into the market and along Wind Street. It's also interesting to visit City's former ground, Vetch Field. (Vetch is a type of legume that grew in the area.) Almost all these old grounds have been turned into housing, and this one may be also. But for right now, some of the entrances and walls are still there, and where the pitch was is now a big grassy area you can walk around in. It's on Glamorgan Street very near the bus station.

Speaking of buses, you should take one to Mumbles. A day pass on the bus system is less than £5, and the 2 bus will take you along a beautiful seaside park and out to the town of Mumbles, which is named for two hump-shaped rocks in the sea, which in turn are named (in local dialect, I guess) for exactly what you'd think a sailor would be thinking about when he sees two hump-shaped rocks in the sea.

It's a cute little town with a nice promenade that leads out to a pier. (I had a good breakfast at the Kitchen Table Café.) Just above the pier, you'll see a stone structure with a staircase next to it; that is part of the 870-mile-long Wales Coastal Path. At the top is an apple-shaped ice-cream stand and some amazing views along the coast. The path keeps going, and you can use the local bus system and path to go for quite an excursion out there.

WEST MIDLANDS / BIRMINGHAM AREA

Aston Villa is a big and historic club with an awesome stadium and giant fan base, and they are back in the Premier League.

LOCATION: In Aston, which is part of the sprawling Birmingham area, just under two hours from Euston station in London

CONTACT: avfc.co.uk, 0333 323 1874, #AVFC

NICKNAMES: Villans or the Villa

WOMEN'S TEAM: Aston Villa WFC play in the top-tier Women's Super League. Home games are at Bescot Stadium, home ground of Walsall FC.

HISTORY: Villa is a massive club: seven league titles, seven FA Cups, five League Cups, one European championship, and one UEFA Super Cup—but none of that since 1996. Their last League Cup was in 1981. Still, they retain a large and loyal following; they're a little like the Dallas Cowboys without the obnoxious owner and gaudy new stadium.

They were born in 1874 and became one of the twelve founders of the Football League in 1888. This is not surprising, since the whole idea came from their board member, William McGregor. (His statue is outside the stadium now, holding plans for the league.) But they didn't just join; they dominated. By 1910 they had won six league titles and four FA Cups, including a double in 1897, the year they moved into the current location at Villa Park.

A decline started in 1920, and relegation came in 1936. The war interrupted their recovery, but by 1957 they were FA Cup winners again. The bottom came in 1967, when they spent a year in the Third Division. New ownership and management arrived, and in 1975 they were back in the top flight and primed for a remarkable run of success.

Villa won the league in 1981, and that meant Europe the following year. Despite a midseason managerial change, they won the European Cup (now called the Champions League)

by beating Bayern Munich in the final at Rotterdam, 1–0. The goal came from Peter Withe, and the moment—specifically the TV commentary of it—is memorialized in a banner across the front of the North Stand at Villa Park: "Shaw, Williams, prepared to venture down the left. There's a good ball in for Tony Morley. Oh, it must be and it is! It's Peter Withe!"

The following year they beat Barcelona to win the UEFA Super Cup. Then came another decline to a relegation in 1987. By 1992 they were up again to be founder members of the Premier League. For the next twenty-plus years they stayed up, losing a few Cup finals but never challenging for the title. Eventually, the rot set in, and they went down in 2016. That summer they were bought by a Chinese businessman, and in 2017–18 they made the promotion playoffs but lost to Fulham in the final. In 2019 they made the playoffs again, this time knocking out local rivals West Bromwich Albion in the semis and Derby County in the final, getting them back to the top tier. In 2020, they stayed up by one point but made the League Cup Final, losing to Manchester City 2-1.

RIVALRIES: Birmingham City is the main rival; the Second City derby goes back to 1879 and has been played 127 times. West Bromwich Albion and Wolverhampton, the other big Birmingham-area clubs, are also rivals. So for this season, the Wolves game will be their most heated, with the Blues and West Brom down in the Championship.

SONGS: They don't have a particular anthem, but they do have some fun songs. They do the same "Hi Ho Aston Villa" thing that Wolverhampton does. They're doing the same "Allez Allez Allez" song as seemingly the rest of the country (see page 353). They sing one about being "on our way to the Premier League" and "You Are My Villa" to "You Are My Sunshine," as well as more than a few about Birmingham City that are filled with obscenities and threats of physical harm.

2020–21 SEASON: 11th in Premier League, 3rd Round FA Cup, 4th Round League Cup

2021–22 SEASON: Premier League (promoted in 2019)

STADIUM: Villa Park, for me, is one of the greats. It combines size with style, history with class, and on a good night has a cracking atmosphere. It has historically been one of the major stadiums in the country as well. It's held sixteen England international matches and fifty-five FA Cup semifinals, from back before they all got moved to Wembley.

The capacity is 42,682, much reduced from the terrace days when the record was more than 76,000. This area was the grounds of Aston Hall, which was owned by Sir Thomas Holte; a stand is now named for him. The hall held gardens and a pond, and in 1897 the pond was filled in to form the same pitch they use today.

The most passionate Villa fans will be in the Holte End behind a goal. Away fans will be in the far end of the Doug Ellis Stand on the side. So if you want a good view of them, sit in the Trinity Road Stand near the North End.

TOURS: Tours were suspended for stadium work at press time; check with the club for the latest.

TICKETS: Last I saw, prices ranged from £30 to £40 and were tough to get, especially against any big club. They have a lot of affordable hospitality options.

GETTING THERE: The closest train station is Witton, about a five-minute walk away. Catch a train there from New Street station in Birmingham. You can also get off sooner at Aston and have a slightly longer walk, unless you're sitting in the Holte End. It's only a few minutes longer to take bus 7 (Short Heath) from Livery Street near the New Street station.

PUBS: There are a few near the ground, including The Witton Arms, which also lets away fans in—unless it's a derby. The Yew Tree, about half a mile the other way from the Witton station, should also have a good mix of fans. One of the finest pubs in Birmingham is also nearby; The Bartons Arms is a protected building on High Street Aston. If you take bus 7, you'll go right by it. If you're coming from the Aston station, you'll pass the Aston Tavern and the historic Holte Pub, both famously packed with Villans pregame.

GRUB: There isn't much around the stadium, other than the pubs. Just make sure that at some point during your time in Birmingham you get a proper balti curry—not the dreck at the stadium, but a real one. Get yourself down to the Balti Triangle and go for it. Balti is a garlic-and-onion curry invented in Birmingham that is fast-cooked in oil then served hot in the pan. It's rather amazing when done properly.

AROUND TOWN: Aston Hall, built in the 17th century, is still there and can be visited from early April to early November each year; see birminghammuseums.org.uk/aston.

Aside from the Balti Triangle and the four football grounds, Birmingham doesn't seem to offer much to the tourist. But with a population of a million people in the city proper and more than twice that in the area, it still bears some exploration. The Birmingham Museum and Art Gallery and the Barber Institute of Fine Arts are both highly regarded.

For some other ideas, check my listing on West Bromwich Albion on page 232.

BIRMINGHAM CITY

A former yo-yo club that has stabilized in the Championship since 2011, Birmingham City is—to outsiders anyway—kind of the forgotten club of the four big ones around Birmingham. But it's a fun and easy place to catch a game.

LOCATION: In Birmingham, West Midlands, ninety minutes north from Euston station in London

CONTACT: bcfc.com, 0121 772 0101, #BCFC

NICKNAMES: The Blues

WOMEN'S TEAM: Birmingham City Women are in the Women's Super League, top tier of the pyramid. Games are at Damson Park, also the home of Solihull Moors FC, in Solihull.

HISTORY: Started in 1875 under the name Small Heath, City had their current name and ground by 1906, when their long story of up-and-down began. Their peak came from the mid-1950s to the early '60s. They were promoted to the First Division in 1955 and finished sixth the following season. They made the 1956 FA Cup final despite never having a home game due to terrible luck in the draw. They lost but made the semifinals again in 1957.

Also in 1956, they became the first British club team to play in a European competition, debuting in the Inter-Cities Fairs Cup. In 1960 they made the final of that Cup, losing to Barcelona. In 1961 they won at Inter Milan (the last English team to do that for forty years) on the way to losing another final, this time to Roma.

They capped off this run in 1963 by winning their first major trophy, beating local rivals Aston Villa to win the League Cup. But after that, decline set in, and the next thirty years saw six relegations and five promotions, leaving them in the second tier. They made the Premier League in 2002, but from 2006 to 2011 they switched leagues five times.

It was during this stretch that they hit their modern highlight, beating Arsenal to win the 2011 League Cup. But they got relegated that year, went out in the group stages of the Europa League the next year, and have languished in the Championship ever since, only once finishing above tenth. They only stayed up in 2020 by two points, finishing twentieth, and last season they were eighteenth.

RIVALRIES: All the other West Midlands clubs qualify as rivals: Aston Villa, West Bromwich Albion, and Wolverhampton. Aston Villa, in the Second City derby, is hated the most. Any of the others would be called a West Midlands derby. This year they get to play West Brom in the league.

SONGS: Their anthem is "Keep Right on to the End of the Road," an old tune that caught on during their 1956 FA Cup run, during which City became the first team to ever make the final without playing a home game. A player named Alex Govan liked to sing it on the team bus, and then he mentioned to the press that he liked it. When the fans started singing it during a semifinal win, he said, "It was the proudest moment of my life."

No matter whom they are playing, you will almost certainly hear "Stand Up if You Hate the Villa" and "Shit on the Villa."

2020–21 SEASON: 18th in the Championship, 3rd Round FA Cup, 1st Round League Cup

2021–22 SEASON: The Championship (relegated in 2011)

STADIUM: St. Andrews, right in the middle of town, is kind of a funny ground in some ways. From the street it looks quite small, but it holds 29,409 people. The Main Stand is actually the smallest and oldest. It runs along one side of the pitch and looks rather outclassed by the rest of the place, which came along in the 1990s. The Kop along the other side and the Tilton Road End behind a goal are connected, and the latter holds the rowdy home fans. Away fans will be in the opposite end, in the Gil Merrick Stand.

I like sitting in the Main Stand but not too low. It feels old-fashioned and has the best views of the impressive Kop Stand.

TOURS: Adults are £12 for this friendly tour led (when I took it, anyway) by a guy who just loves the club and really wants you to see the League Cup trophy. It's offered on most nongame days during the season.

TICKETS: Two seasons ago, tickets were £27 to £40 for adults, and they have frozen those prices for several years running. Even the home derbies didn't sell out.

GETTING THERE: It's about a 30-minute walk from the main station, which is called New Street, and not all of that walk is scenic. A cab from there would be less than £10. You can also walk a few minutes from New Street to the other station, Moor Street, and catch bus 17, 60, or 97.

PUBS: If you're walking over, on the way you will pass the Old Crown on Digbeth Street; it's Birmingham's oldest building and a very cool pub. Closer to the ground, along the main Coventry Road, look for The Roost just past the stadium. It has plenty of Blues stuff on the wall and a patio out back. A few blocks behind it is The Cricketers Arms, more of a small local place. The Royal George Hotel is just around behind the stadium and is a bit more modern. It also has hotel rooms.

Nearer the New Street station, the Wellington on Bennetts Hill is a beer-lovers mecca with sixteen real ales on tap. The Shakespeare, just outside the station, often has folks in it headed for a game at one of the other grounds in town.

GRUB: You'll want to get a balti pie at the ground; it's a curry style invented in town. But the Balti Triangle area, along Ladypool Road in Sparkbrook, is just a half-hour walk away and will offer much better versions of the local delicacy. Otherwise, all the food is in town, like in the cool Chinese Quarter near New Street station.

AROUND TOWN: Birmingham doesn't make most tourists' radar, but there are a lot of nice museums and other cultural attractions around. Check visitbirmingham.com/what-to-do and see what strikes your fancy.

BURTON ALBION

When I started this project, Burton was a tiny club playing in the Championship—then they got relegated. But they are still an impressive story and a very friendly club in the beer-making capital of England.

LOCATION: Burton upon Trent, thirty miles northeast of Birmingham in the West Midlands

CONTACT: burtonalbionfc.co.uk, 01283 565938, #BAFC

NICKNAMES: The Brewers

WOMEN'S TEAM: Burton Albion Women, who are not technically associated with the club but are supported by them, play in the fourth-tier National League Division One Midlands. Home games are at The Lamb Ground in Tamworth.

HISTORY: Starting in the 19th century, there were a few football clubs in town, but it wasn't until 1950 that the current club came into being. They kicked around leagues you will have never heard of (Northern Premier League Premier Division, anyone?) until 1998, when they hired Nigel Clough as player-manager. If you know your English football, you'll recognize the name. Nigel's dad, Brian, is a true legend of the game. He won the title with Derby County in 1972 and then won the league in 1978 and Europe in 1979 and 1980 with Nottingham Forest. You can read more about him in the Nottingham Forest chapter on page 248; Nigel played for him at Forest.

By 2002 Nigel Clough had gotten Burton to the Football Conference, now called the National League, which is levels 5 and 6 of the English league system. He left in 2009, and later that year they were promoted to the Football League for the first time.

In 2006 they gained some notoriety by drawing Manchester United in the FA Cup at home and held them 0–0. This meant a replay at Old Trafford, which they lost, 5–0—but they set the all-time record for away fans there, with 11,000 Brewers fans making the trip.

Their home stadium's capacity: 6,912. Burton upon Trent population: 73,000. Roughly one in six people in town made the trip!

They made League One in 2015, and the next year Clough returned and got them to the Championship. That such a small club got there was remarkable; that Clough kept them up the following year was probably even more amazing. Alas, on the final day of the 2017–18 season, when Bolton Wanderers scored two goals in the last five minutes of their game, Burton were sent back down to League One, where they remain.

RIVALRIES: Back in their lower-league days, they mixed it up with teams like Gresley Rovers, Nuneaton Town, Stafford Rangers, and Tamworth. I know, me neither.

When they made the Football League, their main rivals became nearby (and similar-league) Port Vale, Crewe Alexandra, Notts County, Chesterfield, and Walsall.

In 2016–17, when they got to the Championship, they played their first-ever competitive matches against Nottingham Forest, Derby County, Birmingham City, Aston Villa, and Wolverhampton. All of these clubs are within about an hour of Burton, but they had never been in the same league before. And none of them are anymore.

SONGS: Their go-to seems to be the "na-na-na" from "Hey Jude," followed by "Brewers." They do a version of "Country Road" with the lines "Take me home, Derby Road / to Pirelli, to see the Brewers." They also have a fun one saying that Burton upon Trent is wonderful: "It's full of beer, beer, and more beer."

2020–21 SEASON: 16th in League One, 1st Round FA Cup, 2nd Round League Cup

2021–22 SEASON: League One (relegated in 2018)

STADIUM: The Pirelli Stadium has 6,912 capacity, of which 2,034 are seats. It stands where once there was a Pirelli Tires (or Tyres in the UK) plant. The company donated the land for the stadium in return for naming rights. The seats are all in the South Stand, which also has the club offices, so the rest is terraces. The away fans stand in the East Terrace, known for sponsorship reasons as the Coors Stand (Coors is brewed in town).

TOURS: No tours are available at this stadium.

TICKETS: In 2019-20, it was £18 to stand and £22 to sit.

GETTING THERE: From the rail station, you can walk in about half an hour, unless you get distracted on the way (see Pubs, below). Use Google Maps to see the two different walking routes. You can also take bus 1, 17, or 38 or grab a taxi for about £7.

PUBS: Burton, as a song goes, really is full of beer, beer, and more beer. Along the shortest walking route to the stadium, you'll pass the tiny and über-charming Weighbridge Inn, the local-brewery-owned Alfred, and the Victorian-era, two-room Derby Inn.

If you take the longer route through town and past the National Brewing Centre (see Around Town), you can pass a series of micropubs, several of them award-winning and fabulously named: The Roebuck, The Last Heretic, Devonshire Arms, Coopers Tavern, The Fuggle and Nugget, Burton Bridge Inn, Tower Brewery, Burton Town Brewery, and the Great Northern. I'm telling you, it's beer heaven. Have a pint in each and let's call it the Burton Slam.

GRUB: With all this beer, who cares? Actually, I saw a long line at the Wetmore Road Fish Bar on the longer walking route mentioned above, and the Fish Hut closer to the ground gets good reviews. But I had my fish and chips downtown at Tommy's. Tommy is from Cyprus and has been in town thirty-plus years. Please tell him the American writing the book said hello. And get the haddock.

If afternoon tea is your thing, check out Langan's Tea Rooms.

AROUND TOWN: Beer! Seriously, Burton upon Trent is the brewing capital of England; Americans can think of it as the UK's Milwaukee, Wisconsin.

Beer has been made there since at least the 11th century, when local monks discovered that the water in town was excellent for making strong ale. In fact, the water is of such quality that a word was invented—*Burtonize*—to describe bringing other places' water up to the standard. Combine this with the town having a 12th-century bridge over the River Trent, throw in some canals built during the Industrial Revolution, then railroads, and kaboom: brewing capital!

In 1880 there were thirty breweries in town. Most notable in the town's history was William Bass—yes, that Bass—who combined beer making with industrial practices in the 18th century, and his brewery in town became the world's largest. Two of the three Bass breweries still stand, though sadly now they bear the name Molson Coors. Why does America always export the worst of its culture?

A major by-product of brewing is yeast extract, and it was in Burton that someone figured out a way to consume that: Marmite. It was invented and is still produced in Burton upon Trent. Sadly, no tours are available.

Another item made in Burton, though not invented there, is Bovril, which is kind of like a beef broth drink that doesn't (any longer) have actual beef in it. You are not a proper English football fan until you have warmed yourself on the terraces with a basket of chips and a steaming cup of Bovril.

And finally, Colman's Mustard moved in 2019 to Burton from their home of 160 years, Norwich. They have yet to open a museum or shop in their new home, which is a shame.

If you have kids, they will enjoy the Kandy Factory, where they can make stuff out of chocolate and candy. For artisan shopping in a cool space, see the restored Trinity Church.

St. George's Park, training ground of the England national teams, is nearby. Tours are available, but I can't speak to how interesting it all is.

COVENTRY CITY

A club that is bigger than it currently appears to be, Coventry is being held back by a toxic relationship between ownership and fans.

LOCATION: The city is about twenty minutes by train from Birmingham, a little over an hour from London's Euston station.

CONTACT: CCFC.co.uk, 024 7699 1987, #PUSB

NICKNAMES: The Sky Blues

WOMEN'S TEAM: Coventry City doesn't have a women's team, but Coventry United, a 9th-tier men's club in town, does. They play in the Women's Championship at tier 2 of the pyramid, with home games at Butts Park Arena in Coventry. For more information, see coventryunited.co.uk/ladies.

HISTORY: Coventry City used to be a thing.

They were founded in 1883, took their current name in 1898, and made the Football League after World War I. Legendary manager Jimmy Hill, who also hosted *Match of the Day* on BBC for many years and whose face is on a banner over empty seats at every game, got them to the top tier in 1967, and they stayed there for over thirty years.

Their greatest moment was lifting the FA Cup in 1987, winning at Manchester United along the way, and beating Spurs in the final. The bus they rode around the city in afterward is now in the Transport Museum in town.

They were founder members of the Premier League in 1992, but about ten years later, the trouble began. Relegation, a manager carousel, financial troubles—it's a common story, which in this case wound up with a sale of the club in 2007 just before bankruptcy was to hit. The owners now are a London-based hedge fund called SISU Capital Limited. It's not going well.

In 2012 they went down to League One, and in 2013 they went into administration and were kicked out of the arena where they were playing, with their home games moved for two seasons to Northampton Town, some thirty-five miles away. In 2017 they won the League Trophy but went down to League Two.

There have been protests and a petition by fans and former players begging the owners to sell and go away. A Sky Blue Trust was formed by supporters, with the goal being to get an ownership stake in the club. The last two season's home games were played at Birmingham City's St. Andrews, including an odd situation when the two were drawn together in the FA Cup. The Coventry "home game" was a draw, so in the replay, in the same place, with Birmingham as the "home" team, they won in a shootout.

Despite all this, on the pitch, things have been looking up. In 2018 they finished sixth in League Two then won the playoff to get back into League One. They almost made the playoffs again the following year, and in 2020 they won the (pandemic-shortened) season and are now playing in the Championship.

RIVALRIES: There are many in the area to choose from, and historically it was Aston Villa and Leicester City. But those clubs are in a different world now. Birmingham and Wolves get some mention, and when Coventry City was in the lower leagues, it was more about Walsall and Burton Albion.

SONGS: There are two main ones to know. One is "Let's All Sing Together," also known as "Play Up Sky Blues," which was actually written by Jimmy Hill. The lyrics have been updated to include bigger teams than in the original:

> Let's all sing together
> Play up, Sky Blues!
> While we sing together
> We will never lose.
> Tottenham or Chelsea
> United or anyone,
> They shan't defeat us.
> We'll fight 'til the game is won!
> City! City! City!

There is also a band version of it they play as the teams come out. But I really like "In Our Coventry Homes," with the words:

> In our Coventry homes,
> We speak with an accent exceedingly rare,

You want a cathedral, we've got one to spare,
In our Coventry homes…

We'll get to the cathedral thing later.
They will also sing "Twist and Shout" on occasion.

2020–21 SEASON: 16th in the Championship, 3rd Round FA Cup, 2nd Round League Cup

2021–22 SEASON: The Championship (promoted in 2020)

STADIUM: They are finally done with an awkward groundshare at Birmingham City, so they will be home again at the Coventry Building Society Arena, formerly the Ricoh Arena. At 32,609 seats with a casino and surrounded by parking, it's a perfectly modern stadium.

TOURS: None

TICKETS: Previously at this ground, it was £20 for adults and £7 for under-sixteens. The only way it comes close to selling out is if they draw a big Premier League club in a Cup.

GETTING THERE: Couldn't be simpler: the Coventry Arena Rail Station is right next to the stadium.

PUBS: If you happen to be in Coventry, over by the cathedral, look for the Golden Cross, which dates to 1583 (though it's been massively redeveloped recently) and has a good menu of pub classics. The Artisan Bar and Grill is also nice, and just near the station is a big place called the Litten Tree that looks a standard modern pub with cheap food.

GRUB: There's nothing out by the stadium other than fast food and a Nando's. More options are available in the city center.

AROUND TOWN: If you're into architecture, you may have heard of Coventry. That's because in 1940 their beautiful cathedral was destroyed by a German bombing raid, and they completely rebuilt it. The result is a rare modernist cathedral, opened in 1962 and famous for stained glass and a massive tapestry behind the high altar.

It would appear from the song above that at least some locals don't like it, but I think it's well worth a visit. The ruins of the old one are next door, where two old timbers that landed in the shape of a cross in the destruction were preserved that way.

Museums include Coventry Music, Coventry Transport, Midland Air Museum, and St. Mary's Guildhall, a well-preserved 14th-century building.

Elsewhere around town there are a number of old buildings, especially along Medieval Spon Street, where you can also find a pub dated 1451 called The Old Windmill, with five-foot-tall doors and tiny rooms with a stove in each. It's super cozy.

There is a dash of hipster culture in town as well, particularly at a place called Fargo Village, named for Far Gosford Street where it's located—a street that still has old-school barbers and discount stores but also now has a tattoo place and an artisan coffee house. Gentrification right ahead!

One of those businesses is the Phil Silvers Archival Museum. You have to see this place and meet the owner, Steve. I'm serious; you have to. Who was Phil Silvers? He played Sgt. Bilko, a character in a 1950s sitcom who, should old-timers like me Google him, will be recognized right off. He had a long career as a comedian, actor, and Broadway star and was quite a bit more popular in the UK than in the US, in part because he was in something called "Carry On" films. But I'll let you go to the museum and ask Steve; he'll tell you all about it!

STOKE CITY

Whenever a manager is doing well at a club, commentators will ask a question meant to determine whether his talent is real or just a fluke. The question is, "Yeah, but can he do it on a rainy Tuesday in Stoke?" Somehow that always told me everything about this club.

LOCATION: Stoke-on-Trent, a city of 260,000 in Staffordshire, about a ninety-minute train ride north from London and just over an hour south from Manchester

CONTACT: stokecityfc.com, 01782 367598, #SCFC

NICKNAMES: The Potters

WOMEN'S TEAM: Stoke City FC Women currently play in the Women's National League North, tier 3. Home games are in nearby Smallthorne. See stokecityfc.com/club/women.

HISTORY: Stoke goes all the way back to 1863 and was one of the original twelve in the Football League in 1888. They settled into the Victoria Ground in 1878 and didn't leave it until 1997. They had good years in the 1930s and '40s, mainly because of legendary local boy Stanley Matthews, who represented England for twenty-four years and played competitively until the age of fifty. In 1947 they lost on the last day of the year, ceding the First Division title to Liverpool. It's as close as they've ever been.

In 1972 they beat Chelsea to win the League Cup—their only major trophy—but financial trouble soon followed, exacerbated by a windstorm that damaged the ground so badly, they had to sell players to cover the repairs. They then spent about twenty-five years hiring manager after manager and bouncing mostly between the second and third tiers.

They made the Premier League in 2008 and became the definition of a midtable club for ten years—but the bottom fell out in 2017–18, and they were relegated despite spending a ton of money on players. They have been in the Championship since, but they are not doing well. They spent £50 million on players the first season but finished sixteenth and sacked their manager. In 2020, they got just two wins in the first fourteen games, sacked another manager, and wound up fifteenth. Last year they were fourteenth but didn't sack a manager, anyway.

RIVALRIES: Traditionally, they contested the Potteries derby with local rivals Port Vale, but they have been a couple of divisions apart for years and haven't met since 2002. These days the main rivals are West Bromwich Albion and Wolverhampton Wanderers, but even those aren't too intense compared to many in the country. Derby County draws some ire as well.

SONGS: The official anthem is a song called "We'll Be with You," which was recorded by players for the 1972 League Cup final. It's played before each game as a banner with the same message is passed around above the supporters' heads. They also started singing Tom Jones's "Delilah" about twenty years back during a miserable season, changing the lyrics for a time to "Why, why, why do we bother?" These days it's back to Delilah but with other words changed to include *urine, cigarettes, laughter,* and *penis.* Gotta love football fans!

2020–21 SEASON: 14th in the Championship, 3rd Round FA Cup, Quarterfinals League Cup

2021–22 SEASON: The Championship (relegated in 2018)

STADIUM: While it's officially known as the Bet365 Stadium, many people still call Stoke's home by its original name, The Britannia. Among the fairly recent stadiums, it is at least a little different in that two corners are open. This distinguishes it from all the ovals that have come along lately, but when combined with the fact that the stadium sits on top of a hill, the configuration also exposes fans to rather legendarily cold winds. Away fans will be in the west end of the South Stand behind a goal.

TOURS: Tours are available for groups if you book two weeks ahead. Last year for a group of five or fewer, it was £30.

TICKETS: Two seasons ago they ranged from £30 to £40, and they didn't sell anything out.

GETTING THERE: While the stadium itself is nice, getting there is a pain. It's two miles from the train station and in a kind of industrial park, so a taxi might be the simplest. The club runs shuttle buses (£4 return) from the station. But you'll want to go early, as lines get quite long as kickoff approaches. Check the club website for the shuttle timetable.

PUBS: On the way into town from the station, you'll pass The Glebe, which always has plenty of fans. In town, down near the shuttle buses, look for The White Star and The Wheatsheaf. There is nothing out by the stadium.

GRUB: Aside from the pubs in the town center, all I saw was Hill's Fish and Chips, which was nothing special.

AROUND TOWN: You probably didn't know this, but Stoke has been the traditional home of pottery in England since the 17th century. This is owing to the abundance of clay and coal in the area. In fact, Wedgwood was founded there in 1759 and is still headquartered there. They have a museum with 80,000 works of art, ceramics, and photography; see wedgwood-museum.org.uk for information on visiting.

Also of interest are the city's ceramic collection and the restored plant at the Gladstone Pottery Museum; see stokemuseums.org.uk. And since we're on a pottery theme, the Burleigh company dates to 1851 and still makes pottery the old-fashioned way in historically protected buildings. Tours are available but must be booked ahead at burleigh.co.uk.

And finally, there's a massive indoor water park in town. That's at waterworld.co.uk.

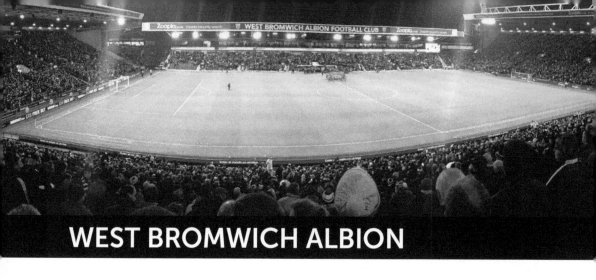

WEST BROMWICH ALBION

One of several big ones in the Birmingham area, West Brom has been a yo-yo club bouncing up and down the divisions for years; their fans also bounce and sing "Boing Boing" when they score. And now they've bounced down to the Championship.

LOCATION: West Bromwich (it's BROM-itch), which to us foreigners seems like just another part of Greater Birmingham, in the West Midlands

CONTACT: wba.co.uk, 0121 227 2227, #WBA

NICKNAMES: The Baggies, perhaps because factory workers in the old days attended games in their baggy work clothes. Sometimes also the Albion; the Throstles, for the bird on their crest; and the Stripes.

WOMEN'S TEAM: The WBA FC Women play in the third-tier National Women's League North. Home games are at Coles Lane in Sutton Coldfield.

HISTORY: West Brom is one of the older clubs around; it was started by workers at a spring factory in 1878. (This whole area was very much ground zero for the Industrial Revolution.) At first they were called West Bromwich Strollers; then in 1880 they became the first team to use *Albion*, a pre-Roman word for the island of Great Britain. (The other big clubs to use it are Burton Albion and Brighton and Hove Albion.) They were founder members of the Football League in 1888 and moved into The Hawthorns in 1900. They were relegated that season, setting something of a pattern.

They were good through the '20s and '30s, then again in the '50s and '60s. They won the League Cup in 1966 and the FA Cup in 1968, on a goal by "the King" Jeff Astle; look for him raising his arms on a very cool gate outside the ground. Another hero of those days, Tony "Bomber" Brown, has a statue nearby. That was their last major trophy, and by the early

1990s, they were all the way down in the third tier. They got to the Premier League in 2001, then got relegated, then got back up and staged a miraculous great escape in 2005, becoming the first team to stay up after being bottom of the table at Christmas. There's a great video online of their last game that season. Then they were relegated the next season anyway. They were back up in 2009, down in 2010, back up in 2011, and down in 2018—classic yo-yo club. In 2018–19 they were knocked out of the playoffs, at home, on penalties, by Aston Villa of all clubs. In 2020 they finished second in the league to go up, then last year they were nineteenth in the Premier League and back down!

They have worn the same blue-and-white stripes for virtually their entire history, and their crest features a cute little bird called a throstle; it used to sit on a crossbar but now rests on a hawthorn branch, a nod to their stadium. Legend has it that in the really old days, the pub where the players dressed kept such a bird in a cage.

About that famous boing-boinging. One theory is that it had to do with all the going up and down through the leagues, but a supporter I met, Nick, had a better story.

"It was about the 1992–93 season, and the story I heard was, in the coach on the way to the ground before a Cup game, there was this young lad who'd had a few pints, and he had his headphones on playing this house music, you know, with the pounding beat. And he's bouncing his head up and down going 'boing boing.'

"Well, the other lads started doing it to mock him, ya know, taking the piss out of it, and they come off the bus doing it, 'boing boing.' And when the Albion scored in that game, they started doing it in the stand. And it bloody stuck!"

RIVALRIES: The other Birmingham-area clubs are rivals, especially Aston Villa and Wolverhampton Wanderers. With the latter they contest the Black Country derby, which goes all the way back to 1886 and has been played 162 times. That matchup—West Bromwich Albion vs. Wolverhampton Wanderers—is said to be the worst nightmare of the person who has about five minutes to engrave the FA Cup trophy with the winners' name. It'd be a cracking final, though.

SONGS: The most random one is the 23rd Psalm. Yes, that one, "The Lord is my shepherd" and all of that. The leading theory traces it to a game away to Everton in 1974; issues with the electricity at the stadium moved the game to Sunday, and since it was the first Sunday game anyone could remember, they decided to get religious. It's now written above the seats in the West Stand at The Hawthorns.

At the other end of the class spectrum, listen for a rendition of "Shit on the Villa," regardless of the day's opponent.

2020–21 SEASON: 19th in Premier League (relegated), 3rd Round FA Cup, 3rd Round League Cup

2021–22 SEASON: The Championship (relegated in 2021)

STADIUM: The Hawthorns has been their home since 1900, and strangely, among the ninety-two Football League clubs, it's the highest above sea level at 551 feet. The site had to be cleared of hawthorn bushes, hence the name.

Capacity is 26,688; it somehow looks smaller from the outside and bigger on the inside. It's a very cozy, enclosed ground and is intimidating to opponents when the Baggies are good. The away fans are behind a goal in the Smethwick End; the hard-core Albion folks are opposite in the Birmingham Road End, known as the Brummie Road End. Between the Brummie and the East Stand is the Woodsman Corner, named for a pub that was there until 2004; look for the giant throstle statue there now.

TOURS: Once every couple of months, the club offers tours. Check the website for dates.

TICKETS: Last time they were in the Championship, adult tickets were £25 to £35 and kids at £10 to £14. Few games will sell out.

GETTING THERE: The closest rail station is The Hawthorns, just a few minutes' walk away. It's about 20 minutes from the main Birmingham station, New Street, with a change at Snow Hill. You can also get there direct from Moor Street, right across from New Street, on West Midlands Trains. A few bus lines stop right outside, and for some games they run the Baggies Barge, a narrow boat on the old industrial canals. Check the website for details.

PUBS: There aren't many near the ground. The Vine is considered the best option and gets high marks for its Indian food. It's about a ten-minute walk away. Also look for The Royal Oak, a similar distance in the other direction. There is the usual FanZone right by the ground.

GRUB: Other than the pubs, there's nothing special in the area.

AROUND TOWN: There's nothing much to see in West Bromwich, really. The sights are all in Birmingham proper and include the Birmingham Museum and Art Gallery, the National Sea Life Centre, and Cadbury World, a chocolate museum. (Cadbury was founded in Birmingham.) The other main sights are related to the Industrial Revolution and old housing. The Jewellery Quarter is worth a walk around, but the real prizes for history buffs are the Birmingham Back to Backs (celebrating a common working-class style of housing) and the twenty-six-acre Black Country Living Museum, which re-creates many aspects of 18th- and 19th-century life.

WOLVERHAMPTON WANDERERS

I used to say what an old-fashioned club Wolverhampton is, and then they turned into giant spenders, stormed the Championship, got promoted, and even made the Europa League twice in the last three seasons.

LOCATION: Wolverhampton, which is officially a city of 250,000 people plus a metropolitan borough, but to me is part of the great sprawling mass that is Birmingham

CONTACT: wolves.co.uk, 0371 222 2220, #WWFC

NICKNAMES: Wolves—even though their name includes *Wanderers*. I don't understand these things.

WOMEN'S TEAM: Wolverhampton Wanderers WFC play in the Women's National League Northern Premier Division, tier three. Home games are played at the CKW Stadium.

HISTORY: Wolves go all the way back to 1877, making them one of the oldest clubs around. They were one of twelve founder members of the Football League in 1888, and in fact played in the first-ever Football League game against Aston Villa. They won the FA Cup in 1893, but they soon faded from prominence.

It was in the 1950s that they hit their glory days. With Billy Wright as the captain and Stan Cullis as the manager, they won the league in 1954, 1958, and 1959. They also staged "floodlit friendlies" with big teams from all over the world. The most famous of these was a 1954 game played at night, live on the BBC, against Honvéd from Budapest, then considered the greatest club side in the world. The Hungarians were up, 2–0, after fourteen minutes, but at halftime Cullis told the staff to water the pitch to slow the opponents down. Wolves scored three in the second half and won it, causing the (British) press to declare them "Champions of the World." The attention afforded that game was apparently the final straw to create the formation of a European Cup tournament, today known as the UEFA Champions League.

Wolves went on to win their fourth FA Cup but got relegated in 1964. Odd historical note: Wolves actually played in and won a 1967 league called the United Soccer Association that was made up of US and Canadian "teams" that were actually foreign teams. The LA Wolves beat the Washington Whips (aka Aberdeen of Scotland) to win it, and then the league became part of the North American Soccer League.

Wolves made the European final in 1971, losing to Spurs, and then the League Cup in 1974. Then they started bouncing up and down, and when they spent a fortune on the stadium in 1979, it almost wiped them out. By 1988 they were all the way down in the Fourth Division, playing teams like Scunthorpe and Newport County.

They got it together and spent most of the 1990s in the top division, then yo-yoed some more until 2012, when they were relegated from the Premier League. The next year they went down again to League One—a double-relegation that has since been called "doing a Wolves." Sunderland did it themselves recently.

In the 2017–18 season, Wolves got back to the Premier League after a Chinese group bought the club and poured money into players for two seasons. They were one of the stories of the following season, finishing seventh and making the FA Cup semifinals. They qualified for the Europa League, made the Round of 16, then did the same again for 2020, getting as far as the quarterfinals. They dropped to thirteenth last season, and then their manager left for Tottenham.

RIVALRIES: By far the biggest rival is West Bromwich Albion, just twelve miles away in another…suburb or whatever…of Birmingham. This is known as the Black Country derby after the region's famous pollution during the Industrial Revolution. They have played 162 times, and in 2008, a national survey of football fans said Wolves–WBA was the fiercest rivalry in the country.

The other area teams, Birmingham City and Aston Villa, are also big rivals. Basically, they all hate each other.

SONGS: Before each game and after each goal, you'll hear a song you'll recognize, even if you don't know the name. It's "Hi Ho Silver Lining" by Jeff Beck. There's a moment when Beck sings, "Hi ho silver lining!" But that's when the music stops and the whole crowd raises their arms and yells, "Hi ho Wolverhampton!" Sheffield Wednesday does this as well, and of course they both claim to have done it first.

Lately they've got an even better one, featuring a reference to their amazingly named manager, Nuno Espirtu Santo, and a star player from Portugal.

Nuno had a dream, to build a football team
With Chinese money and a wonder kid from Porto.
With five at the back and pace in attack,
We're Wolverhampton, and we're on our way back!

2020–21 SEASON: 13th in Premier League, 5th Round FA Cup, 2nd Round League Cup

2021–22 SEASON: Premier League (promoted in 2018)

STADIUM: The Molineux is a 31,700-seater that somehow seems bigger. It is also, like the team's kits, of a striking color. I once referred to this as orange, and I was politely but firmly corrected; it is "old gold." Do not say orange in Wolverhampton!

Its most prominent stand is actually behind a goal; the Stan Cullis Stand, named for a former player and manager, towers over the rest of the place and is visible from all over town. Behind the other goal is the small Jack Harris Stand, where the rowdies sit. There is also a temporary structure next to it, often unused, and known informally as the Gene Kelly Stand; since it's uncovered, folks there wind up "singing in the rain."

On each side are two-tiered, curved stands called the Billy Wright and the Steve Bull. Each of these is named for a club legend, and both the Cullis and Wright stands have a statue of their man outside.

A distinct feature of the place is how they seat the away fans. Normally the away fans are in a corner or behind a goal. At Wolverhampton, they occupy the lower tier of a side stand, all along the touchline. So if their section is full, they stretch from goal line to goal line, with home fans above them. It makes for some interesting banter.

The name Molineux comes from the landowner in the 18th century. He built a hotel that still stands as the City Archives building, and the whole area eventually came to be a big park called Molineux Grounds. Wolves started playing there in 1889.

TOURS: Tours are Friday, Saturday or Sunday and include the museum. It's £17.50 for adults.

TICKETS: With demand so high—they sold out every home game—what they do for foreigners is have you buy a membership, then for each game hold a lottery of foreign members. If there were two of you, you would both need to win the lottery. My broker doesn't have anything to offer here, so if they have this arrangement again, your best bet will be a Cup game or a midweek game against a smaller opponent.

GETTING THERE: One of the reasons I enjoy games at Wolverhampton is how easy it all is. The stadium is about a 15-minute walk from the Wolverhampton rail station, which is about 20 minutes out from Birmingham New Street. You could even get there in two hours from Euston station in London.

PUBS: Another reason to enjoy a game at The Molineux: during that fifteen-minute walk from the station to the ground, you'll go through the historic center of Wolverhampton and pass about 437 pubs. Okay, that was a slight exaggeration, but it's quite the density of boozers:

- The Banks Brewery also offers tours several days a week.
- The Posada is a traditional Victorian pub with no food but plenty of real ales.
- The Goose is a small traditional pub with eight TVs.
- The Hogs Head gets good marks for atmosphere and a big menu.
- The Hooded Ram is a brewery from the Isle of Man with great Indian food.
- Since the Billy Wright is named for a former Wolves player, it would seem to be a good option for a pre-match pint.
- The Bohemian appeared a rather hipster place, advertising cocktails, craft beer, and cider.
- The Prince Albert, super prominent by the station, seemed a bit modern and clubby despite the exterior.
- There is a Wetherspoon on the main drag called the Moon Under Water.

Seriously, that's all in a fifteen-minute walk, and I didn't even cover all of them.

GRUB: Aside from the pubs above, Charlie's Fish Bar looks a proper chippy, and I had a nice, cheap English breakfast at Bethany's.

AROUND TOWN: All of these sights are either right in town or quite nearby:

- The Royal Air Force Museum, which also hosts the British Airways Collection.
- Moseley Old Hall is a fully restored 17th-century manor house where Charles II stayed before he escaped to France during the English Civil War in 1651.
- Wightwick Manor and Gardens is a 19th-century Arts and Crafts manor house that depicts life in Victorian times.
- The Black Country Living Museum is twenty-six acres of restored Industrial Revolution shops, houses, and other industrial buildings.
- Wolverhampton Art Museum dates from 1884 and is known mainly for a collection of pop art second only to the Tate in London, as well as collections of japanned ware and enamels, which Wolverhampton was famous for.

EAST MIDLANDS

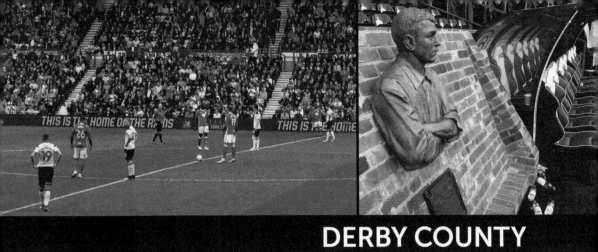

DERBY COUNTY

About as consistent a second-tier club as you can find, Derby County could actually be an easy day out from London or Manchester—with an epic beer scene.

LOCATION: Ninety train minutes north of St. Pancras station in London or east from Piccadilly station in Manchester, and forty-five minutes from Birmingham

CONTACT: dcfc.co.uk, 0871 472 1884, #DCFC

NICKNAMES: The Rams, because of their early association with an army regiment that had a ram as its mascot. Also, to be sure you know it, it's pronounced DAR-bee.

WOMEN'S TEAM: Derby County FC Women, aka the Ewe Rams, play in the Women's National League North, tier 3 of the pyramid. Home games are at Don Amott Leisure Group Arena in Mickleover, on the west side of Derby.

HISTORY: Derby County was formed in 1884, joined the Football League in 1888, and kicked around between the top two divisions—three times finishing second—before World War II suspended everything. When football came back, they won the 1946 FA Cup, and then it was "normal service resumed." After a brief spell in the third tier in the mid-1950s, they were a midtable Second Division side until the late 1960s. That's when they hired Brian Clough (CLUFF).

You might have heard of him; he is one of the all-time greats as a manager and personality. He was an outrageous scorer as a player—251 goals in 274 games for Middlesbrough and Sunderland—but an injury caused him to retire at age twenty-nine. He was hired a couple of years later, in 1967, by Derby, who had just finished seventeenth in the Second Division. He brought along an old teammate from Boro named Peter Taylor, and two years later they won the division. In 1972 they won the First Division. The next year they made the semifinals of the European Cup, losing to Juventus.

But Clough was, among many things, a pain in the ass. The stories are many and legendary, but to the dismay of Rams fans, he and Taylor both left in 1973 amid constant battles with the club's board. (Making things worse, he would wind up with archrivals Nottingham Forest, where he won the league once and Europe twice.) Derby, meanwhile, claimed another league title in 1975 but by 1980 were relegated. They went to the Third Division from 1984 to 1986, and then did the yo-yo with seven league changes in twenty-two seasons.

Last season they flirted with relegation all the way to the final day, while also getting in trouble for financial mismanagement. In fact, their status in the Championship was in doubt for a while after the season, until the Football Association decided to dock them points in the upcoming season. So Wycombe went down after all, and Derby stayed up, but they will start this season in a hole.

RIVALRIES: The biggest rival is Nottingham Forest, which is mostly because they are only fourteen miles apart but also because of the Clough connection. Derby fans weren't happy when he signed up with their rivals, so that added a whole new level to things. In fact, the winner of the East Midlands derby gets to keep the Brian Clough Trophy, currently with Nottingham Forest.

They also dislike Leeds, and again Clough is involved. When he was at Derby, he openly disliked Leeds's playing style and their legendary manager, Don Revie, so the fans took it from there. Leicester City is also disliked because they are thirty miles away; no Clough connection there.

SONGS: Back around the turn of the 20th century, Derby had a superstar named Steve Bloomer. He scored 352 goals in 598 games for them and Middlesbrough, as well as twenty-eight in twenty-three for England. There's a bust of him, with his arms folded, surveying things from next to the home dugout at Pride Park. Well, in 1997 a couple of Derby supporters heard an Australian song called "Up There Cazaly," thought it was cool, and reworked the lyrics. So now they have an anthem that includes the chorus:

Steve Bloomer's watchin',
Helping them fight,
Guiding our heroes,
In the black and the white.
All teams who come here,
There's nowhere to hide.
Everyone is frightened
Of that Derby pride.

2020–21 SEASON: 21st in the Championship, 3rd Round FA Cup, 2nd Round League Cup

2021–22 SEASON: The Championship (relegated in 2008)

STADIUM: Pride Park, named for the 1990s-era business park where it's located, has been their home since 1997. It replaced the Baseball Ground, which was actually built for baseball and so had some seats that didn't exactly face toward the football pitch. The new home, a classic modern rectangle, seats 33,597, with away fans in the southeast corner and the home rowdies in the southwest. So if you don't mind sitting behind a goal, the south end can be pretty fun.

Aside from the statue of "watchin'" Bloomer inside the ground, there is also one outside of former player and manager Dave Mackay emerging from a wall and another of Clough and Taylor. This brings me to the basis for an interesting trivia question: Clough has a statue here and in Nottingham (in town, not at the stadium), making him and Sir Bobby Robson (of Ipswich Town and Newcastle) the only people I know of who have statues at two different clubs.

TOURS: Tours cost £10 and are available a couple of times a month. You can also book a private tour by contacting the club.

TICKETS: Two years ago tickets ranged from £15 to £40 for adults, and in 2019-20 even the derby with Forest didn't sell out.

GETTING THERE: It's a 15-minute walk from Derby railway station and a fairly nice one, with part of it through a greenbelt along the River Derwent.

PUBS: Since it's an office park, there isn't much around for eating and drinking, aside from a Frankie and Benny's. Along the walk from the station there's a Harvester's, which is a chain pub. Another chain, Merlin, has a location just past the stadium on the A6 road.

Derby, however, absolutely shocked me with its collection of high-quality pubs. Lonely Planet called it the best place to drink real ale in the world. I have no idea how it became such a beer-drinker's heaven, but, well, here you go:

- The Brunswick Inn, near the station in a building from 1842, has been called one of the top ten places to drink real ale in Britain and the best pub in Derby two years running.
- Mr. Grundy's Tavern on the Derby Mile is another CAMRA recommendation.
- The Old Bell, dated 1650, has a great patio and second bar out back.
- Ye Olde Dolphin Inn, dated 1530 and the oldest pub in town, has good steaks and a cool patio out back.
- The Falstaff is packed with brewing memorabilia and brews its own beer.

- The Abbey is in a former abbey on the banks of the river.
- Also near the river and the station is The Alexandra Hotel, which has been a top CAMRA pub in town for years.

Trust me, that's not nearly a complete list. For a map of their Real Ale Trail, hit up derbycamra.org .uk/derby-pubs. Derby—who knew?

GRUB: Many of those pubs above have food. Otherwise, there is a wealth of options down in the center.

LEICESTER CITY

You've no doubt heard of Leicester City because they recently pulled off one of the great fairy-tale seasons of all time. And last year they won their first FA Cup. But there's more to the Foxes and their city than memories of two great seasons.

LOCATION: One hour north of London by train and one hour east of Birmingham

CONTACT: lcfc.com, 0344 815 5000, #LCFC

NICKNAMES: The Foxes

WOMEN'S TEAM: LCFC Women play in the Women's Championship, tier 2 of the pyramid. Games are at the Farley Way Stadium in Quorn.

HISTORY: Before 2015, Leicester City's history was that of a top second-tier football club, if that makes sense. Since their founding in 1884, they have spent all but one year in the top two flights of English football, and in fact they are tied for having won the second tier the most times ever—seven. Until they won the 2021 FA Cup Final, they had played in and lost four FA Cup finals, the most by a team who hadn't won it. They have won the (second-tier) League Cup three times, in 1964, 1997, and 2000.

In the 2013–14 season they won the Championship, thus going up to the Premier League. But in March of 2015, they seemed doomed to relegation. With only nine games remaining, they were dead last in twentieth place, nine points below the nineteenth-place team. But they won seven of their last nine games to complete a remarkable great escape.

Then came the 2015–16 season, for which they had essentially the same team under a new manager named Claudio Ranieri, who was on his sixteenth job in thirty years. They were favorites to be relegated and 5,000-to-1 to win the league. But they started that season the way they had finished the last one.

They just kept winning and winning, with a team of castoffs and low-budget finds. But they had a counter-attacking style they were perfectly suited for and a dose of magic about them. Slowly the conversation shifted from "This is goofy fun that won't last," to "Wow, they're really hanging in there," to "Wait, could this really happen?" It was when they whipped Manchester City 3–1 away in February that reality began to settle in. With two games to go, their title was clinched when Tottenham was held at Chelsea in the (in)famous "Battle of the Bridge." The ultra-long-shot Foxes had done it, charming the sporting world along the way and—in a nod to Arsenal's undefeated "Invincibles" team—earning the nickname "The Unbelievables."

They have consolidated since, finishing mid-table or higher in the Premier League. But they suffered a tragedy when, just after a national televised game in October 2018, a helicopter carrying their owner, Vichai Srivaddhanaprabha, and several other people took off from the pitch, lost control and crashed just outside the stadium. No one survived, and the town was shocked by the loss of the popular owner. The entire team attended his funeral in Thailand.

Their FA Cup win got them into the Europa League this year, but they were battling for a spot in the Champions League until the final day of the season, losing out on fourth place to Chelsea—whom they beat in the FA Cup Final—by one point.

RIVALRIES: Any game between Leicester City, Nottingham Forest, and Derby County would be considered an East Midlands derby. There's also a rivalry with Coventry City, at least according to the folks at Coventry City.

SONGS: It's not a song, but you'll want to be in your seats when the team comes out. That's because they are welcomed by a man blowing a fox-hunting horn. It's awesome.

2020–21 SEASON: 5th in Premier League, Winners FA Cup, 3rd Round League Cup, Europa League Round of 32

2021–22 SEASON: Premier League (promoted in 2014), Europa League

STADIUM: The King Power Stadium, named for a Thailand-based duty-free retail company owned by the same people as the club, replaced Filbert Lane in 2002. I wish they would keep the old names. You can visit the site of Filbert Lane nearby and look for Gary Lineker Way; the host of BBC's *Match of the Day* is a local lad and club legend.

King Power holds 32,312 people in a cookie-cutter shape like so many other stadiums. But it can get mighty loud in there. Away fans will be in the northeast corner.

TOURS: Tours are offered on non-home-game weekends for £15.

TICKETS: Like many Premier League clubs, Leicester can be a tough ticket, especially when it's a big game. But with a membership you should be able to get into most games;

the international rate was £20 for adults in 2019-20. Ticket prices for adults run from £26 to £50, and hospitality options are quite reasonable.

GETTING THERE: It's about a 30-minute walk from the main train station, with signs pointing the way. Buses 84, 86, and 88 from the center will also get you to Freemen's Common, a few minutes from the stadium. With all of this just an hour north of St. Pancras in London, you could have breakfast and dinner in London while catching a Foxes game in between.

PUBS: The Blue Boar in Millstone Street is a super friendly real ale pub that also serves sandwiches…I mean, cobs. You'll have to ask them about that! Sir Robert Peel is another fine pub closer to the ground in Jarrom Street. The Counting House on Almond Road—love the tree names!—sometimes allows away fans if they aren't from a rival club. If you're not feeling so adventurous, there is a Holiday Inn basically at the stadium.

GRUB: Aside from the pubs, there are not many options near the stadium. There is a Local Hero chain pub and a Nando's just a block east. Otherwise, eat something in the center.

AROUND TOWN: If English history is your thing, Leicester has some stuff to offer. Its history goes back to pre-Roman days, but the main attraction is the story of Richard III, the last English king to be killed in battle, in 1485. His makeshift grave was discovered in 2012 while ground was being cleared for a parking garage. He was reburied in the Leicester Cathedral, and there is now a visitor centre which tells the story of his life and death near where he was found.

Otherwise, there is a nice medieval quarter where you can find the 14th-century Guildhall and the cathedral, as well as shops and restaurants. If you like ruins, look for the medieval Leicester Abbey a half-hour walk north of the station and across the River Soar from lovely Abbey Park. Also on the river and closer to the stadium is the Roman-era Jewry Wall, which houses a medieval-themed museum. If botanic gardens are your thing, the one at the University of Leicester makes for a lovely walk. Kids might enjoy the National Space Center, with rockets and exhibits and a planetarium.

And finally, this might be of interest just to travel nerds like me, but Thomas Cook got his start in Leicester as well. Cook was instrumental in creating group travel excursions, the first being a special train for five hundred people from Leicester to a temperance society meeting in 1841. By the 1860s he was arranging trips to Europe, publishing guidebooks, and creating train passes and hotel coupons. His son took over in the 1870s and created a worldwide company that only went out of business in 2019.

There's a statue of the elder Cook right outside the train station, and his original office, in Gallowtree Gate, is now a Foot Locker, but there are still a few murals of his earliest excursions on the wall. He ran a temperance meeting room upstairs, by the way.

NOTTINGHAM FOREST

Yes, there is a club named Nottingham Forest, and it's in a very cool city not too far from London.

LOCATION: In the East Midlands, ninety train minutes from St. Pancras station in London or from Piccadilly station in Manchester, an hour from Birmingham

CONTACT: nottinghamforest.co.uk, 0115 982 4444, #NFFC

NICKNAMES: Forest

WOMEN'S TEAM: Nottingham Forest Women FC play in the third-tier Women's National League North, with home games at Eastwood FC.

HISTORY: If you knew nothing of English soccer and you happened to come into contact with Nottingham Forest Football Club today, you might think their history began in 1975 and ended sometime around 1990.

Here is why: in 1975, Forest had just finished sixteenth in the Second Division. In their ninety-seven-year history, they had never won anything except a couple of FA Cups and some lower divisions, and they had finished higher than fifth in the league exactly three times. They were nobody. And then they hired two men to build their squad and run the club: Brian Clough (pronounced CLUFF) and Peter Taylor.

By all accounts, Clough—who had taken nearby Derby County from similar status to the league championship—was a genius at tactics and motivation, as well as being one of the great characters in the game's history. Words like *acerbic* and *biting* and *entertaining* are often applied to him. He was known for quotes such as "When I go, God will have to give up his favorite chair." (I encourage you to watch documentaries about him on YouTube.) Taylor, meanwhile, came off as the voice of reason and calm, with the unfailing ability to spot and attract talented footballers who fit Clough's system.

They got Forest into Division One two years later, in 1977. The next spring they won the League Cup—and then the league! That got them into the European Cup, which they won in 1979 after bagging another League Cup and finishing second in the league. In 1980 all they did was win Europe again!

It's really hard to put this into perspective. Remember Leicester City's fairy-tale league title in 2016? That came after they had been promoted two years before and barely stayed up the year before. Right, so imagine they had gone on to win two straight Champions Leagues. Utterly and completely miraculous.

In the 1980s, Forest got into Europe a few more times, once as far as the semifinals, and won two more League Cups. But Clough's power was fading, his alcoholism was becoming an issue, and he started to alienate everyone around him. In 1993 he retired on a day when mighty Forest was relegated from the Premier League. He died in 2004. Still, he looms over the club.

And in the twenty-seven seasons since Clough left? Forest has had more than twenty managers and spent twenty-one years in the second tier (including the last thirteen), three in League One, and just four in the Premier League—and none since 1999. It's been five years since they even sniffed the playoffs.

But new owners arrived in 2017, and Forest just missed the playoffs in 2020—crushingly dropping from fifth to seventh on goal difference on the last day. Alas, last season they dropped to seventeenth.

RIVALRIES: Derby County is the biggest rival by far, in part because they are fourteen miles away and in part because Derby probably thinks they should have been the ones winning Europe with Clough. The two have contested the Brian Clough Trophy since 2007. Also, Notts County, whose ground is right across the river but who are always in a different league, is a rival. They haven't played since the 2011–12 League Cup, and County aren't even in the Football League anymore. Then there's Leicester City, another East Midlands outfit just twenty-eight miles away. And finally, two Yorkshire clubs: Sheffield United and, to a lesser extent, Leeds United. That's because of a miners' strike in the 1980s when Yorkshire miners walked out but many in Nottinghamshire didn't. (This English stuff gets complicated and multileveled.) I saw Forest play at Leeds once, and the supporters swapped songs about the strike—thirty-five years later!

SONGS: Before each game, to the bagpipe-filled tune of an obscure Paul McCartney and Wings song "Mull of Kintyre," Forest fans stand and sing:

City Ground
Oh mist rolling in from the Trent
My desire is always to be here
Oh City Ground.

2020–21 SEASON: 17th in the Championship, 4th Round FA Cup, 1st Round League Cup

2021–22 SEASON: The Championship (promoted in 2008)

STADIUM: City Ground makes a lovely sight on the banks of the River Trent, especially when you're walking over Trent Bridge from the station. They have played there since 1898, and today's capacity is 30,445. The most impressive stand is, naturally, the Brian Clough Stand, which was built with money from his team's exploits in Europe. It opened in 1980 and was named for him in the 1990s. Two other stands were also rebuilt in the 1990s, leaving the 1965 Main Stand looking a bit worn down by comparison.

The away fans will be in the Bridgford Road Stand behind a goal, over by the Clough Stand. I would sit either in the Clough Stand for comfort or the Main Stand for the view.

TOURS: Tours are offered a couple of times a month and led by the captain of the Europe-winning teams. Cost is £15.

TICKETS: Last I saw it was £21 to £26 for adult tickets, and they didn't sell out a single game.

GETTING THERE: It's a one-mile walk from the station. You can knock most of that distance off by taking a Keyworth-bound bus from the station to the Trent Bridge.

PUBS: As you walk over from the station, you'll pass a Hooters on the right, believe it or not. Just past that on the left, there's a bar at Meadow Lane, home ground of Notts County. They are never at home when Forest is, but their bar is open. Just before the bridge is The Embankment, a 1907 pub now owned by a local brewery. Just across the bridge is the Trent Bridge Inn, a historic pub now part of the Wetherspoon chain.

In town there are three seriously old pubs, each laying some claim to being the oldest around. The Bell Inn, in the middle of town, dates to 1437. Ye Olde Salutation Inn is from 1420! And Ye Olde Trip to Jerusalem, in caves under Nottingham Castle, says it was founded in 1189, but there's no proof of it. The caves were being used to store beer for the castle before that, but the oldest part of the current building is from the 1650s. Still.

Along the restored canal, the Canal Pub is pretty cool, with outdoor seating and lots of food.

GRUB: Behind the stadium on Radcliffe Road you'll find a little cluster of takeaway places, including the popular Bridgford Fish Bar. Further down Bridgford Road is another cluster, including a Pizza Express and a Spanish place called Escabeche. Otherwise, it's all up in town, where I had a nice lunch at the Ugly Bread Bakery and a good burger at Annie's Burger Shack.

AROUND TOWN: So yes, this is Robin Hood country. Dude is everywhere too. Nottingham Castle is really just an art museum now, but the grounds are nice, and there's a good view of the city as well as the old pub mentioned above. And there's a statue of The Man Himself with his arrow drawn.

The 19th-century Lace Market is nice for a walk around. Other things to check out include City of Caves, part of the National Justice Museum; and Wollaton Hall, a country estate and deer park reachable by a city bus.

By all accounts, *the* Robin Hood experience you're looking for, with Maid Marion and the whole gang featuring tours and performances and everything, is offered by Ezekial Bone, at ezekialbone.com. I have never had the pleasure, but even locals say they enjoy it. You'll need to book well ahead.

NOTTS COUNTY

Very much the "other" team in Nottingham to outsiders, Notts County is a wonderful, old-fashioned family club currently in the darkest time of its 130-plus-year history.

LOCATION: Nottingham, in the East Midlands, ninety train minutes from St. Pancras station in London or from Piccadilly station in Manchester, an hour from Birmingham

CONTACT: nottscountyfc.co.uk, 0115 9529 000, #Notts

NICKNAMES: The Magpies, for their black-and-white-striped shirts, or just the Pies

WOMEN'S TEAM: Reborn in 2018 after folding the year before, Notts County Women are in the East Midlands Regional Women's Football League at tier 6. They play their home games at Greenwich Avenue, Basford, which is the home of Basford United.

HISTORY: Here is something I bet you didn't know: Notts County is the oldest professional soccer club in the world. There is an older amateur club—Sheffield FC was founded in 1857—but County goes back to 1862. Yet you may not have even known they exist because they have been below the second tier of English football for twenty-six seasons.

County helped found the Football League in 1888, won the FA Cup in 1894, got relegated in 1926, and then vanished from the top division for more than fifty years. That FA Cup and a few lower-division trophies are all that sit in their very old trophy cabinet.

It was right after World War II that they hit a golden era, but even that was in the Third Division. In the 1949–50 season, home crowds averaged 35,000 as they won the division by seven points—nine over Nottingham Forest. But by the end of the 1950s, they were relegated again and Forest was FA Cup champion. It would be fifteen years before County even got back to the second tier, and 1982 before they briefly made the top tier. But by then Brian Clough had taken Forest to two straight European Cups, and County has been in Forest's shadow ever since.

Notts County almost went out of business in 2003, and in 2006 they stayed in the league only on the last day, finishing twenty-first in League Two. Since then it's been a seemingly constant stream of new owners, chairmen, financial problems, and managers, with the team never getting above seventh in League One. In 2017–18 they finished fifth in League Two, went to the playoffs, and lost in the semifinals.

Bottom was finally hit in 2019, when they were relegated from League Two and thus out of the Football League for the first time in their history. The BBC said they are arguably the biggest club ever to drop out of the league. In 2020, to add to the heartache, they got back into the playoffs and made the final, but lost, 3–1, to Harrogate Town. Last year they lost again in the semifinals.

And finally, something else I bet you didn't know: Juventus, the Italian giants, got their black-and-white shirts from Notts County. They were looking for new colors in 1903, and an Englishman on their staff reached out to a friend in Nottingham, who sent some samples. Juve have worn them ever since. In 2011 Juventus had County over for a friendly to open their 41,000-seat new stadium.

RIVALRIES: Forest, of course, is a rival, but with County in lower leagues, the Nottingham derby hasn't happened since 2012. Lately they've developed hostilities with near neighbors Mansfield Town (fifteen miles away), Lincoln City (forty-five miles), and Chesterfield (twenty-six miles).

SONGS: It seems that in 1988, County were playing at Shrewsbury Town, whose team was up 2–0 and whose fans were singing "On Top of Old Smokey." County fans—either making fun of the locals' accent and country life or celebrating when their team scored two quick goals to get a draw—changed the words to:

> I had a wheelbarrow
> But the wheels fell off.
> I had a wheelbarrow
> But the wheels fell off.
> County! County! County!

They made it to Wembley that year, winning promotion and singing that song all the way. It's been with them ever since.

2020–21 SEASON: 5th in National League (lost playoff semifinal), 2nd Round FA Cup

2021–22 SEASON: National League (relegated in 2019)

STADIUM: Meadow Lane has been their home since 1910, and I would imagine it's the biggest in the history of the fifth tier. Capacity is 19,841 in four separate stands, all built in the 1990s. Away fans get better than usual seats in the Jimmy Sirrel Stand on the side, and home rowdies are in the Kop stand behind a goal. Behind the other goal is the Family Stand.

As you will see if you go to either one, Forest's City Ground is just across the River Trent from Meadow Lane, a straight-line distance of some 300 yards, making them the two closest grounds in all of England.

TOURS: No tours are available at this stadium.

TICKETS: When I saw them in the Football League it was £20 for adult tickets all over the place.

GETTING THERE: It's a very simple 10-minute walk from the Nottingham rail station.

PUBS: There is a supporters club at the ground that lets in everybody who's not an away fan. As you walk over from the station, you'll also pass a Hooters, which seems out of place. If you go past the stadium just a bit, you'll find three modern pubs with good food: the Trent Navigation Inn, The Embankment, and Brewhouse and Kitchen.

For more on food and attractions in town, check the previous chapter on Nottingham Forest.

YORKSHIRE

BILLY BREMNER

1942 - 1997

LEEDS UNITED

1959 - 1976

771 APPEARANCES: 115 GOALS

INSPIRATIONAL CAPTAIN OF THE GREAT

BARNSLEY

Barnsley is historically a second-tier club, nicknamed the Tykes, in a town whose citizens will be surprised but delighted you've showed up for a visit.

LOCATION: In Yorkshire, ninety minutes east of Manchester by train and thirty minutes north of Sheffield

CONTACT: barnsleyfc.co.uk, 01226 211211, #YouReds

NICKNAMES: The Tykes, the Reds, or (more in the past) the Colliers. A tyke seems to be a Yorkshire term for a sly or cunning dog—mischievous, not dastardly. A collier is a coal miner.

WOMEN'S TEAM: Barnsley Women FC play in the fourth-tier National League Division One North. Home games are at Recreation Ground, home of Wombwell Town FC. See barnsleywomensfc.org for more.

HISTORY: A sentence from Wikipedia perhaps defines this club's history perfectly: "Barnsley have spent more seasons in the second tier of English football than any other club in history and have produced some notable talents over the years who have gone on to be successful at other clubs."

They joined the Football League (Second Division, naturally) in 1898 and lost the FA Cup final to Newcastle in 1910. They went back in 1912 and won it, 1–0, over West Brom. After World War I, the league shuffled around a bit, and Barnsley felt they should have been going to the First Division for the first time, but it went to a vote. Arsenal had just moved to a new location in London, and perhaps some bribes went around. Again we hear from Wikipedia: "[Arsenal] duly won the vote and Barnsley were consigned to the second tier of English football for another eight decades."

They didn't actually spend eighty years in the second tier; they went back and forth between second and third, and in the '60s and '70s they spent a few seasons in the fourth tier. They had a good run in the 1980s, finishing sixth in the second tier once.

The peak came in the late 1990s. In 1997 they finished second in the second tier (confusingly called the First Division at the time), thus winning promotion to the Premier League. In their one and only top-tier season, they got relegated, losing seven of their last nine, but made the FA Cup quarterfinals after beating Tottenham and Manchester United along the way. The next year they made the quarters again, and in 2000 they made the league playoffs but lost the final to Ipswich Town.

After financial trouble came in 2002, they stabilized and made a big FA Cup run in 2007–08, winning against Chelsea and at Liverpool before dropping the semifinal to Cardiff at Wembley. The 2015–16 season was also good; they won the League Trophy and beat Millwall in the playoff final to get back to the Championship. They were relegated on the last day back to League One, but the club was sold to a group that includes Billy Beane of the Oakland A's and Moneyball fame. Sure enough, they made it back to the Championship in 2020, stayed up by the thinnest of margins that year, then lost in the promotion playoffs last year.

RIVALRIES: Sheffield Wednesday and Leeds are rivals, although I get the sense neither of them worries about the Tykes much. It would seem to me that any Yorkshire club would qualify as a rival, particularly Doncaster Rovers.

SONGS: None that I can tell, but I want to mention one here anyway. It's not specific to Barnsley, but they seem fond of smuggling a plant pot into the stadium, putting it on people's heads, and singing, "He's got a plant pot on his head." Don't believe me? Google "Barnsley plant pot" sometime.

2020–21 SEASON: 5th in the Championship (lost playoff semifinals), 5th Round FA Cup, 3rd Round League Cup

2021–22 SEASON: The Championship (promoted in 2019)

STADIUM: When I first saw Oakwell on my walk into the upper part of the town, it seemed to fit right into the scenery, as a football ground should. Also, I saw the rusty corrugated iron roof on the West Stand, which dates to the early 1900s. In fact, some of the seats in there are original! Good on the club for keeping these touches around.

The East Stand is on a hillside, so there's quite a walk up to its upper tier. But the view is tremendous, like you're right on top of the pitch, and there is even good legroom. The south CK Beckett Stand holds the hardcore Barnsley supporters, and the North Stand is given to away supporters.

It's a comfortable, modern ground that still feels old—just as I like them. I do have a major complaint though: Yorkshire is known for pies, and Barnsley in particular for pork and goose pies, and the stadium sells…Pukka Pies. Having skipped lunch in anticipation of a local treat, I was disappointed to have to huff down a mass production pie before heading to my seat.

TOURS: No tours are available at this stadium.

TICKETS: Tickets cost from £23 to £36 the last time they were in the Championship, and I can't imagine anything will sell out.

GETTING THERE: It's just a 10-minute walk from the train station.

PUBS: There are a few pubs right around Oakwell, the most football-looking being The Mount on Pontefract Road. It's got a picture of a bulldog carrying a football; I assume that's a tyke. Over on Doncaster Road, the Dove Inn is recommended in the CAMRA *Good Beer Guide*, and kids are welcome (with a £2 entry fee per person) at the Barnsley East Dene Working Man's Club (WMC). Up by the station, look for the simple but classy Old No. 7 and the Irish pub Annie Murray's. The Silkstone Inn is a Wetherspoon outlet.

GRUB: I had heard Yorkshire was known for pies. I saw at the museum that Barnsley Market was famous for goose pies, and in the market there was a vendor who once won the Best Pork Pie in the Country competition. Foolishly, I didn't get one, as I thought they would have some good ones at the ground. Don't repeat my mistake.

I saw a long line at Langdale Fisheries near Oakwell; I take that as a good sign. There's a little cluster of places—Italian, kebab, Indian—nearby on Sheffield Road. And there are two other chippies, Gary's Fisheries and Waldi, in town.

AROUND TOWN: In Barnsley's lovely Town Hall, which now includes a museum, there is a timeline on the wall. One of the entries is "The Romans come and go." I can't think of a better way to summarize an area's attraction. It isn't that Barnsley is unappealing; it's just that even the locals looked at me funny when I said I was visiting from the States.

The Barnsley Market, right by the station, dates to 1249 but these days is a modern place filled with old ladies sipping tea, families shopping together, butchers asking after somebody's mum, and men expressing hope for the football game. I did enjoy walking around and meeting the "Yawk-sha folk," as they call themselves. Noteworthy for being friendly, they also lack cultural diversity around here; Barnsley is listed as 94.7 percent "white British."

I had a nice walk up to Locke Park, where its tower is the highest thing in town and has a nice view of the surrounding area. If you're up for a longer walk, the Trans Pennine Trail passes close to the stadium and offers links to surrounding villages and countryside. In fact, Barnsley is at the hub of the 350-mile network of trails. Check out transpenninetrail.org.uk for maps and guides.

DONCASTER ROVERS

A midsized club in a midsized town in Yorkshire, pretty much in the middle of the country. Rovers are safely one of the best clubs in the history of the third and fourth tiers.

LOCATION: Doncaster, South Yorkshire, about ninety minutes from London's Kings Cross and also from Manchester

CONTACT: doncasterroversfc.co.uk, 01302 764664, #DRFC

NICKNAMES: Donny Rovers

WOMEN'S TEAM: The Doncaster Rovers Belles, believe it or not, used to be the dominant force in the women's game in England. They made eleven of twelve FA Cup finals from 1983 to 1994, winning six! They also won two of the first three league titles in 1992 and 1994, adding the Cup both times. Now they are down in the Women's National League Division One Midlands. See doncasterroversbelles.co.uk for more.

HISTORY: From their founding in 1888 to World War II, Rovers only poked into the second tier for two seasons in the late 1930s. In 1946 they played in the longest match in history. In those days you played until somebody won, and their 2–2 draw at Stockport County lasted 203 minutes before finally being called for darkness. Legend has it people went home for tea and then came back to see the end.

From then through the late 1950s, they spent eight years in the second tier, their best spell in history. The next interesting thing to occur was when their owner, Ken Richardson, drove them off a financial cliff in the 1990s. They were relegated with a minus-eighty-three goal differential, and the fans held a funeral for the club at the ground. Two weeks later Richardson was convicted of hiring three men to burn down the ground for the insurance money! The fire started but was put out after doing moderate damage.

They rebuilt under new ownership and took part in another bit of footballing history. England doesn't really do "sudden death" or "golden goals," but for a brief time they did in the Conference (now National League) playoffs. Rovers were the only team to win promotion with one, taking the 2003 Conference playoff final, 3–2, over Dagenham and Redbridge.

In the 2005–06 League Cup, after beating Manchester City and Aston Villa along the way, they made the quarterfinals and took Arsenal to penalties. Two years later they won the League One playoff final at Wembley (1–0 over Leeds) and spent three years in the second tier, their first time there in fifty years. They spent five of the next six seasons there but have since dropped as far as League Two a few years ago.

They are one of only four teams to win the fourth-tier championship three times, so there's that. In 2018–19 they made the fifth round of the FA Cup, finally bowing out to Crystal Palace, and made the league playoffs but lost a semifinal penalty shootout at Charlton.

RIVALRIES: Yorkshire neighbors Barnsley, Rotherham United, and Scunthorpe United are the main ones, with Chesterfield and the two Sheffield clubs just behind. I saw them play Barnsley when they were top two in the league, and it was a cracking atmosphere with only a few extra police in town.

SONGS: None I noticed

2020–21 SEASON: 14th in League One, 4th Round FA Cup, 1st Round League Cup

2021–22 SEASON: League One (promoted in 2016)

STADIUM: Keepmoat Stadium replaced the old Belle Vue Ground in 2006 and has 15,231 seats. It's also the home of a rugby club and the Doncaster Belles, and the name comes not from some medieval moat nearby but actually from a company that manages council housing. It's basically a perfect rectangle with the South Stand also being known as the Black Bank and housing the ultras group of the same name.

It's not the most exciting place, but it is the only league ground next to a lake, which is bizarrely called Lakeside Lake. It has a trail around it with QR codes you can use to learn more about the nature and history of the area.

TOURS: None

TICKETS: Two years ago an adult ticket was around £20, and even the high-stakes derby with Barnsley I went to didn't quite sell out.

GETTING THERE: It's a mile and a half from the station, so about a 40-minute walk. You can also take First Bus 56 (Rossington) from the station; that stops at White Rose Way, a block from the ground. I took a taxi from the station for £8 and walked back.

PUBS: There are some surprisingly good options for a town this size, starting with the tiny and cozy Draughtsman Alehouse at the station.

Just out of the station, turn right for the Railway and the more traditional Leopard, both designated as away-supporter pubs.

Right in the center, across from the station, there's a Wetherspoon outlet called the Gate House as well as the modern, spacious Angel and Royal. The Yorkshire Grey is a neat older pub with a patio and games on TV. The Doncaster Brewery and Tap has won several CAMRA awards, including the city's Pub of the Year and, in 2018, the Yorkshire Cider Pub of the Year.

There's a friendly bar at the ground called the Belle Vue, which also has pies and sausage rolls. Just down the road is the Lakeside location of the family-friendly Beefeater pub chain with its large menu and abundant seating.

GRUB: Several people recommended the Movida Tapas restaurant on Priory Street next door to the Wetherspoon pub. Same thing for Ada Turkish Barbecue and La Rustica Restaurant. The Clam and Cork Fish Market was also highly recommended but too crowded when I was there—a good sign. I was in a hurry and ate at the ground, so I'm not a lot of use here!

AROUND TOWN: Doncaster very much fits the Standard Northern English Town Story on page 363, with one major exception being that butterscotch was invented there. All praise to Doncaster!

One of the main buildings left over from the old days is the Mansion House, built in 1751 and now home to an art gallery and historical exhibits. Cusworth Hall and Brodsworth House are its country cousins, both with gardens and museums.

Military aircraft buffs will want to book ahead to visit the Vulcan Experience, where they can get up close and personal with a famous Cold War spy plane. Animal lovers may enjoy the Potteric Carr Nature Reserve.

LEEDS UNITED

Once a dominant force in English football—and one known as "Dirty Leeds" for their rough style of play—Leeds wasn't relevant nationally for more than twenty years. But they are back in the Premier League, with a hardcore loyal following making lots of noise in a grand old ground.

LOCATION: Leeds, West Yorkshire, two and a half hours north of King's Cross Station in London by train and one hour from Manchester

CONTACT: leedsunited.com, 0371 334 1992, #LUFC

NICKNAMES: The Whites; sometimes the Peacocks because there is an old pub named The Old Peacock next to their stadium

WOMEN'S TEAM: Leeds United Women play their home matches at Global Stadium, the home of Tadcaster Albion. They are in the Women's National League Division One North, tier 4 of the women's game.

HISTORY: Leeds didn't do much from their founding in 1919 until the 1950s, when a player named John Charles arrived on the scene. He was one of the all-time greats, a six-foot-two giant who excelled at defending and who, upon switching to striker for a season, scored forty-two goals in thirty-nine games. But in 1956 a fire wiped out much of the stadium, and to pay the bills they had to sell Charles to Italian club Juventus. (He is a legend there as well, known as "The Gentle Giant" because he never even got a yellow card in his career.)

By 1961 Leeds were back down in the Second Division. But that's when they hired Don Revie as manager and became one of the great forces in English football. From Revie's arrival until he left in 1974, Leeds won the Second Division, the First Division (twice), the FA Cup, the League Cup, and the Inter-Cities Fairs Cup (basically the current Europa League). But to keep things in perspective, they also finished second in the league five times and lost the

FA Cup final three times. So they were right in the middle of everything, playing a style that was both free-flowing and attacking—and also tough as nails. The leader on the pitch was a Scotsman named Billy Bremner, whose statue outside Elland Road is always decorated for game days. It was Revie, by the way, who switched Leeds to their all-white strip to emulate Real Madrid. He has a statue as well.

Revie left in 1974 and was replaced by Brian Clough, who had won the league with tiny Derby County but was also brash and outspoken, in particular while being critical of Revie and Leeds. So it was an odd appointment—and it lasted for forty-four days. The book and movie *The Damned United* tell this story, sort of. Liberties were taken, but what's clear is that Clough's tenure marked the end of the Revie era; by 1982 they were back in the Second Division and had a reputation for some of the roughest hooligans around.

They had another run in the '90s, even winning the league in 1992 and making the UEFA Cup semis in 2000 and 2001. But money troubles sent them down again, and by 2007 the mighty Leeds United were in League One. They got out of there and back to the Championship in 2010, but you'll still hear "doing a Leeds" to mean handling money so poorly that your team falls apart.

In 2019 under legendary Argentinian manager Marcelo Bielsa (famous for sitting on a bucket during games), they built a fantastically entertaining team that made the playoffs, but they lost a home semifinal to Derby County. In 2020, though, they swept to the top of the Championship, winning the title by 10 points and reaching the promised land.

I strongly advise you to put Elland Road at the very top of your groundhopping list; it truly is the old-fashioned but big-time experience you've been looking for.

RIVALRIES: Mainly their fellow Yorkshire clubs Sheffield Wednesday, Bradford City, and Huddersfield Town are rivals, but they also have rivalries with Manchester United and Chelsea (from the glory days) and Millwall (from the hooligan days).

SONGS: Leeds are one of the few to still sing their old-timey song. Used to be everybody had a Cup song, but "Marching on Together" is a legit good soccer song, and they belt it right out at the beginning of the game, finishing up with the famous, "We love you Leeds! Leeds! Leeds!" The singers on the official recording are the 1972 Leeds team that made the FA Cup final.

2020–21 SEASON: 9th in Premier League, 3rd Round FA Cup, 2nd Round League Cup

2021–22 SEASON: Premier League (promoted in 2020)

STADIUM: Elland Road is absolutely one of my favorites, a combination of old and new, a central location, and what feels like just the right size. Look around for pieces of the old days like brick walls left up near entrances. The site was the home of Leeds City FC before United came into existence, so football has been played here since the 1890s. Today it holds 37,890 people in four stands, the most recent of which was built in 1993.

The Revie Stand is usually called the Kop by fans; it holds 7,000 and is the source of a lot of noise. The grand East Stand holds 14,900, and the 1974 South Stand holds 5,000 including its two corners. One of these was painted yellow and used to house the away fans until it wasn't big enough anymore. It's known as the Cheese Wedge. The 11,000-seat John Charles Stand dates from 1957 and includes the longest TV and press gantry in the country, spanning almost the whole length of the pitch. This is also where the away fans now sit, toward the south end.

TOURS: Occasionally tours are offered on game days, and they sell out quickly. Check the website for details. My tour was led by a longtime staffer named "Sticks" whose Yorkshire accent and storytelling alone were worth the price of admission. Tell 'em you want a tour with Sticks!

TICKETS: Leeds draws very well; even in the Championship every game sold out and prices ran as high as £37 for adults in 2019-20. I sell some hospitality packages; otherwise, if you don't know a longtime season ticket holder, it's gonna be tough.

GETTING THERE: It's a two-mile walk from the station; in the hooligan days, Leeds fans used to taunt the visitors by singing, "You'll never make the station." There is a shuttle bus from near the station for £3 return. You can also take bus 51, 52, or 55 from the center to the ground. You can take a taxi, but getting one after the game is a hassle. The line forms on Elland Road across from the Volkswagen dealership.

PUBS: The most obvious is The Old Peacock right across the road. They have a big tent out back on game days; the loud band isn't for everyone, but pints are reasonable and the wait isn't bad. There's also a bar called Billy's in the stadium.

GRUB: I am told that Graveley's, a chippy right next to The Old Peacock, has excellent fish and chips. I wouldn't know, because both times I have been to Leeds the line was far more than I wanted to deal with. Maybe you can confirm this rumor.

AROUND TOWN: Leeds is a great city, with an old center, a university feel, and lots of new construction going on. It was a major mill center in the Industrial Revolution and today is the third-largest city in England after London and Birmingham. It's also a great base for soccer explorations at one hour from Manchester or Sheffield, two and a half from London, and near many Yorkshire clubs.

Here are just some of the sites I've come across; I can't wait to explore more:

- The old center includes great architecture like Leeds Town Hall, the Corn Exchange, and the Leeds City Museum.
- The Victoria Quarter has lots of fancy shops and arcades—not the video-game kind but the 19th-century-shopping-mall kind.
- There are the ruins of Kirkstall Abbey, a 12th-century monastery.
- The Leeds Industrial Museum is in an old mill building.
- Kirkgate Market (Monday through Saturday) is one of the largest indoor markets in Europe; it includes a farmers market on the first and third Sunday of the month.
- Call Lane is the hotspot for evening entertainment.
- River tours are available.

SHEFFIELD UNITED

The red half of England's Steel City boasts a long history, passionate support, and one of my favorite grounds in the country—and in 2020 became one of the best recent stories in English football.

LOCATION: In South Yorkshire, just over two hours north of London and around one hour east of Manchester by train

CONTACT: sufc.co.uk, 0114 253 7200, #SUFC

NICKNAMES: The Blades, as in swords, because of the city's steel-producing heritage

WOMEN'S TEAM: Sheffield United Women play in the FA Women's Championship at tier 2 of the pyramid. Their games are at the home ground of Chesterfield FC.

HISTORY: Sheffield United's formation sounds a bit like that of Liverpool FC. The ground, Bramall Lane, had a tenant called Sheffield Wednesday (see next chapter). But a financial dispute led Wednesday to depart for another location, leaving the owners of Bramall Lane looking for a club. They started United in 1889.

But since Bramall Lane is the oldest stadium in the world still hosting professional football, let's back up a minute for some perspective. People have been playing football on this spot since 1855! It was an important place. In the early formation of football, there were many sets of rules, the biggest two being the Sheffield Rules and the Cambridge Rules. A series of matches held at Bramall Lane between the Sheffield and London Football Associations eventually convinced everyone that a common set of rules was needed; hence the Football Association was formed (see page 12 for a brief history of all this).

Also, local amateur club Sheffield FC are the oldest club in the world still playing football. They are at level 8 on the football pyramid and are actually now based in Dronfield, Derbyshire.

United's first glory years were right at the start. They won the Football League in 1898 and the FA Cup in 1899, 1902, 1915, and 1925. They lost the final two other times in that stretch. They were in the top two divisions until they bottomed out in the 1970s, dropping as far as the Fourth Division for the 1981–82 season. But they rallied back to the top flight and were founder members of the Premier League in 1992. They were relegated after two years and have only been back in the top league once more, in the 2006–07 season.

Another bad stretch saw them sent down to League One from 2011 to 2017. They failed in the playoffs three times in that stretch, but then, in 2016, cometh the hero. Chris Wilder was born in Sheffield, supported the Blades, played for them, and then became a manager. He got United from League One to the Championship in 2017, and damned if in 2018–19 they didn't go and finish second, getting themselves back to the top tier for the first time in twelve years. Pipping Yorkshire rival Leeds for the second automatic promotion spot, and winning a late-season derby at Elland Road—that I had the pleasure of seeing—was that much sweeter.

And what did this scrappy club do in the Premier League? Oh, just finish ninth and contend for European places until the last weeks of the season, all on by far the smallest budget in the division. Sadly, it all fell apart last season, as Wilder left and they were relegated back to the Championship.

RIVALRIES: United and Sheffield Wednesday (see next chapter) share the Steel City derby, one of the most passionate in the country. With just the two clubs in town, usually nothing major on the line beyond pride, and no one outside Sheffield paying attention, it is strictly personal with this one. It's also incredibly even: In 131 meetings since 1891, United have forty-six wins, Wednesday forty-two, and there have been forty-three draws. It's off again this season, though.

Other Yorkshire clubs, especially Leeds, are also considered rivals. Two other rivalries come from interesting reasons: West Ham because of a legal dispute over West Ham player Carlos Tevez, whom United claimed was signed illegally; and Nottingham Forest, because of a series of miners' strikes in the 1980s when Nottinghamshire miners didn't join in.

SONGS: For me, United sings one of the great songs in football. It's called "Greasy Chip Butty," is set to John Denver's "Annie's Song," and celebrates various pleasures of Yorkshire life:

You fill up my senses
Like a gallon of Magnet
Like a packet of Woodbines
Like a good pinch of snuff
Like a night out in Sheffield
Like a greasy chip butty
Like Sheffield United
Come thrill me again!

To fill in for you: Magnet is a strong beer; Woodbines are strong cigarettes; and a chip butty is considered a defining dish of the area. It is what foreigners might call a french fry sandwich on a white roll with butter. And yes, that's it: a fries sandwich.

2020–21 SEASON: 20th in Premier League (relegated), Quarterfinals FA Cup, 2nd Round League Cup

2021–22 SEASON: The Championship (relegated in 2021)

STADIUM: "Beautiful Downtown Bramall Lane," as the United fans call it, sits square in the middle of Sheffield. It is the longest-serving football stadium in the world; the first game here was played in 1855. Of course, it has been through many changes since, but it still has an old feeling to it. And despite holding 32,702 people, it feels cozy. I was there for the derby with Wednesday once, and I swear my ears rang for a day afterward.

Away fans will be in the lower level of the Bramall Lane stand, with a protective screen over their heads since there are United fans above them. Behind the opposite goal is the Kop, which hosts the most passionate United folk. Try to sit there or on the side. The South, or Main Stand, oddly didn't exist until 1975; before that it was the outfield for cricket matches.

TOURS: Led by the club historian, tours are £6 but not offered too frequently. Check the website for upcoming availability.

TICKETS: Up in the Premier League, tickets ranged from £20 to £30, with most games sold out.

GETTING THERE: It's about a 20-minute walk from the main Sheffield train station. This takes you right through the center of town. A taxi should be less than £10.

PUBS: As it's in the middle of town, Bramall Lane is surrounded by pubs, all of which will be jumping on match day. Look in particular for Sheaf House, Railway Hotel, the Golden Lion, and The Cricketers. As you walk away from the station, you will see The Globe and The Howard.

GRUB: When I got connected with a bunch of Blades fans, they all insisted I have a proper chip butty before a home game. They also insisted I go to a place on London Road called A Salt N Battered. I found the name a bit squirm-inducing and the queue positively un-acceptable. Somebody please tell me how the butty is there (and check below for my butty recommendation). London Road is generally a hub of food and bevvies.

AROUND TOWN: Sheffield is a cool city. It's essentially England's Pittsburgh, which means it was huge in steel—stainless steel was invented here—and then it crashed with the industry. But now it's coming back in the same way Pittsburgh is, with a lot of young professionals moving in to take advantage of its central location, budding social scene, and (in Sheffield's case) the proximity of the Peak District National Park on the edge of town. In fact, technically a third of the city is in the park, and 61 percent of it is green space.

I recommend you walk around downtown for a bit, check out the Winter Garden, and then take a local train or bus out to the Peak District. The village of Grindleford is particularly nice, with lovely walking in the area and a shop in the old train station making a fine chip butty. See visitpeakdistrict.com for suggestions and details.

SHEFFIELD WEDNESDAY

Sheffield Wednesday is one of two great, old-school, and well-supported clubs in the very cool city of Sheffield. Right now, though, they are a cautionary tale.

LOCATION: In South Yorkshire, just over two hours north of London and around one hour east of Manchester by train

CONTACT: swfc.co.uk, 03700 20 1867, #SWFC

NICKNAMES: The Owls

WOMEN'S TEAM: Sheffield Wednesday Ladies are in the seventh-tier Sheffield & Hallamshire Women's County League. Home games are at Sheffield Hallam University. See swlfc.co.uk for more.

HISTORY: Let's start with the name, shall we? Sometime in the early 19th century, a cricket club was formed by a bunch of guys who didn't work on Wednesday, hence the Wednesday Cricket Club. In 1855 they and some other clubs started playing at Bramall Lane, now the home of Sheffield United. On September 4, 1867, they formed a football team to stay fit over the winter—a very common origin story for football clubs. In time, football eclipsed cricket, the two clubs split, the cricket club disbanded in 1925, and now we have Sheffield Wednesday Football Club.

They turned pro in 1880, joined the Football League in 1892, and won the FA Cup in 1896 at the old Crystal Palace. They moved to the suburb of Owlerton in 1899, built a new ground there, and racked up two league titles and another FA Cup in the next ten years. They were good again from 1929, when they were league champs, to 1935, when they were FA Cup winners.

They challenged for a title in 1961 and made another FA Cup final in 1966, but in the '70s they dipped to the third tier. They made a run in the late '80s, winning the 1991 League

Cup over Manchester United—the last team from outside the top division to win a major trophy. In 1993 they lost the league and FA Cup finals (both 2–1 to Arsenal), but in the latter they at least beat rivals Sheffield United in the semis, 2–1 at Wembley.

Then came two more relegations, financial troubles, and two different ownership changes. Last season they got a points deduction for financial mismanagement (their current owner is, let's say, a character), and they were relegated to League One.

RIVALRIES: With United and Wednesday once again in different leagues, the Steel City derby is off again. For us neutrals, it's a shame; I saw numbers 128 and 129 in the 2017–18 season and loved them both. (See "Bouncing Owls and Barmy Blades" on page 274.) It's one of those personal rivalries where people who are friends and coworkers on Friday and Sunday shout "pig" and "scum" at one another on Saturday. Local police spend months planning for the game, and both clubs have many songs about the other. It's also very competitive: forty-six wins for United, forty-two for Wednesday, forty-three draws.

One of the more famous games was that 1993 FA Cup semifinal, originally scheduled at Elland Road in Leeds. With so much interest from Sheffield, the game was moved to Wembley, where more than 75,000 showed up to see Wednesday's win. Of course, Wednesday fans will point to the 4–0 Boxing Day Massacre of 1979 (the hundredth derby) and United fans to 2017's Bouncing Day Massacre (which my story will explain), and then you're down the rabbit hole of memories and accusations.

SONGS: At the beginning of each game and after goals, the PA system plays a song you will recognize even if you don't know its name: "Hi Ho Silver Lining" by Jeff Beck. When it gets to the titular line, the crowd belts out, "Hi ho Sheffield Wednesday!" Wolverhampton Wanderers and Aston Villa do this as well, and I assume they all argue about who did it first.

Wednesday has another one where they all bounce up and down and sing, in a reference to United's nickname, "If you don't fucking bounce, then you're a Blade." They do this no matter whom they're playing.

2020–21 SEASON: 24th in the Championship (relegated), 4th Round FA Cup, 3rd Round League Cup

2021–22 SEASON: League One (relegated in 2021)

STADIUM: Hillsborough is absolutely one of my favorites. It's big, old, classy, and feels much cozier than its 39,812 capacity. It's been Wednesday's home since 1899, and it hosted World Cup matches in 1966 and European Championship games in 1996, but hasn't had much work done since then. The North Stand opened in 1961 (with a friendly match against Pelé's Brazilian club team) and was the first in the country to run the whole length of the pitch. The biggest stand is the Main Stand across the way with more than 11,300 seats.

At one end is the Spion Kop, where 11,210 of the rowdiest home fans sit, and in the other is the West Stand, also known as the Leppings Lane End, scene of the 1989 Hillsborough disaster in which ninety-six Liverpool fans died in a crush. (There's a memorial outside the Main Stand.) Like the rest of the stadium, it's now all seats and hosts the away fans, generally in the upper tier only.

TOURS: The club offers stadium tours on game days only, starting at 10 a.m. and lasting two and a half hours—the longest I've heard of by far. Cost is £15, and demand is high.

TICKETS: In the Championship, tickets went from £42 to £49. They should be cheaper and easier to get this season.

GETTING THERE: It's about three miles from the station, so you may want to take a cab (around £10) or a bus. Look for bus 53 bound for Ecclesfield from near the train station. But the best way is on the Sheffield Supertram. From the main rail station, get on a Blue Line train (Malin Bridge) to the city center, and then switch to a Yellow Line (Middlewood) to the Leppings Lane station right by the ground. You can also hop off at the Hillsborough Park stop for pubs and grub plus a nice walk through the park.

PUBS: The Wednesday Tap is a lovely pub in the stadium, and it offers local ales. Right across the river from the Main Stand is the Riverside Café and Bar, which will be packed with singing locals. A few minutes farther away is The Park, with an outdoor beer garden and live music. Down the main A61 road behind the stadium, the Old Crown also has outdoor seating. If you get off the tram at Hillsborough Park and walk back down the line a few minutes to the river, you'll find several options: a Wetherspoon called The Rawson Spring and two big pubs with views of the river, the Riverside Pub and the Hillsborough Tap.

GRUB: There are a lot of options right around the Hillsborough Park tram stop and another cluster closer to the ground, including two chippies, the Four Lanes and Hillsborough Fish Bar. Lines at both were long when I visited.

AROUND TOWN: For ideas on things to do around town, see the previous chapter on Sheffield United.

BOUNCING OWLS AND BARMY BLADES

Perhaps the reason we go to football games—other than just having a day out and/or acting like children in public—is that we just might have an experience people will talk about for generations. We sit through countless forgettable affairs because someday we're going to see a world-class game-winner, or a stunning upset, or a 5–4 goal fest, or a penalty kick hit a season-saving post, or some seismic shift in the power balance of the game.

Such a moment occurred in the second half of the 2017 Steel City derby. I know I'll never forget it, nor will fans of either Sheffield club, though one set will wish they could. All I know is, I was lucky enough to be there and also to be taking a video when the moment arrived. But we'll get to that.

First, especially for my American readers, please try to grasp what an English football rivalry is like. To be honest, you really can't because nothing like it exists in the States. We have rivalries, but a game like Sheffield Wednesday vs. Sheffield United feels more like tribal warfare. It's generational. Old men and little kids and women and girls—everybody is all in, no moment is mediocre or unimportant, the entire stadium sings and responds to everything on the pitch. Life itself seems to hang in the balance.

When things go well, it's pure bliss, and they aim all of their happiness at the enemy across the way. When things go badly, they slam their fists into the seat, curse their own players like dogs, or just stare into space, shocked as if they've just seen their grandmother killed.

It's insane, of course; it's just football, after all. But somehow it's a lot more than that. It's like our self-worth is based on how the boys in "our" colors do, and they cannot let us down. You can't just let those fucking wankers in that other color feel any joy. *Get after them,* for fuck's sake!

In this case, owing to the clubs being in different leagues, they hadn't done this in six years. Some stuff had built up in the meantime.

GAME DAY IN THE STEEL CITY

Outside the ground, everything seemed calm, even when I watched United fans arrive by bus at the Leppings Lane End of Hillsborough, the home stadium of Sheffield Wednesday. Inside, once the game started, it was a different story. The Wednesday crowd—nervous, excited, afraid, jittery—was like nothing I've ever felt; it was truly a time when I was glad to be a neutral. But I get it. When Portland loses to Seattle, I don't even want to go outside.

And then United scored about three minutes in. Shocked Owls all around me, bedlam among the Blades in the far end. Then a huge roar from the blue side, urging their boys on.

And then United scored again! Shock was replaced by vicious anger; in addition to making it 2–0, this was a stupid goal the defense never should have conceded. Now they're all useless: can't win a header or a second ball, can't pick out a pass, and where

On the same pitch, at last: United and Wednesday face off in Sheffield for the first time in six years.

is the fucking midfield? Fans were practically leaping out of their seats to wave their arms in disgust.

I was actually starting to worry about my neighbors finding out I'm a neutral. Already some of them were arguing with each other about standing up. It was "We can't see" vs. "It's the fucking derby!" and if United scored again, I was pretty sure they would all turn on each other—and therefore me for not caring enough. Honestly, I didn't care who won; I just wanted a proper game, so I considered United's goals to be basically good news, because it meant the home team had to go for it. But it was feeling genuinely ugly in the North Stand. But it was feeling genuinely ugly in the North Stand.

Then Wednesday scored, right at the end of the half. And the roar...my God. It was something felt more than heard. The place was buzzing at halftime, and the Owls came out for the second half and got right to it. They dominated, with the crowd going berserk at every pause. When 30,000 people scream "Come on!" as one voice, the energy is almost scary.

Then they scored again! Absolute madness all around me. I was thrilled; everything I had come to see was happening all around me—a proper game in a proper derby, a sports event like no other. The Owls fans started bouncing and singing, and I started a video with my phone. *The folks at home won't believe this*, I thought. This was a moment!

If you're not…fuckin' bouncin'
If you're not fuckin' bouncin' you're a Blade!

Just as I swung my phone left to the Kop end, I saw out of the corner of my eye that United had the ball and was moving down the field…and that is when an amazing moment became The Moment.

The boys in red swept downfield toward their own fans. There was a split second when you could feel the whole Wednesday crowd stop bouncing and think to itself, *Hang on…what…* And just as I zoomed in that direction, the ball flashed, the keeper flailed, the net rippled, and the red end of the stadium went off like an atomic bomb.

The slamming shut of one door and blasting open of another. Devastation and exultation switching places on a dime. In an instant, 32,000 slumped and 3,000 leaped.

Around me it was stunned silence moving toward anger with the occasional curse—but it was total chaos in the distance. Limbs, as they say. Mental. Again, I was worried my neighbors would pounce on me for not being angry. Good thing they had no idea how much I was loving it!

Inevitably came the taunting chant from beyond the barricades:

You're not bouncing,
You're not bouncing,
You're not bouncing anymore!

And then, a few minutes later, United scored again, a chipped slow roller that barely made it in, leading to another precious football moment: when you realize it's gone in, you know the away fans are going to explode, but it takes just a moment for the sound to reach you. We need a name for that silence. It was shattered by barmy Blades in the Leppings Lane End, and the blue troops began to withdraw from the field in numbers, shaking their heads in disgust and flashing middle fingers at—well, let's face it, their fellow townsfolk.

The starch was out of the Wednesday crowd, and the rest of the afternoon was a Blades party. They sang "Happy Birthday" to their manager (who was a fan and a player before); they sang players' names; they sang how shit Wednesday was; they sang things I honestly couldn't even make out.

They were still singing when I left, out into the streets where little pockets of Wednesday fans were bitching about this player or that tactical decision or the complete lack of urgency and talent. Most of them were simply getting away. I can only imagine what joy the Reds were sharing as they danced off into the streets. It would be a long few months for the blue side of Sheffield until their chance to get back at the fuckers at Bramall Lane.

I just might have to come back for that one as well. After all, this is what I come for. Isn't it what we all come for?

POSTGAME

I tweeted out that video (which is on my YouTube channel) from the lobby of my hotel, hopped on a train to London, and checked into my hotel there. Firing up my iPad, I thought, *Hmmm, I wonder if any United fans noticed?*

Um, yeah. It had already been retweeted over 1,000 times and liked some 3,000. In an afternoon. Pretty soon the messages started rolling in from Blades:

> I've already watched this 100 times and can't stop laughing
> My three favorite films: *Citizen Kane, Godfather,* This
> I want this played at my wedding

And so on.

That night I wrote the above as a blog post, and by noon the next day it had been read 5,000 times and my email was blowing up. Wednesday had once beaten United 4–0 on the day after Christmas, a game known as the Boxing Day Massacre. This was already being labeled the Bouncing Day Massacre.

By the end of that day, I had heard from a reporter at the *Sheffield Star* who wanted to excerpt my blog post and put it on their website.

Also coming in regularly: invitations and encouragement to come see the return leg at Bramall Lane in January—to which I could only say, "Oh, hell yes." I assume it will be more fun than my previous visit to the Lane.

Postscript: I did come back for the return leg at Sheffield United (thanks again, Alan!), and well, it was a 0–0. That's football for you. You should have heard them sing the "Greasy Chip Butty" song, though!

Meanwhile, almost four years later, I still get emails from Blades fans who just wanted to say thanks, and the whole thing blows up on Twitter from time to time.

NORTHWEST / LIVERPOOL AND MANCHESTER AREA

BLACKBURN ROVERS

Blackburn Rovers is a truly traditional club in a classic northern town, with an old-school ground and great uniforms.

LOCATION: Blackburn, Lancashire, an hour north of Manchester's Victoria station

CONTACT: rovers.co.uk, 01254 372001, #Rovers

NICKNAMES: The Riversiders or just Rovers

WOMEN'S TEAM: Blackburn Rovers LFC play in the Women's Championship at tier 2. Home games are at Sir Tom Finney Stadium, home of Bamber Bridge FC near Preston.

HISTORY: Quick: name all seven teams that have ever won the Premier League since it was founded in 1992. The top five are easy: Man City, Man United, Chelsea, Liverpool, and Arsenal. If you've been paying attention lately, you might come up with Leicester City. The other one? Blackburn Rovers, 1994–95. It really happened. I sat next to somebody who saw it in person.

Of course, their history didn't start in 1994. It started more than a hundred years before, when they were founder members of the Football League. They already had three FA Cups, which they had won in consecutive seasons. They got two more by the end of the century, won the league twice before 1920, got another Cup in 1928, and then vanished from trophy world for almost seventy years.

They stayed in the top division until 1936 then after the war got relegated again in 1948. At this point, one of the weirder traditions in all of English soccer got started. A grocer (which Brits call a greengrocer) in the nearby town of Bamber Bridge marked the occasion of Rovers' relegation by filling a coffin with vegetables (which they just call veg) and burying it. When they went back up, he dug it up again. To this day, when Rovers go up or down, so does the coffin in Bamber Bridge, accompanied by a party-atmosphere funeral parade with costumes, speeches, and everything. Preston North End FC, just a few miles away, have started a version of it as well.

After another coffin burial in 1966, Rovers were out of the top flight for twenty-six years, but they were saved by a lifelong fan, Jack Walker, who had made millions in steel and bought his favorite club in 1991. He twice broke the national price record for buying players, dropped £20 million on a stadium rebuild, and put up a new training ground and academy. He hired Liverpool legend Kenny Dalglish as manager, and in 1992 Rovers made the top flight again, this time into the newly formed Premier League.

They won it in 1995, with Alan Shearer banging in the goals, but he was sold to Newcastle in 1996. Rovers went back to being somewhat ordinary. They won the League Cup in 2002 and spent the next ten years in the Premier League. When new owners came along so did two more relegations, and in 2017 they found themselves in League One. They finished second, though, so in 2018 they dug up the coffin again and got started in the Championship.

RIVALRIES: Their biggest rival is Burnley, with whom they share the East Lancashire derby. The towns are only eleven miles apart. Preston North End, just thirty miles away, is also disliked, as are pretty much any of the clubs around Lancashire, which is a nest of footballing antipathy.

SONGS: Their anthem is a rocking adaptation of an Irish folk song called "Wild Rover." In the original the singer says he'll never "play the wild rover" no more. But at Blackburn the lyrics start out:

> I've been a wild rover for many a year
> And spent all my money on this seat right here.

And the famous chorus is adapted as:

> And it's no, nay, never
> No, nay never no more!
> 'Cause I'll stay a wild rover
> Forever and more.

2020–21 SEASON: 15th in the Championship, 3rd Round FA Cup, 2nd Round League Cup

2021–22 SEASON: The Championship (promoted in 2018)

STADIUM: They have played at Ewood Park since 1890, though of course the stadium structure is nowhere near original. Three of the stands were built in the 1990s, and total capacity is 31,367. Also, as an occasional listener to the *Men in Blazers* podcast, I was thrilled to find myself walking toward it on Tweed Street. There is a river behind the oldest and smallest stand (hence their Riversiders nickname), a memorial garden in which you must ask permission before spreading any ashes, and a statue outside of former owner Jack Taylor, identified as "Rovers Greatest Supporter."

Away fans will be in the Darwen End, with home rowdies in the opposite Blackburn End. The main stand is the Jack Taylor. You might want to sit in the Riverside Stand for the old-fashioned feel and a good view of the rest of the place.

TOURS: Tours are offered a few times a month for £7.50; contact the club for details.

TICKETS: The last prices I saw were around £30 for adults, and I doubt any games will sell out aside from perhaps the derbies.

GETTING THERE: It's almost two miles from the station to the ground; you can take bus 1 bound for Darwen across from the station, and it stops right by the stadium. You can also take a local train to Mill Hill and walk about 15 minutes from there.

PUBS: The two closest are the Fox and Hounds, which looks a tiny local pub, and the Fernhurst, more modern and with outdoor seating; it seems to have become the away-fans pub. Better options are in town near the station. There's a large Wetherspoon pub called the Postal Order nearby, and around the other side of a big mall is a historic street where you'll find the Drummer's Arms, the Squire, and the Sir Charles Napier.

GRUB: More than one English person, when I told them I was headed for Blackburn, told me I would find good curries there. This is because the town has one of England's highest ratios, 30 percent, of South Asians in its population. And I did find an outstanding Indian meal on the way to the ground at a restaurant called Thira, right across from the Postal Order. I also spotted what looked a proper sit-down chippy called the Queen Vic on my walk up to Corporation Park. There's a more central, more traditional takeaway chippy in town called the Chippery.

AROUND TOWN: Blackburn, Lancashire: if that town name sounds familiar to you, it's because John Lennon sang about the 4,000 holes there. And that, in turn, is because he read a newspaper article ("I read the news today, oh boy") about 4,000 potholes in Blackburn's streets. So there you go.

Blackburn is the kind of town where if you look on TripAdvisor for the Top 10 Things to Do, you see a park, a museum, a living farm, another park, a historic home with gardens, an art gallery, a shopping mall, and probably another park. It is also the town that inspired me to write my Standard Northern English Town Story on page 363.

I have learned, however, that every place is worth a walkabout before the game. Blackburn's cathedral is right outside the station, as is a big statue of Queen Victoria. There's a nice coffee shop inside the cathedral shop. I walked up through the historic district to the nice Corporation Park, admiring the Town Hall and other 19th-century buildings along the way. I hit up the Lewis Textile Museum to learn about the town's cotton-making past (a mile of cloth every twenty seconds from over 100,000 looms) and admired the art museum, especially the collection of Japanese prints. Then I stuffed myself with Indian food and hit up a really boring third-round FA Cup game against Hull. I came back another time for a more fun local derby with Wigan.

BOLTON WANDERERS

After a spectacular rise and fall over ten years, Bolton nearly went out of business in 2019 and spent last season down in League Two. They are back in League One this year, which is still too low for these former European entrants.

LOCATION: Forty minutes by train northwest of Manchester Piccadilly station

CONTACT: bwfc.co.uk, 01204 673 673, #BWFC

NICKNAMES: The Trotters, which has a couple of explanations that boil down to trotting around being kind of like wandering around

WOMEN'S TEAM: Bolton Ladies FC, no longer affiliated with the men's team, play in the fourth-tier National League Division One North. Check boltonladies.com for details.

HISTORY: Bolton was one of six Lancashire clubs in the original twelve of the Football League, and since then they have set a record they might not be proud of: most years in the top flight—seventy-three—without ever winning it.

They had great success in the FA Cup in the 1920s, winning it three times, including the famous White Horse Final of 1923. The original Wembley Stadium had just been completed, and for the first game there, the authorities decided, "Hey, let's just open it up and let folks in." Estimates range as high as 300,000 in attendance; the crowd covered the pitch and required police on horses, including a famous gray one named Billie, to clear the pitch so the Trotters could beat West Ham, 2–0. (Billie looked white in the films of the event, hence the name.)

The next glory years were the 1950s, when a team built around Nat Lofthouse made two more FA Cup finals, winning one, and finishing top six in the league three times. Lofthouse, who spent his entire fourteen-year career with Bolton, scored 255 goals for the club and thirty for England. His statue outside the ground is adorned with his last words, which begin "I've got the ball now."

The final they lost, in 1953, is another famous one: the Matthews Final. (I'll tell the story here, since I haven't made it to Blackpool yet.) The 'Pool had a player named Stanley Matthews who played 697 games in the top level over thirty-three years at Stoke City and Blackpool. He played so well in the final in question that it's nicknamed for him, even though his teammate had a hat trick. After losing that final, Bolton went back and won it in 1958, with Lofthouse getting both goals in a 2–0 win over Manchester United.

After that Bolton started a long slide, eventually including a year in the fourth tier in the 1980s followed by a spectacular rise in the 2000s. Out of nowhere and on a spending spree, Bolton had some top-ten Premier League finishes. They lost the League Cup final in 2004 and got into the Europa League twice, making the round of 16 in 2008 after getting a draw at Bayern Munich, a win at Red Star Belgrade, and a two-leg win over Atletico Madrid.

And then came the bust. By 2010 they were £93 million in debt. They were relegated in 2012, and in 2016 the debt hit £200 million. I went to a game there that season, one of the more depressing I've seen. One local headline read, "Players Set to be Paid Before Fulham Game." They finished dead last in the Championship, scoring just forty-one goals in forty-six games and winding up nineteen points from safety.

That year the owner forgave all the debt and the club was sold. By 2017 they were back in the Championship. In 2018 they stayed there by scoring two injury-time goals in the last game of the season, a 3–2 win over Nottingham Forest. But in 2019 they failed to pay their players for two months, resulting in a twelve-point deduction in the league for last season, and thence relegation to League Two. Back up and with new owners, there may be some hope brewing in Bolton.

RIVALRIES: Traditionally their rival was Bury, but they haven't seen much of each other lately, owing to being in different leagues, and then in 2020 Bury went out of business anyway. Bolton dislike Preston and Blackburn in particular, so if you see either of those names, as well as Wigan or Burnley, on the schedule, it should be a feisty affair. They play Wigan in the league this year.

SONGS: The teams come out to the Dion song "The Wanderer." There is also "The Manny Road," to the tune of "The Blaydon Races," the anthem up at Newcastle. This one is about people running away from the Burnden Aces. (Burnden is their former home ground.)

2020–21 SEASON: 3rd in League Two (promoted), 1st Round FA Cup, 1st Round League Cup

2021–22 SEASON: League One (promoted in 2021)

STADIUM: University of Bolton Stadium was built in 1997 to replace Burnden Park. It's spectacular from the outside, like a giant, glowing circus tent or something. Inside, it's two levels all around, for a total capacity of 28,723, and it's actually very nice. I am sure it could be rocking if Wanderers ever get it together.

Away fans will be in the South Stand, which when I was there was called, for sponsorship reasons, the Franking Sense South Stand. I just had to look that one up: franking is Britspeak for machines putting postage on stuff.

TOURS: Last year, tours were offered several days a week, £8.50 for adults, but never on game days. Book at least twenty-four hours ahead by contacting the club.

TICKETS: Last time they were in League One, adult tickets went from £26 to £40, and they didn't come close to selling anything out.

GETTING THERE: Couldn't be easier: get on a Preston-bound train at Manchester Piccadilly, get off about 40 minutes later at Horwich Parkway, and there you are!

PUBS: There is a Harvesters chain pub called The Horwich Park right between the station and stadium; it will certainly be mobbed. A few minutes to the right of the stadium on Lostock Lane is The Barnstormers, more of a sports pub. Around behind the stadium is The Bee Hive Pub and Carvery, where a buffet with three meats is less than £10.

There are more interesting options in town, all within a ten-minute walk of the main Bolton station (on the same line from Manchester). The York is right outside the station, the Spinning Mule is a Wetherspoon, and Ye Olde Man and Scythe goes back to at least 1251.

GRUB: Down in town, I had a nice old-fashioned fish and chips sit-down at a place called Olympus Fish and Chip. I told them I was American, and several staff came by to say hello and welcome me. Also downtown is Ciao Napoli, a popular Italian place, and a café called The Kitchen. If you're in a hurry and desperate, the stadium is next to a mall with a food court with a Nando's, Ask Italian, and other chains.

AROUND TOWN: As your Standard Northern English Town (see page 363), Bolton has your standard 19th-century buildings from its standard glorious industrial past. (In their case, milling cotton was the thing.) Most of that is in town by the main station. On the northern edge of town, a few miles out, are two historic homes: Hall i' th' Wood, now a museum, and Smithills Hall, a 15th-century home on the slopes of the Pennines. Both can be found on the museums page at boltonlams.co.uk.

Basically, I'd say swing through town for lunch and a pint, walk around a bit, and then hop back on the train to the game. It should be a fun and easy day out from Manchester.

BURNLEY

From a town of 73,000, with a ground that mixes old and new, Burnley has become a model for a gritty club from a gritty town hanging on in the Premier League.

LOCATION: An hour north by train from Victoria station in Manchester

CONTACT: burnleyfootballclub.com, 01282 446800, #BurnleyFC

NICKNAMES: The Clarets

WOMEN'S TEAM: Burnley Women FC play in the third-tier Women's National League North. Home games are at Arbories Memorial Sports Ground in Burnley

HISTORY: Burnley Rovers started out as a rugby football club, but they switched to Association rules in 1882 and moved into their current home, Turf Moor, the next year. They were one of the original twelve clubs in the Football League, and one of their players got the first hat trick in league history.

After that, it is very much a standard small-club history—early glory, decline, another good run, near ruin, and now a battling run toward the top—all set in a town that is the very definition of the Standard Northern English Town Story (see page 363). They won the league in 1921, going thirty games unbeaten along the way. That's the record Arsenal's Invincibles would break decades later.

After World War II, Burnley built another winning team under the chairmanship of Bob Lord and the management of Alan Brown. Burnley was also an innovator: the first to build a separate training ground, the first to do short corner kicks, and a leader in youth development. In fact, when they won another league title in 1960—grabbing it with a last-day win at Manchester City after not leading the league all season—they did it with two players they bought and the rest they brought up through the youth system. That team had international players and a Footballer of the Year, and they made Burnley's first trip to a European competition.

When those stars retired, the club started to lose the money battle to other, bigger outfits, and by 1971 they had been relegated. By 1985 they found themselves in the fourth tier and needing a last-day win to even stay there. But they rebuilt and popped up to the Premier League for one year, 2009–10, becoming the smallest town to ever host a Premier League team. They still are.

They bounced around between the top two divisions before barely staying up in 2017—the first time they repeated in the top flight in forty years. Since then, under manager Sean Dyche, they developed an outstanding formula for success: be organized, work hard, be tough to beat, and win at home. They had a particular ability to shock the big teams, like when they opened the 2017–18 season with a 3–2 win at defending champions Chelsea. That year they sustained a five-game win streak late in the season that saw them finish in seventh, resulting in a Europa League berth—their first "European tour" in fifty years. They beat a Scottish team before losing to a Greek one, and the effort almost derailed their league campaign. The last two seasons they've finished fifteenth and seventeenth, but by gosh the Clarets are still there.

RIVALRIES: Among all the Lancashire teams, Burnley and Blackburn Rovers agree that they hate each other the most. Those games are called East Lancashire derbies or Cotton Mill derbies, the teams being separated by just nineteen miles and in former mill towns.

SONGS: They have a fun one about Owen Coyle, who played and managed at Bolton and then managed Blackburn Rovers when they got relegated to League One. It includes the lines:

> Owen Coyle's a bastard.
> He wears a bastard hat.
> He was a Bolton wanker,
> He's now a Blackburn twat.

After goals they play "Tom Hark" by the Piranhas. You think you don't know it, but you do. Google it.

2020–21 SEASON: 17th in Premier League, 5th Round FA Cup, 4th Round League Cup

2021–22 SEASON: Premier League (promoted in 2016)

STADIUM: Turf Moor—what a name. I knew I had to go there when I was talking to somebody at a modern new stadium and said I liked the old ones because they're like going back in time. She said, "Well, you ought to go to Burnley then!" She actually shuddered and said, "That's going *way* back in time!" I don't think she meant it as a compliment, but I knew I had to get there soon.

Once there, I found myself sitting on a wood seat next to an older gentleman with pin badges all over his vest. I said I liked the place, and he smiled and said, "It's a proper footballing ground." And indeed it is—all 21,944 seats of it. Their home since 1883 is also the longest continually used stadium ever to be in the Premier League. (And do the math: they average 20,000 a game in a town of 73,000.)

One side and one end were redeveloped in the mid-1990s and are two-tiered, but the other side and end, the Bob Lord Stand and the Cricket Field Stand, date from 1974 and 1969, and both have some wooden seats. Away fans will be in the Cricket Field Stand, with the rowdy Burnley fans in the near end of the James Hargreaves Stand.

TOURS: Tours are on Thursdays and nonmatch Saturdays and cost £10 for adults, preregistration required.

TICKETS: £30 to £40 for adults and usually available with some advance notice, unless they're playing one of the top few teams

GETTING THERE: For getting to Burnley, I recommend you come over from Manchester on the bus. The train ride is fine, and you can take it back for convenience, but the bus is a scenic trip over a hill through villages and sheep country. It's called the Witch Way for some reason and has run continuously since 1948! Catch it at the Manchester Coach Station in Chorlton Street. The Burnley Coach Station is also much closer to Turf Moor.

If you come in by train and arrive at Manchester Road station, it's a 20-minute walk from there. It should be about £5 in a taxi.

PUBS: The closest is a bar in the Burnley Cricket Club right next to the stadium. But that's probably not the vibe you seek. Along Yorkshire Street, the main route to the stadium, look for The Turf Hotel and the more happening—and wonderfully named—Royale Dyche, with a photo of their manager as some kind of medieval prince.

In town and along the walk from Manchester Road station, look for the Bridge Beer Huis, listed in the CAMRA *Good Beer Guide*. Farther away, but worth the fifteen-minute walk, is the Brewers Fayre Queen Victoria, set in the middle of a large park and offering a large menu and plenty of seating; there's also a Premier Inn there. The Talbot is in a six-hundred-year-old building, one of Burnley's oldest. It's on Church Street near the center of town, a ten-minute walk from Turf Moor. Over by the station look for a Wetherspoon called Boot Inn.

GRUB: There's not much by the ground and nothing that looks too spectacular in town. If you want fish and chips, walk a few minutes past the stadium to Norman's Chippy in Lyndhurst Road; it's a proper chip shop that doesn't cook your fish until you order it. Another option for fish is Frydays over near the Bridge Beer Huis. And up by the Manchester Road station, if you want some sugar and caffeine before heading out of town, check out the somewhat goofy Chocstop.

AROUND TOWN: Look, I love the club, they're a great story, and Turf Moor is a favorite. And I met some wonderful people in Burnley—but every one of them couldn't figure out why I was there and assumed I would be leaving right after the game. After the game, when I asked two cops what I should do in town, they actually laughed as if I was "winding them up."

In fact, there is one thing to do. It's called the Singing Ringing Tree, and it's a piece of wind-powered art in the hills above town. Apparently, when the wind hits it right, it sings. Not so when I was there, but the view was nice. You'll need a taxi to get there, and it will be about £20 roundtrip, and from the road the tree is about a ten-minute walk. Have the taxi wait for you.

EVERTON

Everton may have dropped into second position in their hometown of late, but they should be at the very top of your priorities for a visit—soon, before they build a new stadium. "The People's Club" has one of the greatest old grounds left.

LOCATION: Liverpool, two and a half hours from London's Euston station and just under an hour from Manchester Piccadilly

CONTACT: evertonfc.com, 0151 556 1878, #EFC

NICKNAMES: The Toffees or the Blues. Apparently, Toffees comes from there being a toffee shop near the ground way back in the day that sold Everton Toffees. Before every home game, a woman dresses up as the Toffee Lady—think blue-and-white Amish lady—and hands out free sweets to the crowd.

WOMEN'S TEAM: Everton Women are in the Women's Super League, the top tier. Home games are at Walton Hall Park in the Liverpool Soccer (!) Centre. I do love it when Brits say "soccer."

HISTORY: Here is something I bet you didn't know about Everton: they have, by some distance, spent more seasons in the top flight of English football than anybody else in the country. That would be 117 seasons since the Football League was created in 1888. They have only missed four seasons up top and none since 1954.

You might know that they started across Stanley Park at Anfield then moved across to Goodison Park in 1892 over a rent dispute. The split led to the formation of Liverpool FC back at Anfield. The two have been eyeing each other across that expanse of grass ever since.

Everton won two league titles and an FA Cup before World War I, but they hit it big in 1925 when they signed a striker named Dixie Dean. He still holds the record for goals in a league season—sixty in 1927–28—and when he left in 1937, he had scored an incredible

349 goals in 399 appearances. (His statue is outside the ground.) By World War II, they had won three more league titles and another FA Cup.

They had another good run in the 1960s—two more leagues and another FA Cup—and then took off again in the 1980s, winning the league in 1984–85 along with the UEFA Cup Winners' Cup and adding another league win in 1986–87. In both cases they were denied European football the following season because of the ban on English clubs there—ironically because of the behavior of Liverpool fans. In all the years since, they have one FA Cup, two lost finals, and some minor dalliances in Europe to show for another thirty-plus years in the top division.

They also found perhaps England's other greatest striker after Dean: Liverpudlian and boyhood Everton fan Wayne Rooney came through their youth system, scored fifteen goals for the senior team from 2002 to 2004, then left for Manchester United where he became their record scorer with 183 goals. He also retired from international duty as England's all-time leader with fifty-two goals. He returned for one sentimental and not very effective season for Everton, then bolted for MLS in 2018; he's now a player/coach at Derby County.

Their club motto, written on the crest, is "*Nil Satis Nisi Optimum*," which is Latin for "Nothing but the best is good enough."

RIVALRIES: Liverpool, of course, are a rival, but it has frankly become less than competitive in recent years. Going back to the 2007–08 season, spanning thirty-three games, Everton have only two wins in the league (including 2-0 last year at Anfield) and one in the FA Cup. It has been called the Friendly derby because the fans mix together—sometimes families are split over this—but I went to one and it didn't feel that friendly. Less vicious than many, perhaps, but not exactly a love fest.

SONGS: Since 1962 the team has come out to the theme song from an old BBC show called *Z-Cars*. It's based on an old folk song, and it's flute-y and fun. They also do a thing where they just sing "Everton" over and over to, loosely, the home stretch of "Stars and Stripes Forever." They have one called "Grand Old Team" that says, "If you know your history / It's enough to make your heart go worrrrrrr."

2020–21 SEASON: 10th in Premier League, Quarterfinals FA Cup, Quarterfinals League Cup

2021–22 SEASON: Premier League (since 1954)

STADIUM: They call it the Grand Old Lady, and Goodison Park defines many of the things I love about English soccer. It's tucked into a neighborhood so tightly there's a church inside it; there are pubs directly across a small street; it remains beautiful and old-fashioned; its wood seats are cramped; views are obstructed; everybody agrees it has to be replaced; and everyone is sad about that fact. Imagine if you knew the Cubs were about to leave Wrigley. You would hurry up and go, right?

Goodison holds just under 40,000 people, and in today's league, money equals a chance for success. So in 2021, the club got final approval to build the Bramley-Moore Dock Stadium with around 53,000 seats on the Liverpool waterfront. It is scheduled to open in 2024.

Walking into Goodison today is like walking back in time a hundred years. In fact, the main Bullens Road Stand, designed by famous architect Archibald Leitch (see page 356) was built in 1926 and was only worked on in the 1960s for fire safety; it's one of only three that still has Archibald Leitch's distinctive trusses (Portsmouth's Fratton Park is another). The Goodison Road Stand was built in 1971 but isn't actually straight; one end curves in a bit because the property itself isn't square. The Gwladys Street End is another Leitch stand from 1938; that's where the rowdies sit, and the team prefers to go that way in the second half. The Park Stand is from 1994 and replaced a large terrace. Away fans will be in the Bullens Road Stand, so I like to sit in the Goodison Road to see and hear them.

The church inside is St. Luke's, and it was there first. You can go in for tea and a club-themed flea market before the game. Everton actually doesn't play early Sunday games to avoid conflict with services.

TOURS: Tours are available every day except game days and are highly recommended. (Since Everton and Liverpool are never home at the same time, tour one place while you're in town for a game at the other.) It's £15 for adults; the day before a game it's Legends Tours. If your guide happens to be Elle or Lily, tell them I said hello.

TICKETS: Tickets range from £38 to £49, but they can be hard to get. A membership (£30 last year) will help but isn't a guarantee, especially for the bigger games. They also offer hospitality packages, which consistently have the lowest prices of any big Premier League clubs. My broker has a nice option here as well.

GETTING THERE: You may notice this is just like getting to Anfield. They are, after all, less than a mile apart, and the two clubs are never home the same weekend. Right outside the main Lime Street station, you will see a sprawling bus stop area, and one of the first stops will be labeled as the Football Special. It should be bus 19, 20, or 21. There will be stewards hanging around, and they will either sell you a ticket or show you the nearby office where you can get one. Might as well get a return (round-trip) ticket, although some people choose to walk back afterward, such is the traffic.

You can also take a Merseyrail Northern line train from Lime Street to Sandhills station and catch the, yes, Soccerbus from there. Last year you could get a combo train/bus ticket for £4 at Lime Street, so just ask them there.

Or you can just take a taxi, which is around £10.

PUBS: The closest one is about twenty yards from the stadium on Goodison Road. The Winslow Hotel calls itself the People's Pub, and if you can get in there, I recommend it. Just down Spellow Lane, The Royal Oak will also be full of Evertonians. The Brick on Walton Road is an old-fashioned Everton boozer with a view down the street of the Goodison Road Stand. And there will be a Fan Zone at the game.

GRUB: There's a Hot Wok right by the entrance near Stanley Park and some pretty standard fare up and down Walton Road just west of the stadium. I've never seen much worth noting there, so I always eat in the city center.

AROUND TOWN: For the tourist and aside from football, Liverpool is really about the waterfront and The Beatles. I have some detailed recommendations in the Liverpool chapter.

The little tower in Everton's crest is still around. It's officially called Everton Lock-Up, but everybody calls it Prince Rupert's Tower. It's actually an 18th-century jail. The best way to see it is to take a taxi to or from the game and ask the driver to swing by it. Just hope he's not a Liverpool fan!

The folks who own the Liverpool-themed Shankly Hotel now have an Everton version across the street, the Dixie Dean Hotel.

HUDDERSFIELD TOWN

One of my favorite stories of recent years, Huddersfield Town is also one of my favorite examples of a fun, easy, off-the-normal-circuit club to go and visit on a day out from Manchester.

LOCATION: Thirty minutes northeast by train from Manchester

CONTACT: htafc.com, 01484 960 600, #HTAFC

NICKNAMES: The Terriers, which was introduced to honor the fitness and tenacity of a late-1960s side

WOMEN'S TEAM: Huddersfield Town Women FC are in the Women's National League North at tier 3 of the pyramid. Home games are at Stafflex Arena, home of Shelley Community FC.

HISTORY: The club was founded in 1908 and in the 1920s was arguably the best team in the country. They were the first to win the league three years in a row, in 1924–26. Only three other clubs have done it, and no one has won four in a row. They also won the FA Cup in 1922 and lost the final another four times that decade.

After World War II, Town faded, dropping out of the First Division in 1952. They made it back for three seasons in the early 1970s but then spent more than three decades in the lower leagues, at times near extinction. They went into administration (British for "bankruptcy") in 2003 but have come back strong.

In 2011 playing in League One, Town set a remarkable record with forty-four league games unbeaten. At the end of the following season, they were promoted to the Championship after a record-setting penalty shootout in the final of the League One playoffs against Sheffield United. It went eleven rounds and finished with keeper-versus-keeper.

They had just about the lowest payroll in the Championship, and they barely survived; in 2015–16 they were nineteenth. During the 2016–17 season, they set a record that year for one-goal wins, a statement to their fitness and discipline—terriers indeed.

At the end of that season, they went into the playoffs, made the final, and won it—again on a penalty shootout. They spent two years in the Premier League, their first in the top tier since the early 1970s. They were everyone's pick for relegation the first year, but they ensured their survival in the last week of the season by getting draws at Man City and Chelsea. Alas, in 2019 the fun ran out, and they were relegated back to the Championship, where they have finished eighteenth and twentieth the last two seasons.

RIVALRIES: Leeds United, just twenty-one miles away, are the most hated; any game between these two and Bradford City would be called a West Yorkshire Derby. However, Leeds and Huddersfield Town haven't played so often, just eighty times over all the years, with Town winning thirty-three of them. The rest of the years, they haven't been in the same division. I'm sure Leeds, with its proud history and tremendous support, doesn't appreciate Huddersfield calling themselves "The Yorkshire Club."

The same separate-division factor applies to a rivalry with Manchester City, whom they used to play more when City wasn't "all that," like they are now. It's more like different worlds than divisions.

There is also a rivalry with Bradford City, whom they have played more often, having spent more time in the same division. Bradford is just eighteen miles away, but they are currently down in League Two. Barnsley, also of West Yorkshire and the Championship, are a minor rival.

SONGS: Their most famous is "Smile a While," which sprang out of the terraces in their glory days of the 1920s. It was based on a song that was popular during World War I. Here are the lyrics, which aren't typically sung in full, but it's a real treat when they give it a proper go, usually right before kickoff:

There's a team that is dear to its followers.
Their colours are bright blue and white.
They're a team of renown, they're the talk of the town,
And the game of football is their delight.

All the while, upon the field of play,
Thousands loudly cheer them on their way.
Often you can hear them say,
Who can beat the Town today?

Then the bells will ring so merrily
Every goal shall be a memory
So Town play up, and bring the Cup
Back to Huddersfield

We're Yorkshire! We're Yorkshire! We're Yorkshire!

2020–21 SEASON: 20th in the Championship, 3rd Round FA Cup, 1st Round League Cup

2021–22 SEASON: The Championship (relegated in 2019)

STADIUM: The John Smith's Stadium, with 24,500 seats, has been their home since 1994. It replaced Leeds Road, where they played from the club's founding in 1908. The Smith's is a terrific, modern, attractive stadium just a few minutes' walk from the train station. The combination makes it, for me, one of the best of the recently built grounds in the country.

I love that the North Stand is sponsored by a company called Fantastic Media, making it the Fantastic Media North Stand. You want to sit in or near the Chadwick Lawrence (South) Stand, where both the away fans and the hard-core home fans sit.

John Smith's, if you didn't know, is a bitter beer made by Heineken. Naturally, it's for sale inside the ground.

TOURS: Tours are available Wednesday, Thursday and Friday for £5. Call the club for details.

TICKETS: The last prices I saw were adults for £30 and under-18s for £10.

GETTING THERE: It's an easy 15-minute walk from the train station. As always, follow the colors!

PUBS: Right outside the station, which dates to 1850 and is famous for its colonnades, there is a beautiful courtyard area and two great pubs. The one on the right, The Head of Steam, offers food and beer. The one on the left, the King's Head, is more of a traditional pub, just serving beer and cider, but it has a fine selection of each and a very open layout that's been recently renovated. It also, oddly, has in its crest a picture of Jimi Hendrix—the king, I suppose.

On the way to the game, look for the Gas Club on the left as you walk down Gasworks Road. It's basically a community room with beer and TV, for home fans only, with a £2 admission charge. If you skip that right turn and stick with the main Leeds Road, you'll come to the Yorkshire Rose, which has outdoor seating. The Corner, closer to the town center, is a nice, more modern pub with good bar food.

GRUB: As you walk down from the station you'll see a Sharky's Fish Bar; I didn't go in because the line was heinous, which I take as a good sign. In town, I'm told the pizza is good at the Cotton Factory bar. The Sportsman and the Grove are two more pubs with good comfort food.

AROUND TOWN: First, for something to do on the way to town, take the local train from Manchester, the one that stops in Marsden. There, you can visit a unique museum from the Industrial Revolution days.

Back in the early 19th century, a canal opened through a tunnel here, and workers would push barges through it by lying on top of the load on their backs, pressing their feet against the ceiling of the tunnel, and "walking" it through. Today you can visit the museum and take a boat ride 500 meters into the tunnel. In fact, there is even a little twelve-seater shuttle boat from the Marsden station to the tunnel visitor center for £1 per person. Marsden's Riverhead Brewery Tap in town is a highly rated pub for food and bevvies.

Huddersfield itself is really quite lovely. Right outside the station, aside from the two pubs I mentioned above, is an old hotel, The George, sadly now closed. It was built in 1851 and, in 1895, was the birthplace of Rugby League Football. In June 2020, plans were announced to one day house the National Rugby League Museum there.

In the center, be sure to stick your head into the Town Hall, built in 1881, which includes an impressive mural of the town and a gorgeous, 1,200-seat concert hall. It is the home of the nationally renowned Huddersfield Choral Society, which has recorded numerous albums and performed with the best orchestras in Britain.

If you do pop in, see if the caretaker is around, and if he is, tell him I said hello. More specifically, tell him the American working on the book, the one whose team has a mascot with a chainsaw cutting logs on the sideline, says hello. Also, pity him as a Leeds supporter living in Huddersfield.

The other thing you have to do in town is take a taxi up to the Victoria Tower (1899) on Castle Hill. The medieval neighborhood up on the hill, Almondbury, is a treat (you might consider walking through it back down into town.) The view from the top is fantastic, a 360-degree panorama of the town and the rolling, lush, green Pennine Mountains covered in hedgerows and cottages and sheep. A taxi ride from the station, up and back, with about ten minutes spent at the tower, should be around £20.

Finally, as you walk to the ground for the game, stop into the Open Market (which is actually covered) for some local color.

LIVERPOOL

Mighty Liverpool dominated the English game from the 1960s through the 1980s, earning them a worldwide following. They are relevant again, and Anfield remains a must-see stop on a groundhopping tour—if you can get in.

LOCATION: Liverpool is two and a half hours from London's Euston station and just under an hour from Manchester Piccadilly.

CONTACT: liverpoolfc.com, 0151 264 2500, #LFC

NICKNAMES: The Reds

WOMEN'S TEAM: Liverpool FC Women play in the second-tier Championship. Home games are at Prenton Park in Maidenhead, also the home of Tranmere Rovers FC. See liverpoolfc.com/news/women.

HISTORY: In all of England, only Manchester United has more to brag about than the Reds. But if you are younger than forty, you don't remember when Liverpool was winning everything. You probably do remember the Ferguson years at United, so just imagine if after he retired, *another* one came along and did even better, then a former player became manager and won some more. That was Liverpool from the mid-1960s to 1990.

But they almost didn't exist. Everton FC started its life at Anfield but left over a rent dispute in 1892. (They moved barely a mile away, across Stanley Park.) So Anfield's owner, John Houlding, started himself a new club, Liverpool FC. They lost the FA Cup final in 1914 and won the league in 1922 and 1923, but no more trophies came until they won the league again in 1947. By 1961 they were in the Second Division.

But a couple of years before that, they had hired a manager named Bill Shankly. He used the club's boot room as a legendary planning room for him and his assistants, and from that room emerged a dynasty. From 1964 to 1990, Liverpool under Shankly—succeeded by his assistants Bob Paisley and Joe Fagan, and later by player Kenny Dalglish—won thirteen league titles, four European titles (today's Champions League), four FA Cups, four League Cups, two UEFA Cups, and the UEFA Super Cup. From 1972 to 1990 they finished first or second in the league all but one season, winning it eleven times.

It was Shankly who mentioned to the press one day that his wife's favorite song was a Rodgers and Hammerstein piece called "You'll Never Walk Alone" and it would be nice if the fans were to sing it. It is quite possibly now the most famous football anthem in the world. The version you'll hear starting the crowd at the stadium is by Gerry and the Pacemakers, a Liverpool outfit.

Those years were not all good, however. Liverpool's fans were also involved in two of the most infamous stadium disasters in history. In 1985 some of them attacked Juventus fans at a European Cup final at Heysel Stadium in Brussels, causing a wall to collapse and thirty-nine people, mostly Italians, to die. This resulted in all English clubs being banned from Europe for five years (and Liverpool for a sixth). Then, at a 1989 FA Cup semifinal at Hillsborough Stadium in Sheffield, ninety-six Liverpool fans were crushed to death when police mistakes led to massive overcrowding in their end of the stadium. The authorities blamed it on the fans and covered up the reality for decades. No one has ever gone to jail for it, but police forces agreed to a financial settlement with families in 2021. Liverpool fans still sing "Justice for the 96" at almost every game.

Since those memorable years, they have won three FA and four League Cups, and they bagged another European title in 2005 after a memorable comeback from being 3–0 down at a final in Istanbul. In 2018 they made an unexpected run to yet another Champions League final, their ninth, and lost in the final to Real Madrid. The following year they finished second in the league by one point in an epic title race with Manchester City but won the Champions League, beating Tottenham in the final for their sixth European crown.

In 2020, as I am sure you know, they won the league "at a canter." So it would appear the Reds are back, even if the wheels came off a bit last year and they had to rally to make third.

RIVALRIES: Everton, of course, is a rival. The Merseyside derby, named for the local river, has had more players sent off than any other Premier League game, even though in the stands it's known as the Friendly derby. They have played an astonishing 238 times since 1894.

But most Liverpool fans will tell you they hate Man U more. For one thing, the Merseyside derby hasn't been truly competitive for years, but Manchester and Liverpool hate each other for reasons going back to the Industrial Revolution and probably further. (This is England, after all.) United's period of dominance came right after Liverpool's and was highlighted by Ferguson saying he was going to "knock Liverpool right off their fucking perch." And no player has switched from one team to the other since 1964!

SONGS: "You'll Never Walk Alone," which comes before each game and occasionally during it, is certainly one of the most famous songs in world soccer. But it's not their only one by a long shot. They have adapted an Irish folk song, "The Fields of Athenry," into "The Fields of Anfield Road" with lyrics about LFC legends. There are more than a few about all their titles, plus "Ooooh I am a Liverpudlian," and one that says, "We're not racist, we only hate Mancs."

They also take credit for introducing the song of the moment, "Allez Allez Allez," to England. I have more on that on page 353.

2020–21 SEASON: 3rd in Premier League, 4th Round FA Cup, 4th Round League Cup, Champions League Quarterfinals

2021–22 SEASON: Premier League (top flight since 1962), UEFA Champions League

STADIUM: Anfield is one of the palaces of English football, and to their credit, Liverpool in their ambition have not replaced it or ruined it with renovations. Capacity is 54,074 in four tightly packed stands. The most famous is the Spion Kop, one of many around the country named for a hill made famous in the Boer War in South Africa. This stand once held as many as 30,000 people on a single terrace, but in its current all-seater format still holds 12,390 singing, flag-waving supporters. It is often spoken of by commentators as a single entity, as in "The Kop clapped for a returning player."

Away fans will be in the lower level of the Anfield Road Stand, opposite the Kop; it is slated to be rebuilt in the next few years, which will bring the capacity closer to 60,000. Outside the stadium is a ring of statues and gates as well as a memorial shrine to the ninety-six lost at Hillsborough.

TOURS: It's £23 for a self-guided tour with audio and £50 to follow around a legend, which is actually what I recommend. Both include the museum, which you can also do by itself for £10.

TICKETS: As you might imagine, tickets are difficult. To begin with, the normal channels of buying a ticket from the club are not open to you unless you've been buying them for years, and if you're reading this, I assume you haven't been. This means you will need, at the very minimum, one membership (£27 to £44) for each ticket you will want. Even that probably won't do it! It will get you into the ticket resale area of their website, but most of those are snapped up before mortals like us can get at them.

This leaves us, as always, with third parties and hospitality packages. Third parties are abundant and illegal, so you are taking your chances there. Hospitality can come from the club or one of their direct and indirect partners such as yours truly at groundhopperguides.com. Plan to spend hundreds of dollars per ticket, even if it's a lowly Cup game, and up to really scary numbers if they're playing Man U or another big shot. But they have (and we sell) some wonderful hospitality options in their newly expanded Main Stand.

GETTING THERE: Getting to Anfield from the main Lime Street station is pretty simple. Right outside the station you will see a sprawling bus stop area, and one of the first stops will be labeled as the Football Special. It should be bus 17 or 26. There will be stewards hanging around, and they will either sell you a ticket or show you the nearby office where you can get one. Might as well get a return (round-trip) ticket, although some people choose to walk back afterward, such is the traffic.

You can also take a Merseyrail Northern line train from Lime Street to Sandhills station and catch the, yes, Soccerbus from there. Last year you could get a combo train/bus ticket for £3 at Lime Street, so just ask them there.

Or you can just take a taxi, which is around £10.

PUBS: There are quite a few pubs right around the ground, and they will all be packed. The Albert, right outside, is a shrine to the club, with posters and scarves and banners covering every space. The Park, right across the street, is less decorated but no less crowded and loud; same for the Twelfth Man just down the road past the Albert. The designated away-fans pub, last I heard, was The Arkles, just a few minutes away, or the Flat Iron down Walton Breck Road. There is a large Fan Zone outside the stadium as well.

GRUB: Liverpudlians are known, in addition to that wonderful term, as Scousers. I always thought it sounded like a putdown, but in fact Scouse is the local dialect, which was named for a stew of lamb or beef with potatoes and other vegetables—typical exciting traditional English food. I had some near the ground that was so awful that all I will say is beware any cafés you can see from outside the Kop.

A bit of quick internet research for better options turned up a café called Maggie May's in the center and a pub called Baltic Fleet down on the water. The Ship and Mitre, also in the center, is said to have good scouse and the biggest selection of beers in town. Clearly, more research is required.

Up by the ground it's all the standard fare, except that in the Fan Zone I saw some local food trucks with better-looking options than usual.

AROUND TOWN: The waterfront area is great for a walk around, in particular the Albert Dock. It was remade after its industrial heyday with food, drink, shopping, and museums like the Maritime Museum and Tate Liverpool. Liverpool also has the second biggest Chinatown in the world after San Francisco.

If it's Liverpool FC you dig, you should check out the Shankly Family Experience at the Shankly Hotel. They offer tours of the city and their own memorabilia collection.

Otherwise, it seems to be all about The Beatles, who, of course, started in Liverpool. There are numerous tour companies in town that do Beatles tours among many other kinds of tours. I had a great walking tour of the waterfront and some of The Beatles stuff from BeatlesWalk.com. Liverpool Cycle Tours has a biking Beatles tour among others. And Brilliant Liverpool Tours has many great options, some of which can be customized.

MANCHESTER CITY

The club once called "noisy neighbors" by Man U's manager is now one of the biggest and baddest teams in the country. With their new worldwide following plus a nice, modern stadium in a cool city, they should be a major attraction for groundhoppers.

LOCATION: Two and a half hours from London's Euston station

CONTACT: mancity.com, 0161 444 1894, #ManCity

NICKNAMES: Citizens, Sky Blues, and just City, which owing to the local accent is often written as "Citeh"

WOMEN'S TEAM: Manchester City WFC are in the top league, the Women's Super League, and they are one of the best teams in it. They finished first or second the last six years and won the FA Cup in 2017 and 2019. Home games are at the Man City campus in the Academy Stadium.

HISTORY: Manchester City have always been the city's second team to most people, although I get a sense that it's more like Manchester United are the world's team and Manchester City are the city's. I probably hear that from City fans, granted, but if somebody has been a City fan for more than ten years, it's because they genuinely love them, not because they signed up for a front-runner like so many recent Man U fans.

Founded in 1880, City became the first Manchester club to win the FA Cup in 1904, but then financial troubles, highlighted by a fire at their ground, led to struggles and a new home, Maine Road, in 1923. They won another Cup in 1934, then the league in 1937, then declined before winning the Cup again in 1956. That final was famous because their goalkeeper, Bert Trautmann, played the last twenty minutes despite breaking a bone in his neck. Granted, he didn't know he had broken it, but still.

They had good years in the late 1960s to mid-1970s, winning another league title and FA Cup as well as a couple of League Cups and the UEFA Cup Winner's Cup. But the 1980s were a disaster, and despite being founder members of the Premier League in 1992, by 1996 they were in the third tier—today's League One. They also went from 1990 to 2003 without ever beating Man U.

As recently as 2008, they were in financial trouble. Then they were bought by some very wealthy oilmen from Abu Dhabi, and they immediately started throwing the money around. They won the FA Cup in 2011—their first trophy since 1976—and have been a force since then. They won the league in the last minutes of the 2012 season, when Sergio Agüero (their all-time scoring leader) scored in injury time to take the title away from Manchester United. The official time of the goal was 93:20, which explains why you see that number all over the stadium. They have since won the league four more times, including last season; won the League Cup six times (and are the current holders); and won the 2019 FA Cup. In 2019, they were the first to win the league, League Cup, and FA Cup in the same season, and last year they made the Champions League Final, losing it to Chelsea. They are becoming the standard by which the league, much less that other club across town, measure themselves.

RIVALRIES: United, obviously, is their biggest rival. The Manchester derby goes back to 1881, and of the 185 matches, United have won seventy-seven and City fifty-five. The most famous perhaps was the "Denis Law game" in 1974, when the former United legend scored a backheel goal at Old Trafford to relegate them. He famously declined to celebrate, but City's fans made up for it.

SONGS: Their most famous song, by far, is "Blue Moon." They will probably even carry a giant blue moon onto the center circle before the game, and you'll hear the song throughout the game. This apparently started after a 1989 loss at Liverpool.

You will also hear "I'm City Till I Die" and "You Are My City" to the tune of "You Are My Sunshine." And they have a fun one for their manager, Pep Guardiola. They sing "We've Got Guardiola" to the tune of "Glad All Over."

They also do a simple "City, City, the best team in the world," and they are on the "Allez Allez Allez" bandwagon. See page 353 for more.

2020–21 SEASON: 1st in Premier League, Semifinals FA Cup, League Cup Winner, Runners-up UEFA Champions League

2021–22 SEASON: Premier League (promoted in 2002), UEFA Champions League

STADIUM: Officially it's the City of Manchester Stadium, and the area around it Sportcity, but everybody just calls it The Etihad because that airline cut a big ol' check. It opened in

2002 for the Commonwealth Games then became City's home in 2003, when they left Maine Road after eighty years.

When it opened it held 42,000 people, but it's now up to 55,097 after a second expansion in 2015. They are actually reducing capacity slightly this season, then they plan to bring it up to about 63,000. Its facilities, inside and out, are second to none, even if the atmosphere, for me, is sometimes lacking.

Away fans will be in the South Stand, often stretching into all three tiers.

TOURS: There are a few options, including limited game-day tours. The basic tour is £25, another with the academy tour is £35, and a Legends Tour led by a former player (they're all "legends") is £70.

TICKETS: Like all the big Premier League clubs, tickets can be tough, but City—with their fairly recent big-time status and large stadium—seem to be a little less difficult than the other big six. Tickets range from £30 to £50. A membership (£20 to £35) will certainly help. They also have great and relatively affordable hospitality options that I can help with.

GETTING THERE: It couldn't be easier getting to The Etihad; there is a tram stop right there. It's called Metrolink, and the stop is Etihad Campus. At Piccadilly station's Metrolink stop, look for line E going to Ashton-under-Lyne—or, as always, follow the colors. They have lots of staff around the platforms on game days to answer questions and sell tickets.

I am told a taxi from Piccadilly is about £10. You can also walk there in about 25 minutes.

PUBS: There isn't much around the stadium except for City Square right outside it, where they have a pub called Summerbee Bar and a family-friendly place called Blue Moon Cafe. Both will be completely nuts before the game. There will also be music and contests and a big screen and everything. It's quite a scene.

There are still some old-school Man City pubs near the ground. Mary D's on Gray Mare Lane is a traditional favorite, as is the even less glamorous Townley around the corner on Albert Street.

If you're looking for lunch and/or a pint before the game, you should do that in town. I most highly recommend two pubs in the terrific Northern Quarter part of town: Tib Street Tavern is the more traditional option (just don't wear any football jerseys at all), and Second City is a little more hip. If you fancy some billiards or indoor golf while you watch the game on TV, go to The Green just outside the Northern Quarter.

GRUB: There is a cool new development called The Printworks near Victoria station with a pub of the same name. Across from that is a Nando's, which has really good peri peri chicken. There is also a Wagamama in there; that's an Asian bowl place with lots of tasty options, including vegetarian and vegan.

After the game, or at some point during your stay, I highly recommend two particular areas: Chinatown and the Curry Mile. Chinatown is right downtown, just a few minutes from Piccadilly Station. I have had two very good meals at Happy Seasons. A more famous and fancy place, though it's hard to get into, is Wing's. It's kind of a thing in soccer world, with players and coaches dropping in on occasion.

The Curry Mile is just something to behold. It's a long strip of road where Arabic is the main language and every business seems to be a curry house, sweet shop, or men's barbershop. I ate at MyLahore, simply because it looked like the most approachable to a white guy traveling alone. It was delicious. I also had an outrageously good Indian meal next door at Mughli Charcoal Pit. And I hear very good things about Shere Khan. Afterward, go to Sanam Sweets, get something to go, and just walk up and down the street.

The best way to get to the Curry Mile is probably by cab. There is a city bus, but it takes a bit; Google Maps will tell you how that works.

AROUND TOWN: I talk about sites around town in the chapter on Manchester United. Manchester also makes an awesome base for soccer explorations; see "Make Manchester Your Base" on page 362.

MANCHESTER UNITED

Manchester United is a giant club with a giant stadium, a collector of championships, and a global brand that is loved all over the world and hated all over England. They have also been, by their standards, a bit of a mess lately.

LOCATION: Manchester, which is two and a half hours from London's Euston station

CONTACT: manutd.com, 0161 868 8000, #MUFC

NICKNAMES: The Red Devils, Man U, or simply United

WOMEN'S TEAM: For some reason it took until 2018, but they finally have a women's team. Manchester United started that year in the Women's Championship at tier 2—and they won it! So they are now in the Women's Super League, with home games at Leigh Sports Village, where the men's youth teams also play.

HISTORY: United have won major trophies in multiple decades, but they have not actually been a consistent record of massive success. They were founded in 1878 as Newton Heath FC, changed their name to the current one in 1902, won the league twice and FA Cup once by 1909...and then disappeared. They almost went bankrupt in 1931.

But in 1945 they hired a manager named Matt Busby and embarked on a great period of success. They won three league titles in the '50s and became the first English club to compete in the European Cup (now Champions League). But that team, known for its youth as "Busby's Babes," was decimated by a plane crash in Munich on February 6, 1958. Twenty-three people died, including eight players. There is still a clock outside the stadium that is part of a memorial to that team.

Busby rebuilt the team around legends Denis Law, Bobby Charlton, and George Best—the "United Trinity" whose statue faces that of Busby outside the stadium. All three were European Footballers of the Year at various points, and together they won league titles, FA Cups, and the club's (and England's) first European Cup in 1968. But Busby retired in 1969, and in 1974 United was relegated. Yes, this actually happened; Law, playing for Manchester City by then, scored the goal that did it—and refused to celebrate.

They got back up in a year but essentially floundered for another decade before hiring Alex Ferguson in 1986. They almost fired him, but he won the 1990 FA Cup and got to stay on. All he did after that was win thirteen league titles (including three in a row twice), five FA Cups, four League Cups, and two Champions League titles—one of which came in the famous "treble" season of 1998–99, when they also won the league and FA Cup.

Ferguson retired in 2014, and another period of floundering began. They have won each domestic Cup once since then, but for their legions of fans, that's not good enough. The fear is that they will suffer the same fate as their great rival Liverpool, who won everything in the '60s to '80s but then didn't win the league for thirty years.

In 2020, United made the Europa League semifinals, trying to rebuild under manager Ole Gunnar Solskjaer, who scored the winning goal that got them the Champions League title in the '99 treble season. Last season they were in the Champions League but dropped out of it to the Europa, where they lost the final to Villarreal of Spain. This year, they will be back in the Champions League after finishing second in the league.

RIVALRIES: Fans disagree on who the bigger rival is. Manchester City, whom Ferguson once referred to as "noisy neighbors," has obviously become a major force. But Liverpool, so often the great rival for trophies, is probably still the biggest. Leeds United was a great rival in the '60s and '70s, so older fans will still resent them as well.

SONGS: "Glory Glory Man United" is a mainstay, but there are many others. Still, opposing fans like to taunt the Old Trafford atmosphere as resembling a library, and the club has even tried to put in a "singing section" at some games. They will also do a looping, repetitive "Bring out United" just before the teams come out.

2020–21 SEASON: 2nd in Premier League, Quarterfinals FA Cup, Semifinals League Cup, Group Stage Champions League, Runners-up Europa League

2021–22 SEASON: Premier League (promoted in 1975), UEFA Champions League

STADIUM: Old Trafford, also known as the "Theatre of Dreams," is a palace of English football. It holds 74,994 people, making it the biggest club stadium in the country. Named for the neighborhood it's in, it has been their home since 1909—although the stadium now certainly bears no resemblance to what it was then.

It's basically three very large sides and one smaller one. The last is the Sir Bobby Charlton Stand, which they would like to expand, but the engineering challenges are immense. Across from that is the Sir Alex Ferguson Stand, the largest in the country with 25,500 seats. The East Stand (aka Scoreboard End) is behind one goal (away fans are in the corner between this and the Charlton Stand), and behind the other is the Stretford End, traditionally home to the most diehard fans. United likes to attack that end in the second half.

If you have any choice in the matter, try to sit in the Charlton Stand, as it has the best views of the other three towering structures, or in the Stretford End for atmosphere.

TOURS: Offered all day every day, except for game days. The standard version (£25) includes the stadium and museum, but some tours are led by former players, some include food, and some include a boat ride on a canal from Central Manchester. If you do, they will probably be low behind a goal. Check the website or call 0161 826 1326 for more info.

TICKETS: Best of luck. Along with Liverpool, Arsenal, and Chelsea, these are among the toughest tickets in the country to get. They have made a club membership a requirement; these range from £20 to £60…and *then* you can pay £41 to £53 for tickets, which you probably can't get anyway. If you do, they will probably be low behind a goal. And you will definitely never get an away ticket to see them play somewhere else.

Scoring one or two seats for a home game against a lowly team is one thing. Getting more than that together will only happen at Cup games against nobodies, and getting anything against a big club simply won't happen. This means you have to go with hospitality packages or the secondary market, in which you're on your own.

See "I Can Help" on page 373; Groundhopper Guides is a reseller of several hospitality packages here.

GETTING THERE: It couldn't be easier. You go to any Metrolink train station in the center—there is one at the main Piccadilly station—and take a train bound for Altrincham. It stops at Old Trafford, at which point the entire train will empty out. It's about a 10-minute walk from there and the definition of "you can't miss it." A return ticket in 2019 was £3.20, and there will be assistants all over the Metrolink stops in the center if you have questions.

PUBS: There are really only three choices out by the stadium. As you walk in from the Metrolink station, you will see The Trafford on the right and The Bishop Blaize on the left. The Trafford is more traditional; The Bishop Blaize is more modern and has an outdoor patio. Both will have a line to get in, and you will need to produce a home-section match ticket for admission. The same is true at Hotel Football on the other side of the stadium; it's a hotel owned by former players, including Ryan Giggs, and it has a couple of bars.

There is a convenient, if not too exciting, pub one stop before the stadium. Hop off at Trafford Bar, walk up to street level, and check out The Tollgate. It will be manageably crowded, anyway. And in town, there's a United-themed pub called the Old Nag's Head that is popular with local fans.

Another thing that I get asked a lot is "Since we can't get (or afford) tickets, where can we watch the game in town?" There are, of course, a million pubs, many of which show games. I checked out quite a few, and I most highly recommend two in the terrific Northern Quarter part of town. Tib Street Tavern is the more traditional option—just don't wear any football shirts at all—and Second City is a little more hip. If you fancy some billiards or indoor golf (seriously) while you watch, go to The Green just outside the Northern Quarter.

GRUB: All the pubs listed above have food, although service will be challenged on game days. You really should just count on eating in town (see below) or as part of the hospitality package you probably had to buy. You can also take the Metrolink to Media City UK and eat at one of several places over there, then walk about twenty minutes to the game.

AROUND TOWN: Manchester is, to me, an undiscovered attraction in England—especially for the football fan. It has many of the modern conveniences and historic and cultural attractions of London but without the crowds. There are great tours available in the center, which is highly pedestrian friendly on its own.

There is also, of course, another pretty big football club in town (see previous listing) as well as the National Football Museum, which reopened after a remodel in 2019. And there are many other clubs in the surrounding area, some reachable by Metrolink. This makes Manchester a fantastic base for a northern football-themed adventure. Within ninety train minutes of Piccadilly station, you can see a game at Huddersfield Town, Rochdale, Wigan, Bolton Wanderers, Macclesfield Town, Barnsley, both Sheffield clubs, Burnley, Bradford City, Leeds United, Blackburn Rovers, Preston North End, and Stoke City—and that's not even to mention that Liverpool is just under an hour away by train.

Back in Manchester, I recommend several parts of town in particular. Manchester's Chinatown is fantastic and filled with restaurants; my favorite is the relatively subdued Happy Seasons. The Northern Quarter—like Chinatown, just minutes from Piccadilly station—is rapidly becoming hipster central. Turtle Bay is a chain that does some good Caribbean food, and Canal Street is the center of the vibrant Gay Village.

And perhaps the coolest is the Curry Mile, a neon-lit stretch of Wilmslow Road in Rusholme that is lined with curry shops, kebab houses, sweet shops, and barbershops. It is said to be the largest concentration of South Asian restaurants outside of South Asia, but it's also starting to attract a lot of Middle Eastern places as well. I have had particularly good meals at the Indian restaurant Mughli Charcoal Pit and the curry shop MyLahore. Afterwards, hit up Sanam Sweets for takeaway desserts and enjoy the street scene.

That is all within about a twenty-minute ride on several bus lines, or roughly a £10 taxi fare, from the city center.

OLDHAM ATHLETIC

Such an approachable club that you might be able to hear the pregame team talk from the parking lot.

LOCATION: Oldham is basically a suburb of Manchester, about twenty-five minutes out from the center on the city's Metrolink service.

CONTACT: oldhamathletic.co.uk, 0161 624 4972, #OAFC

NICKNAMES: Latics, which, as at Wigan, apparently comes from the Lancashire accent taking on the word *Athletic*

WOMEN'S TEAM: They only have a youth setup for women, with the highest level being Under-18.

HISTORY: I have always had a soft spot for Oldham. In the spring of 1990, I was backpacking around Europe and found myself in a London pub watching football highlights. One guy near me turned to another, they both shook their heads, and one of them said, "Look at Oldham!" I asked what about (and really, what is) Oldham, and he said, "They're in the quarterfinals of the Cup, mate. Oldham!"

I didn't know what any of that meant, of course, but it was my first glimpse of English football beyond Liverpool and the World Cup, my first sense that in this game, little clubs could do big things that people all over the country talked about.

Turns out I had brushed up against Oldham at their all-time high point. I bet you didn't know that little Oldham Athletic, currently in League Two and not above the third tier for twenty-three years, was a founder member of the Premier League in 1992.

Sure, it was only their second season in the top tier after seventy years outside it, but they were on a high. Two years before, just after I was in that pub, they had taken Manchester United to a replay in the 1990 FA Cup semifinals, losing the second leg to an injury-time goal. The same season they lost the League Cup Final to Nottingham Forest, 1–0—their only game ever at Wembley. In 1991 they won the Second Division (now Championship) title with a last-minute winner of their own, a penalty by Neal Redfearn at home against Sheffield Wednesday. (I mention his name so you can ask your seat neighbor if they saw that goal.)

That got them into the top tier, which in 1992 became the Premier League. That year, they needed to win their last three games to stay up. First they won at second-place Aston Villa, ending their title hopes. Then they beat Liverpool at home. Then they beat Southampton, 4–3, and stayed up. Look at Oldham!

They crashed out the next season, spent the next three in the second tier, and that was that. They've bounced between the third and fourth tiers ever since, much as they did for many decades before. Financial trouble came in the early 2000s, but disaster was averted when a trio of American businessmen bought the club.

They sold it in 2018, and things seemed to not be going well, starting with their relegation to League Two in May of that year. They faced "winding up" orders that could have sent them into administration late in 2019 and early in 2020, and prospective owners are circling.

They were nineteenth and eighteenth in League Two the last two seasons.

RIVALRIES: This area of Lancashire is just a nest of football clubs. Rochdale, Salford City, and both the Manchester clubs are within ten miles of Oldham, and half a dozen more are within twenty miles. Rochdale are the most disliked, with Bolton and Huddersfield Town just behind them.

SONGS: When I saw them, they came out to "Fanfare for the Common Man," which didn't seem to get people too stirred up. Could also be it was freezing cold and an FA Cup tie with Burton Albion…

2020–21 SEASON: 18th in League Two, 3rd Round FA Cup, 2nd Round League Cup

2021–22 SEASON: League Two (relegated in 2018)

STADIUM: Boundary Park holds 13,513, all seated, and is famous for being on top of a hill, which in Lancashire during football season means cold. One former manager referred to it as "Ice Station Zebra." I was there in December on a sunny day that was just above freezing with a stiff breeze—to which the locals reacted with borderline glee that it wasn't raining.

Home rowdies will be behind a goal in the Chadderton Road ("Chaddy") End, with visitors opposite in the Rochdale Road End.

It's all so small-time and homey that when I was walking around before that FA Cup tie, admiring the coaching staff's two parking spaces right up against the Main Stand, I heard a big shout come from inside and wondered what it was. A few minutes later, my phone blew up with Twitter notifications of a spectacular goal in another FA Cup game, and I realized I had heard the Oldham players in their dressing room watching the game. That's the kind of place Boundary Park is!

TOURS: None

TICKETS: Last I saw it was £18 for adults, but I got into that FA Cup game for £6 cash on the day.

GETTING THERE: The nearest Metrolink stop is Westwood, on the Rochdale line from Manchester Victoria; it's about a 20-minute walk from there to the ground. If you're going into Oldham's center first, that's a 30-minute walk from the ground, but you can take bus 409 to Royal Oldham Hospital and knock most of that time off.

PUBS: The closest to the ground is the Clayton Green, part of the Brewers Fayre chain with unexciting food. In the center, the old Town Hall Tavern looks newer and a bit brighter than the more traditional Old Bank, which had more people in it.

GRUB: Parliament Square looked a proper café, and I had a nice fish and chips at the old-fashioned sit-down Lever's. There's a historic marker at Tommyfield Market, which makes a bold claim: that Oldham invented the fried chip, thus fish and chips, and thus pretty much the entire fast-food industry. I will not wade into this particular debate. But the fish was good.

There's also, I am told, a traditional dish in the area called "rag pudding," which is meat and onions wrapped in a suet (basically lard) pastry and cooked in cheesecloth. Apparently, British cuisine didn't have enough variations on meat and onions in a pastry.

But we need to talk about the chicken places. England has this (to me) eternally fun habit of naming fried chicken takeaway places for various North American locales. I guess you can't use Kentucky, but it seems everything else is up for grabs. Ever since I spotted Maryland fried chicken in Nottingham, I have been collecting photos of these places—there's a fun punch-card game in here somewhere—but nothing prepared me for what I saw in Oldham.

Just on a walk of a few minutes in the town center, I saw chicken places named for Toronto, Virginia, Orlando, Montana, Florida, and Michigan. And for kicks, they threw in a Havana Burgers, because nothing says Cuban food like a burger. Somebody there is managing to get away with a burger (and chicken) place called Arbeez. And then I topped it all off with a nice cup of Rhode Island coffee. What the hell is going on in Oldham?

AROUND TOWN: I mean, it's a nice enough place, and the people are friendly, and there's a chance you could get fried chicken from a place named for your home. The Dove Stone Reservoir looks nice, but you'd need a car or a taxi to get there. And Stonerig Raceway looks like fun for kids who want to race model cars or drive simulators. But let's be honest—you're coming out on a day from Manchester, if at all, right?

The thing to do in Oldham, then, is get something to eat, have a pint, and go up to Boundary Park. With a jacket.

PRESTON NORTH END

Almost the definition of a traditional, well-supported, and mostly second-tier club, Preston also has a lovely modern ground, a convenient location, and butter pies.

LOCATION: Preston is about an hour by train north of either Manchester or Liverpool.

CONTACT: pnefc.net, 0344 856 1964, #PNEFC

NICKNAMES: The Lilywhites, after their shirts

WOMEN'S TEAM: In 2020, the club's women's team came back to life after a previous version split off. Preston North End Women's FC debuted last season in the sixth-tier North West Women's Regional Football League.

But we must pause to discuss Dick, Kerr's Ladies FC, arguably the first women's football team in the world. Founded in Preston in 1917, they played 833 games over the next forty-eight years, occasionally beating pro men's teams in the early days. The name comes from the company whose employees started it, a locomotive manufacturer called Dick, Kerr and Company.

Their 2–0 win over a French team in 1920 is considered the first women's international. That French tour led to much publicity and then to a crowd of 53,000 for a game at Goodison Park. Incredibly, the Football Association couldn't take it; they rescinded the Ladies' certification later that year and banned women's football from FA club members' grounds for the next fifty years. Men are pigs. The team changed their name to Preston Ladies FC and played another forty years on non-FA grounds.

There's a memorial about this outside Deepdale.

HISTORY: This club has one thing it is very well known for. When the Football League was formed in 1888, North End were founder members. Earlier that year they had lost the FA Cup final, so they were a top team. Then, in the league's first season, they played

22, won 18, and drew 4. They won the league by 11 points, and they won the Cup without conceding a goal.

I have often wondered if people thought, *Right, well done to them*—not realizing it would be 115 years before anybody (Arsenal in 2003–04) went through a top-flight season unbeaten again. In the next seventy-five years, only one other club (Aston Villa in 1897) pulled off a league-Cup double until Tottenham did it in 1960–61.

So while Preston's "Invincibles" earned and have their place in history, I wonder how long it took for people to realize how amazing it was. (Americans need only think of the 1972 Miami Dolphins, still the only team to go unbeaten through an NFL season, including the Super Bowl.)

And since then? Well, they won the league again the next year, finished second three straight years after that, and then were regular top-flight residents through the 1950s. They won lower divisions a few times and brought home another FA Cup in 1938, with future Liverpool manager Bill Shankly making one of 297 appearances for the club. But they haven't been top-flight since 1961, which honestly surprised me. They seem like a bigger club than that, especially with such a nice stadium.

There were a few highlights along the way. In the 1950s, with the legendary player Tom Finney, they twice finished second in the league and lost a memorable 1954 FA Cup final, 3–2, to West Bromwich Albion. In 1964, as a Second Division team, they got back to the Cup final and again lost, 3–2, this time to West Ham.

A lowlight was in 1986, before promotion and relegation were automatic. They finished last in the Fourth Division and had to apply (successfully, as it turned out) to stay in the league. In the late 1990s, defender David Moyes turned player-coach, and then just coach, taking them to a 2001 playoff final that would have gotten them into the Premier League; alas, they lost to Bolton. Moyes left for Everton and elsewhere (currently West Ham), and Preston again lost the playoff final in 2005.

They have spent sixteen of the last twenty-one years in the second tier, with their biggest success coming when they won the League One playoff final in 2015 to get where they are now: in the Championship.

About the name—there are no other teams in town, nor have there ever been really, so the whole "North End" thing seems funny to me. If only there was a Preston South End, that would be a derby!

RIVALRIES: Mainly it's about Blackpool, which is less than twenty miles to the west. It's the West Lancashire derby and has been played ninety-four times in all four top divisions. The two teams haven't played each other since 2013, but with Blackpool back in the Championship, the wait is over!

Otherwise, any of the other Lancashire clubs—mainly Blackburn Rovers and Burnley at this point—would raise local temperatures.

SONGS: Nothing in particular I noticed

2020–21 SEASON: 13th in the Championship, 3rd Round FA Cup, 3rd Round League Cup

2021–22 SEASON: The Championship (promoted in 2015)

STADIUM: I was really impressed by Deepdale. There have been games on the site continuously since 1878, making it one of the longest-used football venues around (this topic is a minefield of argument, by the way). But it was all rebuilt starting in the 1990s and today is a modern, cozy, convenient ground that I would imagine can get pretty loud during a big game.

Its capacity is 23,404 in four separate stands. One is named for the Invincibles, and the other three for former players: Bill Shankly (the "Kop," where up to 6,000 away fans will be), Alan Kelly, and Sir Tom Finney. Each stand even has its own player's likeness on the seats. I would try to sit on the side fairly close to the away fans.

Outside you'll find a tribute to Dick, Kerr's Ladies FC, and a statue of Sir Tom Finney that is truly one of a kind. Finney, known as the "Preston Plumber" because that was his non-soccer business, is shown nearly horizontal in a fountain. It's based on a famous photo from 1954 at Stamford Bridge in a game that would never be played today because of the amount of water on the pitch.

TOURS: None

TICKETS: Last I saw, adult tickets were £24 to £30.

GETTING THERE: It's about a half-hour walk from the station through the city center, but you can make it easier on yourself by taking bus 19 (Sharoe Green) to the Football Ground stop right outside Deepdale. Catch it at the bus station (via bus 111 from the train station) or by walking to Lancaster Road in the center.

PUBS: There are some proper old pubs in the center of Preston. The Old Black Bull looks a little cooler on the outside than the more modern inside, but the Black Horse is legit old school and in a Grade II historic building. The tiny and cozy Market Tap may be older than that. The Guild Ale House has a neat atmosphere and great ale selection.

If you fancy a walk by the river, the Continental has a big menu and lots of beer selections.

Out by the ground, supporters will be in the Princess Alice, the White Hart, the Moorbrook (good outdoor seating), or the Moor Park.

GRUB: Some of the above pubs have food, as does the Wellington Inn in the center. I also got tasty takeaway from Roast in Orchard Street downtown. The barista at Town House Coffee, where I had a nice break, told me North End players occasionally pop in.

But let's talk about butter pie, two words whose coming together caused no shortage of excitement when I did my Preston research. It's your basic pie in structure, but instead of meat and sauce, it has potatoes, onions, and butter. Apparently this goes back to when Preston had a lot of Catholics who didn't eat meat on Friday. Take out the meat, put in butter? I say yes. I read one review that called it "pure, unrelenting, delicious fat," and I agree.

Get one at Deepdale, where fans insisted they come back to the menu after a local producer folded in 2007, and you'll see what I mean.

AROUND TOWN: Avenham Park along the River Ribble is quite nice if you're up for a peaceful walk. The city center is worth a walk around as well, especially since it's on the way from the station to the ground. The old Preston Dock area now has some shopping and a couple of pubs, plus a nice walking path. The Harris Museum has art and natural history displays.

TRANMERE ROVERS

If you're in Liverpool for a game at one of those "other" clubs, do yourself a favor: take a ferry across the Mersey and go see a traditional game of football at Prenton Park.

LOCATION: Tranmere is a neighborhood in Birkenhead, which in turn is in a place called The Wirral Peninsula. But Rovers are not in Tranmere; they are next door in Prenton. All this is just across the River Mersey from Liverpool.

CONTACT: tranmererovers.co.uk, 3330 144452, #TRFC

NICKNAMES: Just Rovers

WOMEN'S TEAM: Tranmere Rovers Ladies play in the North West Women's Regional League at tier 6 of the pyramid. Home games are at the club's training complex in nearby Wallasey.

HISTORY: For their first hundred years after forming in 1891, Rovers spent all of one season above the third tier, finishing last in the 1939 Second Division. In all that time, they were best known for developing and then selling top players, most notably Dixie Dean, who went on to be a legend at Everton.

Their glory years hit during the 1989–90 season, when they won the League Trophy—still their only major title. They lost the playoff final for promotion to the second tier that season, then went back and won promotion the next season after losing another League Trophy final. So that was four trips to Wembley in a year!

Home attendances, which had been under 2,000 just a few years before, swelled to over 8,000, and they stayed in the second tier for the next nine seasons. Three times they made the playoffs for a shot at the Premier League, and three times they lost in the semifinals. They capped off this fine run in 1999–2000, when they made the quarterfinals of the FA

Cup and final of the League Cup, which they lost to Leicester City, 2–1, after having a man sent off.

If you've read much of this book, you almost know what's coming now, don't you? The magic ended, relegation came, and with it the financial trouble, which brought more relegations. By 2015 they had dropped out of the Football League entirely, for the first time in ninety-four years.

They got back up in 2018, then made League One the following season. But when the pandemic hit in March 2020 and the season ended, the league switched to a points-per-game table, which meant Tranmere were back in League Two.

In the 2019-20 FA Cup, Rovers were involved in two of the more entertaining stories. First, they hosted, in the second round, Chichester City of the eighth-tier Isthmian League South East Division, 104 spots below Rovers in the pyramid. The game was broadcast nationally, and I just had to go. Chichester, a team of all amateurs, held Rovers off for over an hour before tiring and giving up five quick goals. But in injury time, in front of hundreds of their fans (probably most of them, to be honest), Chichester scored off a corner, setting off wild celebrations and an ovation from many of the home fans. After the game, their players posed for pictures with the fans, who stood and sang well into the night. (Search groundhopperguides.com for Chichester for a full description of this one.)

In the next round, Rovers went to Watford and were down 3–0 after just half an hour. But they stormed back, got a 3–3 draw, then won the replay at home through a 104th-minute winner. Then they drew Manchester United at home and lost, 6–0, but hey, this is what the FA Cup is supposed to be about.

One nice tradition of late is Liverpool playing a preseason friendly at Prenton Park, presumably to share the wealth by giving Rovers a sellout crowd. The July 2019 game was the fourth straight, a 6–0 Liverpool win capped off by a "pitch invasion" that looked on video like a bunch of kids trying to get Liverpool players' autographs.

RIVALRIES: Liverpool and Everton are the closest geographically, but they never play Rovers in a real game. Rovers supporters say the biggest rivals are Bolton Wanderers and Oldham Athletic, so try to get to Prenton Park when Oldham are in town.

SONGS: I've been to a lot of games in a lot of places, and Tranmere Rovers gave me one of the weirdest experiences of the lot. I was taking my usual video of the teams coming out when something in the music sounded familiar. It took me a minute to place it, then I couldn't believe it, but it was true: they were playing the theme from *The Rockford Files*!

If you're under fifty, you might not even know what that means. Back in the 1970s, American television was dominated by detective shows, with James Garner's portrayal of Jim Rockford being one of the biggest. (Remember the voicemail messages?) The theme song was this electric bluesy thing with harmonica and guitar that seems totally out of place in English football.

How did this happen? Like so many things in football, there's no clear answer. The best-sounding theory to me is that in the 1970s, in an attempt to draw more fans, Rovers started playing home games on Friday nights, putting them in competition with *The Rockford Files* on "the telly." When attendances disappointed, their chairman quipped that apparently people would rather watch the show than their club, so to get a laugh at the next game, the PA guy put the record on. They must have won that game, because some forty years later, it's still the pregame anthem!

2020–21 SEASON: 7th in League One (lost promotion playoffs), 3rd Round FA Cup, 1st Round League Cup

2021–22 SEASON: League Two (relegated in 2020)

STADIUM: Prenton Park is bigger and nicer than you would probably expect from a club this size. It holds 16,587 people, and three of the four stands were built or redeveloped in the 1990s. Home rowdies are in the Kop behind one goal, and away fans are opposite in the Cowshed, which housed the home fans until about twenty years ago and got its name because its predecessor looked like something from a farm.

TOURS: The only reference I've seen is a VIP Matchday Experience for up to 15 people, which includes a tour. Check the website for the latest.

TICKETS: Last I saw, adults were £18 to £21, and even the home Cup game with Man U didn't quite sell out.

GETTING THERE: There are a couple of ways to do this, assuming you're starting in Liverpool. You can take Merseyrail from Liverpool Central to Hamilton Square in Birkenhead, then hop bus 423 (Seacomb) to Highpark Road, a few minutes from the ground. But what you really should do is take a Mersey Ferry from Pier Head in Liverpool (down by the Beatles statue) to Woodside, which is just a few minutes' walk from Hamilton Square Station. Grab bus 423 from there.

PUBS: Right where you're catching the 423 bus, there's a really cool pub called Gallagher's Traditional that's filled with Royal Air Force memorabilia. There's also a decent option called the Birch Tree right next to the ground, another called Prenton Park right around the corner, and a supporter's club under a tent at the ground with cheap food.

GRUB: The pubs mentioned above have basic fare. There's pretty good Thai at Sawasdee near Hamilton Square. Really, all the food options are over in Liverpool.

AROUND TOWN: Put it this way: When I went, I just got something to eat, hit the game, and went back to my Liverpool hotel. And when I Googled "see and do in Wirral" just now, I came up with Birkenhead Park (the world's first publicly funded civic park and an inspiration for Central Park), an island with a bird sanctuary, and a bunch of sites in Liverpool. I'm sure there are other interesting things happening in the Wirral, so if you find any, please let me know!

WIGAN ATHLETIC

For years a story of plucky overachievement topped off with a remarkable moment of success, Wigan have crashed onto hard times. Mired in financial chaos, they were relegated to League One in 2020 and stayed there by one point last season.

LOCATION: Wigan is between Manchester and Liverpool, about thirty minutes from each by train.

CONTACT: wiganathletic.com, 01942 774000, #WAFC

NICKNAMES: The Latics or just the Tics. Apparently this is based on the pronunciation of *Athletic* in the local accent.

WOMEN'S TEAM: Wigan Athletic Ladies compete in the North West Women's Regional League at tier 5; see walfc.co.uk for details.

HISTORY: Compared to many clubs in this book, Wigan is quite young. They go back "only" as far as 1932, when the club emerged from a series of other local clubs from the previous forty years. The town was always better known for its rugby club—and indeed the one athlete honored by a statue in the area is a rugby player—but the Latics were considered one of the top non-league football clubs in the country. Still, they were so small that their colors changed in the '40s from red to blue because the local sports shop ran out of red shirts.

They kicked around a lot of local leagues before finally making it into the Football League in 1978, and in just three years got up to the Third Division. But the main event in their modern history occurred in 1995 when the club was purchased by local businessman Dave Whelan.

Whelan grew up in Wigan and played for Blackburn Rovers. He appeared in the FA Cup final but broke his leg—hold that thought—and soon after retired to concentrate on his business ventures. He started with a market stall in town, built that into a chain of ten groceries, then sold that and went into sporting goods and fitness centers. That is now a nationwide chain of stores. When he bought the club in 1995, he said he would take it to the Premier League, and in 1999 he laid out the £30 million for their new stadium.

They won the Third Division in 1997, won the Second Division in 2003, and in 2005 made the Premier League. Their first year they finished tenth and made the League Cup final, and for the next eight years they were a model for a small club from a small city hanging on in the big time. In the 2012–13 season, they ran into big trouble in the league but made an amazing run in the FA Cup. They got to the final and faced mighty Manchester City; Whelan himself led the team out. Incredibly, they won it 1–0 on an injury-time Ben Watson header off a corner kick in front of their own fans. The television announcer famously said Watson had won it for Wigan and Whelan. There's a statue of Whelan holding the Cup outside the West Stand.

Sadly, Wigan also became the first club in history to win the FA Cup and get relegated in the same year—three days later, in fact. Two years after that they dropped down to League One. They got back up in 2016, went back down in 2017, and in 2017–18 won the league, putting them back in the Championship.

Unfortunately, they've been hit by a financial storm. A majority share of the club was sold to Hong Kong investors in June 2020, but three weeks later the club went into administration (bankruptcy). This led to a twelve-point deduction penalty, which in turn led to relegation to League One. They were bought by a businessman from Bahrain in 2021, so we'll see.

RIVALRIES: There are so many clubs around (see "Make Manchester Your Base," page 362) that Wigan—despite having a short history with all of them—consider Bolton Wanderers (especially), Preston North End, Oldham Athletic, Blackburn Rovers, Burnley, and Rochdale as rivals.

SONGS: In the pregame buildup, you'll hear The Monkees' "I'm a Believer." This comes from the 2012–13 season, when the football team's success in the Cup and the rugby team's claiming two trophies led to a citywide "Believe in Wigan" campaign.

2020–21 SEASON: 20th in League One, 1st Round FA Cup, 1st Round League Cup

2021–22 SEASON: League One (relegated in 2020)

STADIUM: The DW Stadium is pretty much the epitome of the modern English football stadium: clean, comfortable, without much character, and next to a shopping center. It holds 25,138—a little odd since the official record crowd is five people fewer than that. The away fans will be in the North Stand, and the South Stand is the family section. The rowdy Wigan fans will be in the north end of the East Stand, making for some decent banter with the away supporters. There is always a drum in that end of the East Stand, though. You've been warned.

TOURS: Tours are not available at this time.

TICKETS: The last prices I saw were £20 to £25, which were frozen from the previous League One season. I doubt they will sell out a game unless they draw a big boy in the FA Cup.

GETTING THERE: Both Wigan stations—for some reason, a town of 100,000 people has two train stations across the street from each other—are about a 30-minute walk from the stadium. From the stop right in front of North Western station, take bus 628 or 641 to Montrose Avenue, and then follow the colors. Blue Star Taxis has an office on the main road; you might want to arrange something for after the game as well.

PUBS: There are several good options right in the town center. The Swan and Railway is just across from North Western station and is a pretty traditional pub. Up the street away from the tracks are the Moon Under Water, the Clarence Hotel, and the Berkeley. The Red Robin (not the American burger chain) is a modern pub in the shopping center by the stadium and hosts away fans as well. The two best options are The Anvil, run by a local brewery and just a few minutes from the station, and Wigan Central, a more modern spot just past the tracks and on the left. Both have great beer selections.

GRUB: Wigan is nationally famous for meat pies. Every December, Harry's Bar hosts the World Pie Eating Championships. Apparently, the story goes back to a 1920s strike when the locals were the first back to work, thus having to eat "humble pie." In fact, folks from Wigan are often called Pie Eaters or Pie Men. Asking which pie is best is like asking somebody from Philadelphia about cheesesteak sandwiches, so let's just say that the three most convenient and highly rated options are Galloways across from Wallgate station on the main drag, Greenhalgh's a few minutes north on Market Street, and Poundbakery, also on the main drag.

Of course, this being England, somebody decided that a pie (like so many other things) would be even better if you put it on buttered white bread! It's called a pie barm, or a Wigan kebab. You can also have them pour pea juice on your pie; this is called having it "pea wet." I dare you to order that.

If you're looking to gain even more weight, Wigan is also the home of Uncle Joe's, purveyor of famous mint balls (which "Keep You All Aglow"). Their shop in the town center closed, but look for the mint balls around town—including the two-billionth one made, which is in the Museum of Wigan Life.

If you'd prefer fish and chips, look for Mr. Chips over behind the church. And if you want Indian, check out The Raj on Woodhouse Lane, about a ten-minute walk from the stadium. Vegetarians will like The Coven in the center.

AROUND TOWN: Honestly, aside from the pie and the mint balls and the beer and the football, there's not a lot to do in Wigan. There was a world-famous disco called Wigan Casino back in the 1970s, but it was replaced by the Grand Arcade. There are still a number of nightclubs along King Street. There is the Wigan Pier, actually a docks area along the Leeds and Liverpool Canal made famous (for being awful) in a book by George Orwell. It's been adandoned for a while, but a group is trying to bring it back to life; check canalrivertrust.org.uk for more.

Get yourself a pie (barm), a pint or two, some candy for the trip back, and head out to the game.

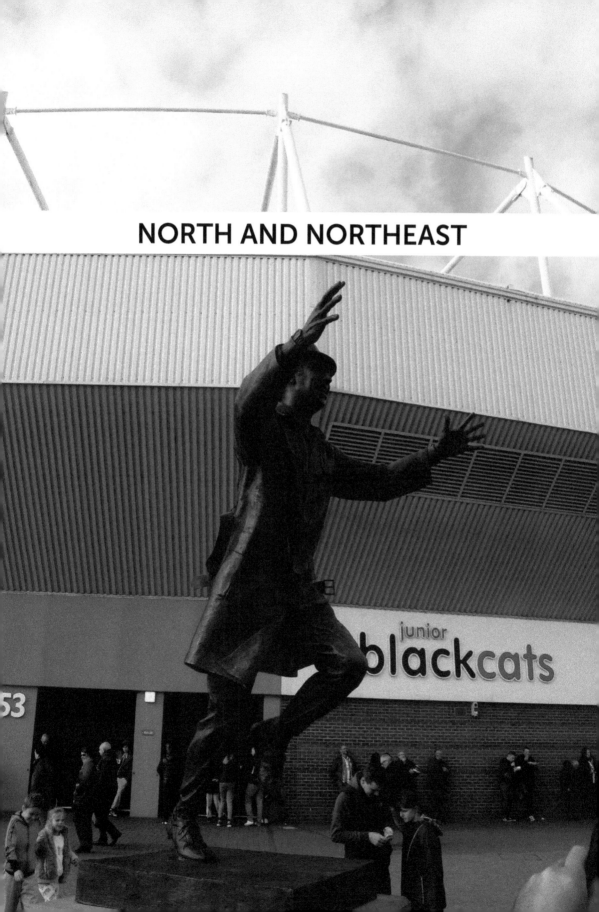

NORTH AND NORTHEAST

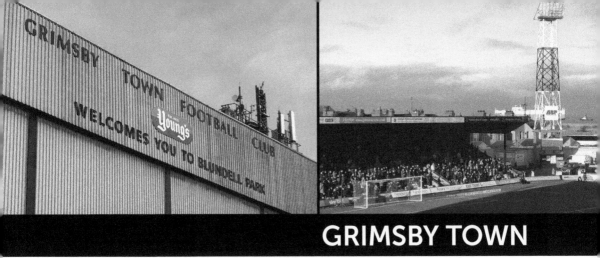

GRIMSBY TOWN

Way out on the edge of the country, and now out of the Football League, there's a club who famously "only sing when they're fishing."

LOCATION: Grimsby is two and a half hours by train east of Manchester and just over three hours from London.

CONTACT: grimsby-townfc.co.uk, 14726 05050, #GTFC

NICKNAMES: The Mariners, because Grimsby was home to the world's largest fishing fleet as recently as the mid-20th century. A fishing vessel even adorns the club crest.

WOMEN'S TEAM: The Grimsby Town Women's FC, in just their third year in existence, will play this season in the East Midlands Regional Football League Division One North at tier 6. Contact the club for fixture locations..

HISTORY: I love regional rivalries, the kind where nobody from more than ten miles away cares and nothing is on the line except local pride. In the first lines of the Grimsby Town page on Wikipedia, which we can assume was written by a Mariners supporter, it says Town is "the most successful of the three professional league clubs in historic Lincolnshire, being the only one to play top flight English football. It is also the only club of the three to reach an FA Cup semifinal (doing so on two occasions). It has also spent more time in the English game's first and second tiers than any other club from Lincolnshire."

Take *that*, Scunthorpe United and Lincoln City!

I won't get into this debate, and I haven't been to the other Lincolnshire clubs, but I will point out that the Mariners haven't been in the top tier since 1948, they haven't been above the fourth tier since 2004, and after least season they even dropped out of the Football League.

Town's best season was certainly 1997–98, when they won the League Trophy, beating Bournemouth in the final on their first-ever trip to Wembley. Their second trip to the national stadium was just four weeks later, when they beat Northampton Town in the playoff final to get back to the second tier.

They lasted four seasons there before the wheels came off; they suffered two straight relegations into League Two, and in 2010 they dropped out of the Football League entirely. They made it back in 2016 and lasted five years.

And now I'll tell you about my trip there. I am working my way through the ninety-two league clubs, so I had to get there eventually; they were in League Two at the time. (And yes, Scunthorpe and Lincoln, I'll get there too!) Also, since I spent a few summers in the Alaska fishing fleet, I have a fondness for fishing towns. And as you might imagine, everyone assured me the fish and chips there would be excellent.

So I waited for a derby to pop up, and sure enough, I got to see the 2019 visit of Scunthorpe United, from just thirty miles up the road. A River Humber derby! I eagerly read the stories about extra police coming on, and about trouble that popped up at previous games, and about the 2,000 supporters making the trip from "Scunny."

I rolled in the night before, got some excellent fish at St. James Fish by the station, and the next morning set out to explore. A few hours before the game, I was over at the ground, where I asked somebody in the club shop for another chippy recommendation. (I might be a fried fish addict.)

This is the kind of experience you have at clubs like this: The man walked me fifteen minutes down the road to a wonderful place—Ocean Fish Bar in Cleethorpes—while regaling me with tales of Grimsby glory and expressing constant incredulity that I even knew about the Humber derby, much less came to see one. I offered to buy him lunch, but he declined, wished me a pleasant day, and then walked back to the ground.

I checked out Cleethorpes for a bit (it's the seaside entertainment district) and then decided to follow the seafront back to the ground. Shops were closed for the season, and all was quiet—until a train pulled up to the Cleethorpes station. Out poured "the Scunny lot," many hundreds of loudly singing (and I presume highly intoxicated) visiting Irons heading for the game along the seafront.

For half a mile of open space, it was literally just me and them, with the latter closing in behind me. They didn't appear menacing, but then again they could easily have assumed I was a local. So I walked faster and thought of the most "dumb American" thing I could possibly say should they catch me.

There's a point where you have to take a footbridge over the railroad tracks to get to the ground, and that bridge was crawling with cops. So I was briefly between the cops and the Scunny lot, not wanting to be associated with either. I got there ahead of the crowd just as they started coming up the steps behind me. As I approached, the officers had a stern look, to say the least.

I looked at the first one and said, "Is it this way to the SOCK-er game?" Half of them laughed, the other half looked confused, and I knew I would be okay. They waved me on, then started shouting instructions at the throng behind me. I went in for a cracking game of football.

Scunthorpe won it, 1–0, sang their guts out the whole time, threw flares onto the pitch, and then burned Cleethorpes to the ground. Okay, I made that last part up. But I do love me a derby, and especially a small, petty regional one that nobody else in the world gives a crap about. See you next year, Scunny!

RIVALRIES: You guessed it: Scunthorpe United and Lincoln City. Hull City would qualify as well, but they are now three leagues above them and haven't played Grimsby Town in more than twenty years.

SONGS: There's this song that supporters across the country taunt each other with: "You only sing when you're winning." Grimsby Town, in a masterpiece of English self-deprecation, sing about themselves: "We only sing when we're fishing." You'll see it on scarves and posters around as well.

They also sing a slightly modified version of the Greasy Chip Butty Song from Sheffield United, replacing the gallon of Magnet with a barrel of Tetley's. See the Blades' listing for the rest of the lyrics.

2020–21 SEASON: 24th in League Two (relegated), 1st Round FA Cup, 1st Round League Cup

2021–22 SEASON: National League (relegated in 2021)

STADIUM: They have played on this spot since 1899, and this is a proper old ground. The latest major renovations were in 1982, when the two-tiered Young's Stand opened. Opposite that is the old Main Stand, much of which dates to 1901; it's considered perhaps the oldest stand in the country.

Away fans will be behind one goal in the Osmond Stand (built 1939), and home rowdies are opposite in the Pontoon Stand (1961), which gets its name from the old fishing days. While much of that industry is gone, if you sit in the Upper Young's like I did and look out over the Pontoon, that big building you see is one of the largest frozen-fish storage facilities in the world.

TOURS: None

TICKETS: Back in their League Two days, adults were £18 and £20, and I even managed to get one for the derby.

GETTING THERE: Cleethorpes is actually the closest station at about a 20-minute walk. Trains run only from Grimsby Town Station, though. When I was there, trains arriving here were packed with away supporters, but if it's not a derby, I can't imagine this is an issue. From there, walk the main road or the seafront. Grimsby Town Station, the main one in town, is over two miles. Bus 10 (North Sea Lane) from Old Market Place, just outside the station, will get you there in under 20 minutes, but getting a bus after the game is a hassle with traffic. A taxi is less than £10 each way.

PUBS: Right outside Grimsby Town Station is a Wetherspoon called the Yarborough Hotel. The closest pub to the ground is the Blundell Park Hotel, right across the street. And there's one inside the ground as well. There are also several good ones in Cleethorpes, which were full of away fans when I visited. These include the Coliseum Picture Theatre and the smaller Scratching Post.

GRUB: Fish and chips! They're everywhere, especially over in Cleethorpes. I was very happy with what I had at Ocean Fish Bar over that way, as well as at St. James Fish behind the Grimsby Town station. Mariners over by the ground is more of a traditional pregame chippy. I'm sure there's other food in town, but I didn't eat any of it.

AROUND TOWN: I wish I could say that you can stroll the docks among the rusty boats and crusty fishermen, hearing tales of the sea and learning bawdy songs in steamy pubs. Actually, it's a major industrial port that you can't really visit. The most famous building in the city is the Grimsby Dock Tower, which is rarely open to the public.

You can get a sense of the glorious past at the Grimsby Fishing Heritage Center, a large museum, and you can tour the Ross Tiger, a fishing vessel converted to a museum in 1992. Model railway geeks (hand up here) will love the tiny Immingham Museum.

Otherwise, Cleethorpes is worth a walk around for an old-timey beach tourist feel with about a dozen fish and chips places. And then you're off to the ground!

MIDDLESBROUGH

A classic yo-yo club, Middlesbrough have spent all but two seasons since World War II in the top two tiers but have just one major trophy to their name.

LOCATION: Teesside, named for being along the River Tees, is three hours north of London by train, two and a half hours from Manchester, and one hour from Newcastle.

CONTACT: mfc.co.uk, 01642 929420, #UTB

NICKNAMES: Boro, even though their name isn't Middlesboro; these things confuse me. Also, in the local accent it comes out more like "burra" than boro. Sometimes local people are called smoggies, a name that Sunderland fans gave Boro fans because of the air quality in town.

WOMEN'S TEAM: Middlesbrough WFC play in the Women's National League North at tier 3. Home games are at Bedford Terrace, the home of Billingham Town FC. Find out more at middlesbroughwomenfc.co.uk.

HISTORY: Much of Boro's history is standard fare: formed in 1876, did well in the First Division for a while, got interrupted by the wars, and had some good players and good (second division) seasons in the 1950s. One of those players was local boy Brian Clough, who scored an amazing 204 goals in 222 games before leaving for Sunderland. He later managed Derby County and Nottingham Forest to great success, and all three cities now honor him with a statue.

By the 1960s Middlesbrough had spent a year in the third tier, but by the mid-1970s manager Jack Charlton had them back in the top division. Then more decline set in, and in 1986 they came within ten minutes of going out of business. They were saved by another local boy, Steve Gibson, who made a fortune in trucking and still owns the club.

In the 1996–97 season, soon after moving into their new stadium, they lost the finals of both the FA Cup (0–2 to Chelsea) and League Cup (0–1 to Leicester City in a replay), and were also relegated that year.

They have stabilized since then, finishing as high as seventh in the Premier League in 2003–04. Their one major trophy was the 2004 League Cup, which got them into the following season's UEFA Cup, now called the Europa League. They made the final sixteen that year, and in 2006 made the final, losing 4–0 to Sevilla of Spain.

RIVALRIES: North East neighbors Newcastle and Sunderland. Each city has its own river, and therefore name, for the derby. In Middlesbrough, on the River Tees or just in Teesside, it's the Tees-Wear derby and the Tyne-Tees derby.

SONGS: Before games, they play the same song, "Papa's Got a Brand New Pig Bag," also used by Queens Park Rangers. I will make no attempt to sort out who did it first. They also seem quite fond of "You Are My Boro," sung to "You Are My Sunshine."

2020–21 SEASON: 10th in the Championship, 3rd Round FA Cup, 2nd Round League Cup

2021–22 SEASON: The Championship (relegated in 2017)

STADIUM: The Riverside is yet another perfect example of the perfectly rectangular modern stadium. It seats 34,742 people and has been their home since 1995, when they moved over from the old Ayresome Park. One nice feature is that the old gates from Ayresome Park are outside the main entrance.

There are statues of Wilf Mannion and George Hardwick, two local lads who played for Boro in the 1940s and '50s and made the England team.

Away fans will be in the southeast corner, with the home rowdies (known as the Red Faction) in the nearby south end.

TOURS: Offered on Mondays, Thursdays, and Sundays for £10 by the club's charitable foundation. Book ahead at mfcfoundation.co.uk.

TICKETS: Last I saw, an adult ticket was £34 to £39.

GETTING THERE: It's a pretty easy walk of just under a mile from the station.

PUBS: The closest pub to the station is the roomy but unexciting Isaac Wilson. On the way to the stadium, look for the fancier and more modern La Pharmacie, also with good food, and Doctor Brown's, which will host the away fans. Closest to the ground is the Six Medals, a big and family-friendly place with a large menu and outdoor seating.

But the beer-lover's action is in the city center, where a thriving microbrew scene has taken hold. Look for the tiny Infant Hercules, the refurbished Twisted Lip, the very cozy Slater's Pick, and the simple but nice Sherlock's.

GRUB: I had a lovely meal at Fork in the Road Café, with a good variety of main dishes up to £15. It's also a nonprofit that is staffed by people who have come through their job-training program. Al Forno was recommended by locals, as were Fellini's for Italian and Barbarossa for pizza.

There is also a local dish called parmo, which is a fried pork (or sometimes chicken) cutlet covered in béchamel sauce and cheddar cheese. You might think (as I did) that it was done with parmesan, but not so. It is also said to have been invented by an American who opened a restaurant there after serving in the area as an army chef in World War II.

AROUND TOWN: Let's talk about this Transporter Bridge, because you'll be hearing a lot about it anyway. It seems to be The Main Thing in Middlesbrough. It's obviously not a Transformer bridge that turns into a monster, though that would be cool. It is, in fact, a 1911 ferry bridge officially known as the Tees Transporter Bridge. It's a ferry in that up to two hundred people and nine cars can ride in its moving part across the river in ninety seconds, but it's a bridge because the "car" isn't on the water. I struggled to figure out the amazingness of it, and I didn't take a trip on it, but people sure seem excited about it.

Middlesbrough was, during the Industrial Revolution and up until the middle of the 20th century, a center for iron, steel, and shipbuilding. Its nickname was Ironopolis. This means that much of the city was destroyed during World War II, leaving a fairly modern city center.

You can go down to Albert Park and see the statue of Brian Clough; I am pretty sure he's the only football person honored with a statue in three cities. The park is also a nice place for a walkabout, and it's where you'll find the highly rated Fellini's restaurant. Southfield Road is a hip area near Teesside University. The Captain Cook Birthplace Museum honors the life and explorations of the famous explorer. And outside the Institute of Modern Art lies the rather striking *Bottle of Notes* sculpture.

It's not the most exciting place. But if you are into exploring the countryside, you are very close to a real treasure: the North York Moors National Park. I took a train on my day off from Middlesbrough to the beautiful coastal town of Whitby, passing through fantastic little villages along the way. You can hop on and off the train for walks and pubs and bike rides, but Whitby itself is a treat. The fish and chips at The Fisherman's Wife are outstanding, as is the view of the beach. The park's website is northyorkmoors.org.uk.

There is also, at certain times of the year, a steam-powered North Yorkshire Moors Railway (founded in 1836) that goes deep into the countryside and runs steam trains. Their website is nymr.co.uk.

ST. JAMES' PARK

Home of the Toon Army

NEWCASTLE UNITED

If you're measuring clubs by stadium size and fan base—as opposed to, say, recent success—then Newcastle is one of the biggest clubs around, with an amazing stadium and supporters who keep getting screwed by ownership drama.

LOCATION: Newcastle-upon-Tyne, in the northeast, about three hours from London and ninety minutes from Edinburgh

CONTACT: nufc.co.uk, 0844 372 1892, #NUFC

NICKNAMES: The Magpies, for their traditional black-and-white-striped shirts. Their fans are known as the Toon Army, based on how the word *town* is pronounced in the local accent. Locals are also referred to as Geordies.

WOMEN'S TEAM: Newcastle United WFC are in the Women's National League Division One North (tier 4) and play at Druid Park, which I need to visit just for the name.

HISTORY: There was an earlier club playing at St. James' Park in 1886, and it merged with another to form Newcastle United in 1892. They quickly became a national power, winning the league three times and making five FA Cup finals by 1911 (they lost four of them). They won the Cup again in 1924 and 1932, but were relegated in 1934. After World War II they surged again, winning three FA Cups in the first half of the 1950s, then were relegated again for a few years in the '60s.

They were then pretty ordinary until the '90s, when they signed a man—nay, a god if you ask the locals—named Alan Shearer. He was a Newcastle boy who used to stand on the terraces, and he had just helped Blackburn Rovers win the Premier League. From 1996 to 2006, Shearer scored 206 goals in 395 games, occasionally leading the league in scoring and setting a Premier League record with eleven hat tricks. And yet, it must be pointed out, in all those years Newcastle never won a trophy. Still, the image of him running around with his right arm in the air after scoring is the equivalent of Joe Montana sticking both arms up in the air after tossing a touchdown pass.

He is now a regular commentator on BBC's *Match of the Day* (see page 351).

After Shearer retired, another decline began: relegation in 2009, finishing above tenth in the Premier League only once, and getting relegated again in 2016. But, as in 2009, they crushed the Championship and came back up in a year. They also broke just about every away attendance record in the Championship; hardly anybody travels like the Toon Army.

The problem appears to be the owner: a businessman named Mike Ashley at the time of this writing. He made his money running the Sports Direct empire, and he has a reputation of somewhere between odd, difficult, and obnoxious. In any case, the fans hate him, and he keeps saying he wants to sell the club. But deals keep falling through. In 2020 it emerged that a Saudi group was going to buy, and the deal seemed more set than usual, but then it also fell apart. The poor Geordies deserve better than this. And in fact, they have launched a bid to buy a share of the club themselves.

RIVALRIES: Sunderland, just eight miles away, is the other half of the Tyne-Wear derby. Of course, it's the Wear-Tyne derby in Sunderland. In fact, they both use a phrase from the northeastern dialect, "Howay the Lads." At least, that's how it is written in Newcastle. In Sunderland it's *Haway*. They have played 154 times since 1883. If you ever heard a story about a fan punching a police horse, that was a Newcastle fan on derby day.

SONGS: "Blaydon Races" is a Geordie folk song written in the 19th century by, yes, Geordie Ridley. It sounds very happy and makes one want to dance around. It's pretty much the anthem of the city and refers to races that happened in that town until 1916. The lyrics are in Geordie dialect:

> Ah me lads, ye shudda seen us gannin',
> We pass'd the foaks alang the road just as they wor stannin';
> Thor wis lots o' lads an' lassies there, aal wi' smiling faces,
> Gannin' alang the Scotswood Road, to see the Blaydon Races.

After singing this as the team comes out, they then blast out Mark Knopfler's "Local Hero."

2020–21 SEASON: 12th in Premier League, 3rd FA Cup, Quarterfinals League Cup

2021–22 SEASON: Premier League (promoted in 2017)

STADIUM: It's hard to think of another city so dominated by its football stadium. St. James' Park is the biggest thing in Newcastle on the highest hill in town and is said to supplant the local cathedral in significance—it has a bigger congregation, anyway. It holds 52,405, making it the seventh-largest soccer stadium in the country.

Newcastle has played there since 1892, and they have apparently been arguing about expansion since it opened. Today it has a rather odd appearance—three massive sides and one small one—because the apartment building next to it is protected, limiting expansion in that direction. They have talked about moving a couple of times, but I don't see it.

Another funny thing about the stadium is that the pitch slopes just a little bit. I would never have noticed had I not taken the tour and the guide pointed out that at one end, the advertising boards are right on the pitch, and at the other they are about a foot off it. Newcastle does score more goals going downhill.

If you're wondering, this is the Newcastle of Brown Ale fame. The brewery was the shirt sponsor for years, and that's the official name of the southern stand. But everyone calls it the Gallowgate, as it's close to where the old city gallows were. Across the way is the Leazes End (close to a park of that name), which is officially named for manager Sir Bobby Robson. He also has a statue outside—and at Ipswich Town. Away fans have to sit way up top of this stand; the climb up the steps is known all over the league.

That leaves the Jackie Milburn Stand, named for a hero of the 1950s team, and the East Stand, the small one. I like to sit in the East Stand so I can get the full palatial aspect of the rest of it. It is simply a beautiful stadium, with apologies to my friends in Sunderland (see page 342).

Above all this is a spectacular roof made of glass to let the sunlight through. It's the largest cantilever structure in Europe, and occasional stadium tours include a walk up there!

TOURS: Tours are offered Friday, Saturday and Sunday at various times. Last I saw, it was £15 for the usual tour, £20 for that tour with lunch, and £20 for the rooftop tour on weekends from April to October. There are also less frequent Legends Tours led by former players you will have never heard of unless you're a Geordie. Check with the club for the latest.

TICKETS: Around £30 to £35 last season. I also have a couple of good hospitality options here.

GETTING THERE: It's only a 15-minute walk from Newcastle Central station; go through Chinatown on the way and get something to eat. You can also find Grainger Street just outside the station and take bus 71 or 87.

PUBS: The Strawberry is right across the street and is so significant that a corner of the stadium is named for it. It's been there since 1859 and is a proper pub adorned with drawings and photos of Toon legends. It will, of course, be mobbed on game days.

The Head of Steam near the station has an absurd selection of beers, and both the Duke of Wellington and the Old George are proper old pubs down in the center.

GRUB: As I said, Chinatown sits right next to the stadium; locals almost brawled when I asked for the best place, so just follow your nose. There's also a proper chippy near the station called Clayton Street Chippy.

AROUND TOWN: What an amazing city. Newcastle was the center of shipbuilding for decades, and its riverfront is still spectacular. There are several bridges over the Tyne, including the Gateshead Millennium Bridge, which lets boats go through by hauling itself into the air. Take a boat tour from River Escapes—some of them even go out to the sea—or a walking tour from Newcastle City Guides. There's even a small (and sure, artificial) beach and bar down there called Quayside Seaside.

Make sure you also see the nearly-200-year-old Grainger Market, a really cool indoor market with over a hundred stalls and famous scales where you can get yourself weighed. Also make sure you swing by the all-football bookstore called The Back Page. You can get lost in there.

And finally, there is the 1838 Grey's Monument, down in the architecturally rich old center. That would be the local earl and legislative hero who directed his staff to make a tea that covered the (then poor) taste of the local water—hence, Earl Grey Tea. You can even go up a spiral staircase inside the monument.

SUNDERLAND

A club that was just hanging on in the Premier League for years finally lost it three years ago. And then they dropped out of the Championship in 2018. Like their hated neighbors up the road in Newcastle, this amazing group of supporters deserves better.

LOCATION: In the northeast of England, about four hours by train from either London or Manchester

CONTACT: safc.com, 0371 911 1200, #SAFC

NICKNAMES: The Black Cats, apparently because of a black cat that lived in their old stadium

WOMEN'S TEAM: Sunderland Ladies play in the Women's Championship, the second tier. Home games are at The Eppleton Colliery Welfare Ground in the southern part of the city.

HISTORY: If you used measurements like top-flight titles, FA Cups, support, and stadium capacity, Sunderland would be a right big club. And indeed, they used to be—eighty years ago. Now they languish in League One after playing in the Premier League from 2007 to 2017. Eight managers in six years underscore the chaos at the club.

The club was founded in 1879 and has since spent eighty-six years in the top flight (winning six titles) and thirty in the second. Last season was only their fourth in the third tier, but the third in a row. The last league title was in 1936, and the following year they won their first FA Cup. Then came forty pretty dry years before they won another FA Cup in 1973 while playing in the second tier. That has only been done by two clubs since.

In that 1973 final, they beat Leeds United—the best team in the country at the time—1–0 on a famous goal by Ian Porterfield. Even more famous was a double save made by their keeper, Jimmy Montgomery; it was so amazing, the BBC announcer thought the ball had gone in. But the most famous image was of their manager, Bob Stokoe, who at the final whistle took off running straight at Montgomery to give him a hug. The image of him strid-ing across the pitch at Wembley is preserved in his statue outside the Sunderland stadium. Such was the importance of that win that Stokoe has a statue despite being the manager for less than four full seasons.

Their next major highlight was in 1985 when they made the final of the League Cup, which back then was called the Milk Cup. They drew Norwich City, and it was the height of the hooligan days. Both sets of fans were determined to put on a proper show of good behavior, and the result was what's often called the Friendly Final. The supporters mingled and drank together before, during, and after the game; swapped scarves as souvenirs; and fed mints to the police horses. They also played a game of football in the parking lot that was said to be at least fifty versus fifty.

Norwich won the real game, 1–0, on a Sunderland own goal. On the trains after the game, Norwich fans sang, "We Won the Cup" and Sunderland fans sang back, "We Scored the Goal." Such was the goodwill from that day that ever since, when they play each other, they contest the Friendship Trophy. Sunderland has it at the moment after a win and a draw in the Championship in the 2017–18 season. And since they are now in different leagues, the Black Cats will likely have it for a while.

Two seasons of a Netflix documentary called *Sunderland 'Til I Die* document, in excru-ciating detail, their fall to League One and then their loss in the playoff final to get back up. Along the way, they also lost the 2019 League Trophy final at Wembley to Portsmouth. They won the League Trophy in 2021, but their fans couldn't even be there to see it.

RIVALRIES: Newcastle United, which is about twelve miles away, is the main rival—and it's positively tribal. They can't even agree what to call it. Sunderland is on the River Wear, Newcastle on the Tyne. So Sunderland call it the Wear-Tyne derby and Newcastle the Tyne-Wear. Each club has won it fifty-three times, and there have been forty-nine draws. Middlesbrough is also considered a rival; that's the Wear-Tees derby.

SONGS: Not so much a song as a chant, you will regularly hear fans yell, "Haway the Lads!" It's northeastern dialect, but of course in Newcastle it's spelled *Howay*. They also sing "Can't Help Falling in Love" and another that says, "Things Can Only Get Better," which they adopted during a great escape year in 2013.

2020–21 SEASON: 4th in League One, 1st Round FA Cup, 1st Round League Cup

2021–22 SEASON: League One (relegated in 2018)

STADIUM: The Stadium of Light holds 48,707, but since they are in League One, they close the upper tiers for home games. It is yet another example of a fairly bland, fully enclosed oval—just bigger than most. The name comes from the city's long mining heritage. A light would be left on at the top of the mineshaft until the last miner was out. This became a symbol of the city's commitment to its workers and football club, and today there is a light outside the stadium.

TOURS: Several days a week (not match days) for £10

TICKETS: The last prices I saw were £20, and I can't imagine they will sell anything out unless they draw a big Premier League club in a Cup.

GETTING THERE: From the Sunderland train station, you can walk it in just over 20 minutes. You can also take the Metro tram's Green Line to St. Peters and walk just under half a mile. That line also continues on to a stop called Stadium of Light, but it's a little farther away. The Metro also connects into Newcastle. Note that after the game, trains from the Stadium station will only go north, and from St. Peters they only go south.

PUBS: There are several good options right around the stadium. The Colliery Tavern and The Victory are both popular. The Harbour View is a nice option on the seafront, about a 20-minute walk down Roker Avenue from the main stadium entrance.

Over by the station, south of the river, the Dun Cow has received awards from CAMRA for good beer selection, and it's right next door to the famous Empire Theatre. On the other side of the theater is Revolution, which has better food options. There's a Wetherspoon pub called the Lambton Worm next to that.

GRUB: There's not much near the stadium except the pubs listed above. As you walk up from the station, turn right on High Street W for a Frankie and Benny's and a Nando's.

AROUND TOWN: They've put a lot of work into the riverbank in Sunderland, including a sculpture trail. The National Glass Center has exhibits and glass blowing. You can download a map of the South Tyneside Heritage Trail from visitsouthtyneside.co.uk; use it and Metro to explore local towns and sites, including the 1871 Souter Lighthouse. A few miles up the River Wear—and of interest to Americans, anyway—sits Washington—as in George. His family was from here, and the Old Hall where they lived is now a National Trust location. Tours are £5; see nationaltrust.org.uk/washington-old-hall.

South Shields is a famous old-school seaside town that has been remade as a renowned hub of Indian food. There is a park and pier on the water, and the Indian places are all lined up along the main road from there. South Shields has a Metro stop that's about forty minutes north of downtown.

As you wander around the footballing landscape, occasionally you bump into the most amazing stuff. And sometimes, when you think it can't possibly happen again, it does! So it was when I, as an honorary Mackem, saw Sunderland get a totally improbable win over Chelsea at Stamford Bridge.

But it started at Old Trafford. I needed to tick Manchester United's home ground off the list, and I happened to be there during the dreaded David Moyes season, when the post–Alex Ferguson hangover was just settling in. It was a Tuesday night in January, second leg of a League Cup semifinal against Sunderland, and I managed to get a killer seat for £56. For Man U, it was barely a thing; but for Sunderland, it was massive. Going to Old Trafford with a shot at Wembley? They were all in. They brought 9,000 people to the game, a singing, jumping, red-and-white wall of humanity like nothing I'd ever seen.

And they won! They scored a late goal that looked like the winner—I got a great video of that with their fans in the background—and then moments later United tied it (of course), Sunderland won in a penalty shootout. Again, that happened in front of their fans, and again I videoed the whole thing, then shared it online. This led to tens of thousands of hits on the video, many thousands on my blog, and dozens of Mackems—the nickname for Sunderland folk—telling me I had captured the greatest moment of their lives.

And this, in turn, led to me meeting up with some of them when Sunderland came down to London to play at Chelsea. José Mourinho was back with the Blues and hadn't lost a home game in sixty-something outings. Sunderland was battling relegation and sitting dead last in the table. I met with Mackems Steve and Scott at a pub before the game, and we hit it off. Then it was off to the game—for, we all assumed, a thorough beating at the hands of the mighty and title-chasing Blues.

As we made our way through a sea of blue shirts toward Stamford Bridge, Steve and Scott agreed it would probably be a long day, another nail in Sunderland's relegation coffin. As Steve said, "We'll just make it a ninety-minute sing-song!" This began on the concourse of the Shed End at the Bridge, where my previously polite and humble new friends turned into fountains of song and enthusiasm, their arms held wide and high, their throats filled with defiance. The mood in the red end was "We're here, we're probably doomed, but by God, we will be heard!"

I sat with the more relaxed folks in front, as I am more of a sitter and watcher for the most part. The game started about as expected: Chelsea dominated possession and scored fairly quickly. Waves of scorn came our way from the home fans, also as expected, but the singing in the red corner hardly wavered. They had chants of "Haway the Lads," whatever *haway* means, as well as a rendition of "Red-White Army" which, considering its speed and the alcohol blood level of its singers, sounded like "REH-wia-MAY!" They sang that things

The author got his Sunderland scarf and helped entertain the staff at Stamford Bridge.

were gonna be all right; they sang that Sunderland is by far the greatest team the world has ever seen, that its fans are the loudest the world has ever heard; and they sang more than one that I couldn't make out at all, despite my being surrounded by at least 2,000 of them. I had not encountered such fans as those of Sunderland in any sport.

And then the Black Cats scored, and absolute mayhem broke out all around me. Young men leaped around and tore their shirts off, grown men hugged each other, women flashed obscene gestures at the Chelsea people. *Carnage* is a word I hear to describe it, and it's the right one. Any sense of decorum and restraint flew away, and then my goodness did they sing for the rest of the match! The Chelsea manager argued with the refs, and we sang for him to sit down, along with other two-syllable suggestions. We taunted "injured" Chelsea players, bellowed for cards whenever one of our boys hit the ground, swapped offensive chants with the locals, and never sat down or shut up. In short, we were proper football fans.

And I say "we" because when the Sunderland goal went in, my marra Steve—*marra* is what they call a mate up in Sunderland—draped his scarf over my shoulders, and I decided it was time for me to join them younger fellas in the stand-up section. I might have let slip a few curses along the way, aided by my affection for Fulham FC and therefore disgust for the Blues. (Fulham has a song called "Stick the Blue Flag Up Your Arse.")

The battle raged on, in the stands and on the pitch, and then a critical moment occurred right in front of us (did I mention the gods of sport?). A Chelsea defender slipped, and Sunderland's Jozy Altidore (an American now with Toronto FC) pounced and headed for goal. Then the defender took him out from behind! We bellowed as one, and the beloved referee, truly a pillar of vision and sound thinking, pointed to the spot—a penalty for Sunderland to take the lead!

Fabio Borini, a hero of the season, calmly walked up and—incredibly, amazingly—put Sunderland up, 2–1.

Yes, we had a lead—a moment only enhanced by some kerfuffle along the Chelsea bench and one of their staffers being thrown out of the game for trying to get at the ref. Buncha punks, those Blues. And now there was not much time to go. The singing went on, ever more fevered but now with an element of nerves. Were they really going to do this thing? It would be a truly historic win and incredibly valuable in avoiding relegation, but Sunderland winning at Chelsea? Do we dare to dream?

With about two minutes to go, I just decided to start filming. I wanted to capture the mood as much as possible and perchance the celebration. You'll have to go watch the video on my YouTube channel, but what I love about it, other than the final outcome, is the nervous pacing and nail-chewing, as well as the suggestions from my neighbors that the referee might consider blowing his whistle—or words to that effect.

And then the moment actually arrived: victory!

The gods of sport apparently love something about the combination of me and Sunderland. Needless to say, they have exquisite timing as well. In fact, it was just after I shot the video that one of the stewards remembered that the use of camcorders is illegal in Premier League grounds and asked me to put it away. Perfect timing, sir!

As our jumping and screaming gave way to huge sighs and "I can't believe that just happened," the stewards began gently walking us toward the exits, letting slip the occasional "Well done" and then "Now it's off to Sunderland with you." The look on one gent's face as I posed for my victory photo says it all: a bemused yet fatigued sense that at least he can go home now and be released from the company of these merry lunatics.

We sang our way out to the streets, and on the way my friends suggested I might remove the scarf for safer travel. I did so and walked them over to the buses that would take them back to their suddenly happy section of the Northeast. Word that Newcastle had gone down, at home no less, to a last-minute Swansea winner provided a little icing on our winning cake. With a round of handshakes and hugs, and with thanks from me for the £40 ticket Steve wouldn't accept payment for, I said farewell for now to the mighty and crazy fans of Sunderland.

Sunderland actually stayed up that year, and even though "normal service" has long since resumed—that is, Man U and Chelsea are in the Champions League, Sunderland is in League One, and Newcastle is in the Premier League—they'll never take away me and my fellow Mackems' big day at the Bridge.

THROW-INS

Its music is recognizable to probably everyone in the UK. Watching it is more of a tradition than anything that exists in America. Arguments about its running order are almost as passionate as about the games themselves. And it is so old-fashioned that before it comes on about six hours after the last game, the BBC sportscasters give a heads-up before they show—but don't announce—the scores of that day's games lest viewers have the surprise ruined. In 2021!

Match of the Day is so deeply embedded into the British sporting consciousness that people always look at me funny when I point out that it actually covers *all* the matches of the day, so maybe they should change the name. Silly American.

Match of the Day is the BBC highlight show that comes on at 10:30 every Saturday evening, with a *Match of the Day II* on Sunday. It started in 1964, when every week they would pick one game to show highlights of; owing to pressure from clubs worried about ticket sales, they never announced which game they would be showing. It has since expanded to include all games, averaging about ten minutes of highlights for each. It now has a viewership of around seven million people—most of whom are angry about which game is shown first.

The current host, former England striker Gary Lineker, has run it since 1999, making him slightly longer-serving than the legendary Jimmy Hill. Lineker, who grew up in Leicester and played for Leicester City (and later Everton, Barcelona, and Spurs), famously tweeted during the 2015–16 season that if Leicester City won the title, he would present *Match of the Day* in just his underpants. They won it, and he opened the next season's show in boxers only, with his fellow commentators doubled over in laughter behind him.

Perhaps the most famous thing ever said on the show was by commentator Alan Hansen, who said of a young Manchester United team in 1995, "You can't win anything with kids." Unfortunately for him and the league, those kids included Ryan Giggs, Phil and Gary Neville, Paul Scholes, and David Beckham—the Man U academy's famous Class of '92. They won the league and FA Cup that season, then won a famous treble of those plus the Champions League in 1999.

For about twenty years now, England has been engaging in a slow-motion bad idea—similar to something America did in the 1960s and 1970s. They are tearing down old grounds full of character and history, but lacking in space and facilities and corporate boxes, and replacing them with clean, comfortable, sterile, and utterly crap stadiums that everyone seems to agree are better and necessary as well as boring and awful.

In the States, think about the Polo Grounds giving way to Shea Stadium, or Comiskey Park giving way to wherever the White Sox play now. Or just contemplate Wrigley or Fenway coming down.

I recall a moment at Reading FC and their oval 1998 Madejski Stadium, on the edge of town between a Costco, an expressway, and a business park. I asked my neighbor about their old home, Elm Park, where they played for 102 years. His eyes misted up a little, and he said, "It was cramped, it smelled like stale beer and piss and cigarettes.... It was great." Such is the English attitude toward the modern stadium.

Want to see what I mean about these modern stadiums? Go to Southampton, Stoke, Sunderland, Reading, Leicester, or Swansea.

Want to see what's being replaced? Get yourself to Everton, Burnley, Crystal Palace, Watford, Fulham, Leeds, Norwich, Portsmouth, or either club in Sheffield. Brits will tell you it isn't the same since the terraces went away (see "The Taylor Report," page 365), but for us foreigners, it's a trip back in time to when the nature of the place was an essential part of the club's character. What would the Cubs be without Wrigley or the Red Sox without Fenway? Ask a West Ham fan.

Let's hope they figure it out. America certainly has. Consider what baseball has done since Camden Yards opened in Baltimore, or what MLS clubs are doing now, building "soccer-specific" stadiums in the middle of town, modeled on—that's right—the old European places. The fact is, you can build modern, safe, comfortable stadiums with good food and facilities that still feel like an old-fashioned ground.

The new place at Tottenham seems to have gotten this right. With Chelsea, Everton, and many other clubs looking to expand or replace their homes, may they remember to add some class and character! And may you get out to the old grounds while you still can.

If you pay attention to the singing at English soccer games, you will have heard a particular song spread all over the game the last year or two. The chorus and the name are "Allez Allez Allez," accompanied by much hopping and waving of scarves, and the lyrics vary from club to club.

It started, at least in England, during the 2017–18 season when Liverpool were making a run in the UEFA Champions League. They played a game at Porto in Portugal, where the locals were singing a tune adapted from an old Italian dance number called "L'Estate Sta Finendo" ("The Summer Is Ending").

It had made its way through the Italian leagues before Porto picked it up. Liverpool fans started singing it, and then back home a local musician added these lyrics:

> We've conquered all of Europe
> We're never gonna stop
> From Paris down to Turkey
> We've won the fucking lot.
> Bob Paisley and Bill Shankly
> The fields of Anfield Road
> We are loyal supporters
> And we've come from Liverpool.

It became their signature tune that year, and then it spread around the UK. But it started as mockery. You see, Liverpool (going for European title number six) lost the final that year to Real Madrid in Kiev. The winning goal came from Welshman Gareth Bale, and Liverpool's star player Mo Salah was famously injured ("accidentally," of course) by Madrid defender Sergio Ramos. This inspired Manchester United to start singing lyrics first tweeted out by their legend Gary Neville. It refers as well to United's 1999 team that won the league, FA Cup, and Champions League:

> They thought they'd conquered Europe,
> Celebrating six,
> Thank you, Gareth Bale,
> Made them look like dicks,
> The 26th of May,
> Always in our heart,
> United won the Treble,
> The Scousers fell apart.

Manchester City came in with their own version:

All the way to Kiev
To end up in defeat
Crying in the stands
And battered on the streets
Ramos injured Salah
Victims of it all
Sterling won the double
The Scousers won fuck-all!

To keep the fun going, in the 2018–19 season City made a run in Europe as well, but they lost at home to Spurs when Sterling's apparent winning goal was waved off by video review. Cue Tottenham fans:

City thought they won it
But Tottenham pulled it back
Wanyama in the middle
Llorente in attack
Sterling scored the winner
The Etihad went mad
The ref went to the camera
But it was disallowed.

I've found and heard versions of this all over England, so I put up a post on my website to track them. If you hear somebody singing it and want to know the lyrics, check tinyurl.com/allezengland. Likewise, if you find one that I haven't posted yet, please let me know!

THE LAST DAY: "TOTAL CHAOS"

Since the British have this funny idea that a season's championship should be decided over the course of a whole season—as opposed to a tournament at the end—and since they have another quaint notion that the worst teams in the league should be punished with relegation to a lower level, the last day of their season can have a lot of stuff riding on it.

It could be the title on the line. It is often promotion and relegation decisions made on the last day. A fourth-place European or promotion playoff spot could still be up for grabs. And occasionally there is everything to play for, with "results elsewhere" taking on massive significance. In 2019 Manchester City had to win on the last day at Brighton to beat out Liverpool by one point. They did, but when Brighton scored first in that game, grounds all over the land (especially Anfield) were buzzing.

It is for this reason that on the last day of each league's season, everybody plays at exactly the same time. If a club facing relegation knows it's safe, they could send out a bunch of reserves, thus handing critical points to their opponent and knocking somebody else out of, say, Europe or the league.

Teams and players also get prize money for their finishing spot in the table, so on the last day there could be millions of pounds at stake, even for a team that won't win a trophy or promotion.

This has led to some barnstorming final days, perhaps most famously at the end of the 2012–13 season when Manchester City scored two goals in injury time at home against QPR (who were battling relegation) to snatch the title from Manchester United, who had won their game at Sunderland and were champs for about three minutes. It's an incredible video to watch; just Google "Agueroooooooo." (I swear you'll never see anything like it ever again!)

In other memorable last days, Man U won the title by a point over Arsenal in 1999; in 1989 second-place Arsenal won at Liverpool 2–0 (with an injury-time winner) to take the title from the Reds on goal difference.

There have also been dramatic great escapes with one team's survival depending on another team's late goal across the country. See "Notable Great Escapes" on page 369 for more on that.

And there have been completely random results, like an already-relegated Newcastle destroying Tottenham at home, 5–1 in 2016. What's Geordie for "cathartic"?

Even without all of this happening, there is a festive and crazy last-day-of-school vibe when there's nothing to lose, the weather is great, and big rivalries are never scheduled so everybody just goes for it. It tends to be the highest-scoring day of the season, and with one last day to cheer on the lads before the summer break, folks make it a great day out. It's highly recommended as a time to visit and a fun day to watch telly back at home.

This season's last Premier League day will be May 22. The Championship and League Two wrap up the weekend of May 7 and 8, League One the week before.

I am a total stadium geek, and as I read about the old grounds I so admire, I kept coming across this name Archibald Leitch. So I thought I would introduce you to him as well.

Leitch (pronounced LEETCH) was born in Scotland in 1865 and became an architect, first of factories. He designed his first football ground for Scottish club Kilmarnock in 1899, then more famously at Ibrox Park, home of Rangers FC in Glasgow.

But it almost ended right there, as on opening day in 1902 a section of the Ibrox Park bleachers collapsed, killing twenty-five people. Inferior wood was blamed, but Leitch learned the lesson and redesigned the terracing that was then the basis of all grounds. Instead of bleachers, Leitch designed layered earthen banks, and on the surface he put metal crush barriers meant to stem the flow of people. You can see one of these from the old Liverpool Kop (which Leitch designed) in the club's museum.

His first jobs after Ibrox were Craven Cottage at Fulham and Stamford Bridge at Chelsea. Although terraces are long gone due to safety improvements, much of Leitch's design at Fulham still exists, most famously the cottage itself and the Haynes Stand with its gabled roof.

Over the next thirty years, Leitch's firm would build grounds at dozens of clubs; in fact, in the late 1920s Leitch had designed sixteen of the First Division's twenty-two grounds. You can still see his work at many clubs, including Aston Villa (the Holte End), Rangers (South Stand), Everton (Bullens Road and Gwladys Street), Sheffield Wednesday (South Stand), Crystal Palace (Main Stand), and Portsmouth (South Stand).

Leitch, who died in 1939, also influenced many stands and grounds that have since been rebuilt or replaced, including at Liverpool, Sheffield United, Manchester United, Blackburn Rovers, and Arsenal. At Aston Villa, his masterpiece, the old Trinity Road Stand, sadly was demolished in 2000.

What's left of Arsenal's old stadium, Highbury, still shows Leitch's design. To see how to visit it, check the Arsenal chapter.

Every club has some version of a family area in its ticketing and seating scheme. Sometimes this just means an area where, in theory, there is less standing, drinking, and cursing. Sometimes it's an area where no alcohol is served. Sometimes, though, we're talking about a full-on play area behind the seats, so if your little one gets bored with the game there are board games, table games, and video games, and the club mascot will come in to say hello.

I haven't listed this for every club in here, but I wanted you to know it's an option. When you're buying tickets online or calling in to the ticket office, look or ask for the family section.

You don't have to leave the kiddos at home; just beware of taking them into the club shop!

WAYS TO SAY "THAT GAME SUCKED"

Let's face it: not every game is a thriller. In fact, some of them are really no fun at all. At a game like that, other than the supporters having a go at one another, the only fun thing to do is try to figure out which word or phrase the media will use to describe this shit show.

Here are the ones I've collected over the years from both print and broadcast:

Damp squib
Desultory
Dire
Dismal
Dour
Drab
Dreadful
Forgettable
Grim
Lacking in clear-cut chances
Lackluster
Less than stirring
Limp
Low-quality
Muted
Slow burner
Sorry
Sterile
Turgid
Uneventful

The short answer here is "try not to."

Many stadiums—starting with Wembley after it hosted NFL games, but spreading to more and more clubs—are now saying you can't bring in a backpack. What they mean by that word varies; some of them go with dimensions (and who knows the dimensions of their pack?), while some say things like "nothing bigger than a purse." I don't know about you, but I've seen some damn big purses in my day.

Conveniently (wink wink), should you show up with something too big to bring in, they have a very handy place to store it during the game for a small fee. That usually works pretty well, but why bother?

If you plan to hit the club shop before the game, don't worry: *that* bag is more than welcome! Shop bags are all transparent now to make sure yoau don't have something illicit in there, so you could probably put some other personal items in there as well.

Bottom line: Keep it to a small purse when you can, and otherwise travel light.

Also, if you happen to have one, don't say "fanny pack" to an English person unless you want to shock and entertain them. *Fanny* in the UK means…well, something different from what it means in the States.

One of the first differences many of us Americans notice when exploring the world of soccer is that everybody else does scorelines differently. Basically, ours always look like this:

Ale and Pilsner United 0
Groundhopper FC 5

In America, that means Ale and Pilsner went to Groundhopper and got a whipping. But in England, that game happened at A&P; the home team is always on top. Also, they would use a configuration you'd never see in the States for the same result: Ale and Pilsner 0:5 Groundhopper.

Again, the home team is first in that listing.

Also, when an English PA guy reads "scores from around the country" at halftime, he always says the home team first, no matter who is winning. In the States, where the team in the lead always comes first, if you hear "at halftime, Chicago 2...," you know that Chicago is ahead or even, but you don't know where the game is being played. In England, if you hear "Everton 1...," all you know is that Everton is playing at home and has a goal. (And they would say "Everton are home to" somebody.)

Their system leaves a bit of suspense in it, and sometimes there's a delicious moment when the announcer lets that first score hang for just a second, and then there's the slightest change in his voice if, for example, after saying "Everton 1" he says "Southampton 3." Bit of a surprise, that!

And now, back to your halftime beer.

I assume you'll be in London at some point. I also assume that even dropping down below the Premier League will, for many of you, seem like an adventure.

If you want to go deep into this thing, check out one of these non-league clubs around town. For simplicity, I am keeping this to levels 5 and 6 of the pyramid (see my guide to the leagues on page 17). Also, I will trust that you can work the internet to determine where they are and when they're playing. I would also be happy to help; reach out at groundhopperguides.com.

All of these are within about an hour by train from London Bridge. I had to draw the line somewhere!

National League (Tier 5):

- Barnet
- Boreham Wood (see page 81)
- Bromley (see page 87)
- Dagenham and Redbridge
- Wealdstone
- Woking

National League South (Tier 6):

- Dartford
- Dorking Wanderers
- Dulwich Hamlet (see page 106)
- Ebbsfleet United
- Hampton & Richmond Borough
- Hemel Hempstead Town
- Slough Town
- St. Albans City
- Welling United

If you're a typical tourist, you will probably be spending much, if not most, of your English trip in and around London. And well you should; it's an extraordinary destination and an incredible football city.

But allow me to briefly make a case for Manchester, in particular if you are building your trip around soccer games.

Manchester is a vibrant, entertaining city, one that is growing like gangbusters and attracting many young professionals. It's like Seattle and Portland combined—and with the same weather. For outdoorsy folks, the Pennines and Peak District National Park are just outside town, and the Lake District is a couple of hours' drive away.

But let's talk about soccer. Even I was astounded to realize how many Football League clubs are so close to town.

Right in town, obviously, are Manchester United and Manchester City. Liverpool is less than an hour away by train, adding Liverpool and Everton to the Premier League possibilities. On Manchester's Metrolink light-rail system, you can reach Rochdale and Oldham.

Within ninety minutes from Piccadilly station by train, you can get to Huddersfield Town, Wigan, Bolton Wanderers, Crewe, Barnsley, both Sheffield clubs, Burnley, Bradford City, Leeds United, Blackburn Rovers, Preston North End, and Stoke City. Even Derby County and the Nottingham clubs are around ninety minutes away, but at that point you should just stay in Nottingham.

With any of those clubs playing a 3:00 p.m. game, you could have a leisurely morning in Manchester, hop on a train, have a pint or two, catch the game, and be back for dinner. And honestly, in most of those cases, you'd have a lot more fun staying in Manchester anyway.

Allow me to introduce you to the Standard Northern English Town.

I have seen this in every northern town I've visited, and you will as well, so we might as well get it out of the way.

1. There was a forest with people living here and there.
2. The Romans came through, and if the place was important, they built something. A smidgeon of said something remains around here somewhere.
3. There was a monastery. Perhaps a bridge.
4. There was a plague that killed pretty much everybody.
5. The Dark Ages happened, and we don't know shit about them.
6. The town was mentioned in the Domesday Book, and it had a name kind of similar to what it's called now.
7. In medieval times, there were weavers/cobblers/carpenters/whatever working in their homes. There was trade, and the place was kind of important.
8. There was something—wood, textiles, beer, pottery, something—for which the place was famous.
9. There was a battle or something nearby during the Civil War.
10. The Industrial Revolution happened, during which:
    - Canals were dug.
    - Machines took over and enabled massive production.
    - There was resistance to machines.
    - The machines won.
    - Fortunes were made.
    - Parks and big homes and brick and stone buildings were built, and art was collected.
    - The town was important, and famous people were here, if briefly.
    - An entertainer whom old English people will have heard of grew up here.
    - It was a polluted, miserable shithole for 98 percent of the poor, wretched people living here.
11. The Industrial Revolution petered out because…competition, technological advances, karma, whatever.
12. The wars came, and lots of people died. They were very brave, and there are monuments to them in town.
13. The last of the industry died.
14. The town almost died.
15. Lots of people from South Asia started moving here.

16. Now it's coming back as, well, tourism? Hipsterism? Art colony? Resort area? Something like that.
17. Or it's not really coming back.
18. They pedestrianized part of the downtown area.
19. There is a large rejuvenation project going on.
20. There's a Christmas festival.
21. Most of the locals voted for Brexit.
22. The local football club won the FA Cup in about 1923.
23. They kind of suck now, but we still love them.

One of the great misconceptions foreigners have about English soccer is that there are still roaming bands of violent hooligans beating people up, smashing windows, and peeing in fountains. You can find traces of that if you'd like, mostly at international games or big derbies, but basically it ended with a thing you will often hear references to: the Taylor report.

After the 1989 Hillsborough disaster, in which ninety-six Liverpool fans were killed in a crush at an FA Cup semifinal, a report was sanctioned to suggest ideas for greater safety at games. Specifically, the Hillsborough Disaster Inquiry, chaired by Lord Taylor, blamed Hillsborough on the police. It went on to make many suggestions that transformed the game—certainly for the better, though some old-timers would like to see parts of it undone at least a little.

The biggest change suggested was that terraces—open areas for standing—be replaced with an all-seater configuration. Also done away with were the fences that were supposed to keep people from invading the pitch or attacking each other but which, at Hillsborough, penned people in and caused many of the deaths.

Although many changes took additional Acts of Parliament, the Taylor report also led to the banning of alcohol within seating areas and more effective use of turnstiles.

All of that, plus closed-circuit television and fans having to create some kind of identity online to purchase tickets, has led to greater accountability, much less violence, and very few pitch invasions.

The banning of alcohol within the seats and the elimination of terraces have never quite sat well with many fans. In fact, many Brits take footballing vacations to Germany, where terraces and beer are common. Terraces are now allowed in leagues below the Premier League, and they may make a comeback there as well. This is what they are talking about when you hear "safe standing areas" mentioned.

Still, we can thank Lord Taylor and Parliament—plus generally improved economic conditions, higher ticket prices, and other social factors—for the fact that your chance of going to a soccer game and winding up in a street rumble are quite close to zero.

One of the entertaining things to watch during a game how a referee communicates with players. One assumes he speaks, and one would love some of the responses, but unless you can read lips, you are left with various gestures. With thanks to my Timbers seatmate Andrew for his encyclopedic mind, here are some ref gestures to watch for.

- A flat hand and shaking head: "You don't get to speak to me."
- The wagging finger: "No, you were not fouled. Don't give me that."
- Both hands out flat, pushed down: "You're getting a little carried away; take it down a notch." This is also warning number one.
- A shrug of the shoulders: "I don't know why you're talking to me; you're the one who fouled him."
- Whipping his arms wide apart, like "incomplete" in American football: "Some of you thought there was a foul there, but I saw it, I'm the ref, and *no*. Play on!"
- The "get up" motion with his hands while running away: This is the same as just above but with an added "Get your embellishing arse up and play" element.
- Two arms held out up and forward is actually an official sign meaning he's "playing the advantage." This is when he saw a foul, but the team that would get a free kick has the ball anyway, so play on. Sometimes they lose it quickly, and he "pulls it back" for a free kick.
- The standard "come over here" signal: somebody is about to get warning number two. Sometimes he makes the captain come over as well. "Talk to your boy, here."
- Pointing at the player several times, then a shorter, more compact version of the "no foul" arm-whip means "You've committed a couple of fouls now. The next one is a yellow card, so *stop it*." This is warning number two.
- Talking to one player from each team: These are probably the captains, and he's probably telling them to tell everybody else to calm the hell down.
- Pointing toward the seats: "You've been sent off. This conversation is over. Go away." Sometimes you can clearly read his lips saying, "Go away."
- Pointing at his watch: "Stop wasting time." This can be when a player is leaving the field too slowly or a goalie is taking too long on a goal kick. It also means the ref is adding to injury time because of your nonsense.
- Calling a player over, pointing with one hand at three places on the field, while reaching for his pocket with his other hand: "Right, you committed a foul there, there, and there, and I already gave you the 'stop it' signal, so now you get your yellow card." This is the wonderfully named persistent infringement violation.
- Pointing at his ear: Head for the loo; he's hearing from the video referee.

When you think of English soccer, you probably think of the Premier League. It's rather hard to miss in the culture, and it is a tremendous league filled with world-class players in every club. But there are several reasons why I prefer watching the Championship, essentially the AAA baseball of English soccer.

These reasons also apply to Leagues One and Two, but for me, the Championship is the sweet spot of talent, club size, and all these advantages:

Different winners: The Premier League championship is, essentially, a private club of big-money, big-city clubs: Arsenal, Chelsea, Manchester City, and Manchester United. Liverpool are back in there, but before 2020 they hadn't won the league since 1990. For Tottenham, the other big six club, it's been since 1963. Only two other teams have ever won the title since 1993—Leicester City and Blackburn Rovers once each.

But in the Championship, at the end of each season the two best teams literally vanish, having been promoted to the Premier League; a third joins them via the playoff. And since three other teams drop down from the Premier League, who on earth knows who's going to win the title?

Total number of clubs to win the second tier since 1993: twenty-three!

Easier, cheaper tickets: You can probably count on your hands the number of sellouts in the lower leagues each year, and tickets usually max out around £40.

Playoffs: Brief but intense, the Championship playoffs consist of two-legged semi-finals leading to a final at Wembley. You want something on the line? The winner of that game gets ridiculous TV money and spends the next year playing all the big clubs in the country; the loser goes back to playing in Preston and Middlesbrough. No disrespect, of course.

That final, by the way, is known as the richest game in football. The 2019 game, won by Aston Villa over Derby County, was said to be worth about £170 million ($216 million) to the winners.

Big clubs down on their luck: I have been to some of the coolest stadiums in the country and seen some of the best fan bases while their teams were in the Championship. This was true at the time of Carrow Road (Norwich City), Hillsborough (Sheffield Wednesday), and Ewood Park (Blackburn Rovers), and this year you can probably get a ticket to see Sheffield United at Bramall Lane.

New clubs coming up: When teams come up from League One, sometimes they are genuine fairy-tale stories, like when Burton Albion with their 6,000-seat stadium came up to the Championship. Other times they are former powers like Leeds fighting their way back up the pyramid. This year it's Blackpool climbing back up from an ownership disaster.

Derbies coming and going: There is something thrilling to me about seeing a derby that hasn't been happening of late. Liverpool play Everton every year, but in 2019 Swansea City and Cardiff City hooked up for the first time in five years. That kind of built-up excitement can make for some real drama. This year I can't wait to see Blackpool play Preston North End for the first time since 2013.

New clubs and towns to explore: By kicking around the second tier of English soccer, I have managed to visit the brewery capital of England in Burton, the medieval city of Norwich for their heated derby, the fabulous city of Bristol, the Victorian seaside town of Brighton before they went up, and the amazing city, stadium, and fans at Newcastle United when they were down.

Proper English football: I don't want to overstate this, but there does feel like a big difference between attending a game in the Championship, especially outside London, versus being yet another tourist, especially at one of the big six Premier League clubs. One of my goals for this book is to get you out beyond the lines that most foreigners don't cross and into a proper English footballing experience. I hope that you'll meet fans who will genuinely appreciate that you've shown up at all, much less learned something about their club, explored their town, and maybe learned one or two of their songs.

Everybody loves a great escape—well, except the folks who didn't get out.

A great escape is simply a team staying up when they seemed doomed. In the Premier League era, here are a few of note:

Coventry City 1997: As Sunderland and Middlesbrough both failed to win on the last day, Coventry won at Tottenham, 2–1, and went from nineteenth to seventeenth. There's a famous image of a Boro player named Juninho weeping after their game at Leeds United.

West Brom 2005: At kickoff on the last day, nobody was definitely down. West Brom had been bottom at Christmas and hung on. They led at home but needed a goal elsewhere to stay up. After the game they had to nervously wait to see what happened in a Charlton vs. Crystal Palace game, which finally broke their way, leading to mayhem at The Hawthorns. Look up the video online and enjoy.

West Ham 2007: They were ten points from safety with ten games to go, went on a run, and still had to win at Man U the last day to stay up. They did indeed win. But Man U had already won the title, so they played a weak side against West Ham, which got them fined. In the end, it was Sheffield United that went down.

Fulham 2008: The Cottagers were six points from safety with five games to go. They won one, lost one, then trailed 2–0 at Man City with twenty minutes left. They scored three in that one, then gutted out a 1–0 win at Portsmouth on the last day and beat the drop.

Sunderland 2014: In the drop zone in April, with away games left against Man City, Chelsea, and Man U, Sunderland manager Gus Poyet said it would take a "a shock, a miracle." And shock they did: they drew at City, won at Chelsea and Man U, won two home games, and coasted on in.

Leicester City 2015: Forget Christmas: Leicester was bottom at the end of March. All they did was win seven in a row to get to fourteenth—and then they won the whole league the next year!

A few from other leagues:

Luton 1983: They won at Man City on a last-minute goal, staying up and sending City down.

Torquay 1987: They were about to go out of the league entirely and needed a late goal—when a police dog bit one of their players. I'm serious. They regrouped while he got treatment, scored a late equalizer, and stayed up.

Carlisle 1999: Goalie Jimmy Glass scored in extra time on the last day.

Bournemouth 2009: The Cherries were almost out of the league, but a late goal by Steve Fletcher in the last home game kept them in it. Six years later they were in the Premier League.

CONNECT WITH PAUL

Ultimately, my goal with all of this is for you to go to games, know more about what you're experiencing and how it all works, and have a great time. That is why I have written this book. But I can offer more than the book. Here's a quick summary of how I can help:

Consulting ("The Phoner"): Even with this book and my website, you might still have questions about your specific trip, so you can reserve some time with me on the phone. After trading a couple of emails to see what you have in mind, I will answer all your questions and make a bunch of suggestions. Two-thirds of the money you pay for this goes toward future ticket purchases.

Custom Itineraries ("The Planner"): In addition to the above, I can send you a comprehensive and link-filled document detailing my suggestions and all the options for your upcoming journey. I will also include tips on hotels, trains, food, drink, etc. Half of what you pay for this service goes toward future ticket purchases.

Hospitality Packages: As I described in the "Getting Tickets" section on page 46, one option for attending games is what's known as a hospitality package—essentially a ticket plus some other benefits like a buffet, lounge access, stadium tour, and so on. I am an official reseller of these, so get in touch with me to see about options for the games you're interested in.

Guiding: Should I happen to be in the UK when you are, and should you like to have me show up at your hotel and accompany you through the day or game—making the experience that much easier and, I hope, more fun—we can work this out as well. Perhaps you and your group would like me to arrange more than a single game.

"Groundhop" Tours: This could be a one-day event with a crew going to a game or a longer tour with a game or two, tours, meeting fans, etc. Check my website for the latest.

Find out more on all of this at tinyurl.com/soccertrips.

CONNECT ONLINE

I am continuously working on this project—going to more clubs, updating ticket info, telling stories, and answering questions. The best place to keep up with all of that is on my website, groundhopperguides.com. Posts are organized by topic and club.

Another great way to follow along is to subscribe to my "Groundhopper" newsletter, which is easily done from the home page of the website.

I am also on other social media, all linked from the main website:

Twitter: @groundhopguides
Facebook Page: facebook.com/groundhopperguides
Facebook Group: facebook.com/groups/groundhoppersoccerguides
YouTube: tinyurl.com/hoppervids
Instagram: @groundhopper.soccer.guides

I would also love to hear from you directly via paul@groundhopperguides.com.

Paul Gerald grew up in Memphis, Tennessee, and still has an NASL Memphis Rogues pennant somewhere. He had a very brief career as a decent goalkeeper until around the age of fifteen, at which point his strong tendency toward laziness kicked in and he decided to write about sports instead of playing them.

When he got to Southern Methodist University, he started writing in sports for the student newspaper. He eventually had jobs at the *Dallas Times Herald*, the *Memphis Commercial Appeal*, and the *Memphis Flyer* before fleeing the southern summers for Portland, Oregon in 1996.

Since then, he has written sports, travel, and outdoors articles for publications all over the country and is the author of five guidebooks for Menasha Ridge Press, including Portland's best-selling hiking guide, *60 Hikes within 60 Miles: Portland*. He has guided hiking trips in Oregon, California, Colorado, Italy, and Nepal.

Along the way, since writing never really pays the bills, he has also worked for nonprofits, restaurants, tour companies, an insurance company, Radio Cab Company in Portland, and on Alaskan fishing boats. And that's just what he can remember. He lived in Portland until 2021, when he became what the kids call a "digital nomad."

Since his first English soccer game in 2011, he has seen more than a hundred contests at more than sixty different grounds. Back at home, he's a Portland Timbers season ticket holder and a dues-paying member of the Timbers Army; he hates nothing in life more than the last ten minutes of a game when the green and gold are ahead by one goal. His neighbors in section 217 can attest to this.

CPSIA information can be obtained
at www.ICGtesting.com
Printed in the USA
BVHW062258211221
624600BV00002B/7